MW00532376

"Science gradually answered the questions religion used to answer. The unraveling of Christendom with the Reformation brought about the 'disenchantment of the world.' These are just two ideologically-driven narratives that Joseph Minich deconstructs. Instead, he employs phenomenological analysis to help us understand why we all feel the absence of God in our 'gut' even before we consciously believe or disbelieve in God's existence. This book not only explains and informs but puts a finger on the sore spots, how even believers *feel* God's presence very differently than their predecessors. If you found Charles Taylor's analysis persuasive, I think you'll find Minich's even more so."

—MICHAEL HORTON,
J. Gresham Machen Professor of Systematic Theology and Apologetics,
Westminster Seminary California

"A work of insight and nuance, featuring a myriad of interlocutors, Minich's perceptive and clever analysis of the plausibility structures that have given way to the possibility of such an impersonal reality as unbelief is penetrating and clarifying. Our world has recently changed, Minich shows us. We now live in a realm where reality is 'manipulable material, meaninglessly arranged' unless the human mind does the work of meaning-making. How did this happen? While disenchantment narratives abound, Minich makes apparent that the move from enchanted ancestors to disenchanted descendants is not primarily ideological. Rather, the answer to the how and why lies nearer the phrase 'God's existence is no longer felt to be obvious.' This is now the go-to work to find out the relationship between this felt divine absence and the development of modern atheism. Written with elegance and a delight to read, Minich also offers a path forward in our age of unbelief, of 'lost faith,' an age of fractured selves in a technocratic world."

—CORY BROCK,
minister at St. Columba's Free Church of Scotland in Edinburgh;
author, *Orthodox Yet Modern: Herman Bavinck's Use of
Friedrich Schleiermacher*

"Minich has written a wonderfully scintillating treatment of the spiritual condition of modernity; it's culturally perceptive and psychologically astute. Being especially attentive to the material factors that have rendered atheism so thinkable and attractive, his account offers insights lacking in many ideological fall narratives and resists the temptation of nostalgic laments over disenchantment. His concluding section presents a theological framing for the modern condition that is suggestive and daring, which I will doubtless be reflecting upon for some time."

—ALASTAIR ROBERTS,
adjunct senior fellow, Theopolis Institute

BULWARKS OF UNBELIEF

BULWARKS OF UNBELIEF

ATHEISM AND DIVINE ABSENCE
IN A SECULAR AGE

JOSEPH MINICH

LEXHAM
ACADEMIC

Bulwarks of Unbelief: Atheism and Divine Absence in a Secular Age

Lexham Academic, an imprint of Lexham Press
1313 Commercial St., Bellingham, WA 98225
LexhamPress.com

Print ISBN 9781683596752
Digital ISBN 9781683596769
Library of Congress Control Number 2022944271

Lexham Editorial: Todd Hains, Tim Perry, Andrew Sheffield, Katrina Smith, Mandi Newell
Cover Design: Joshua Hunt; Brittany Schrock
Typesetting: Abigail Stocker

For Οὖτις, my mentor and friend

Contents

Foreword

Charles Taylor notes in *A Secular Age* that, while one can today believe in the same things as a Christian in the year 1500 (e.g., the Trinity, the Incarnation, the Resurrection), one cannot believe them in the same way. In 1500, such belief was intuitive, resting upon bulwarks of belief that made denial of Christianity, if not strictly impossible, really very difficult. Today, however, the opposite applies: one chooses to believe in the Christian faith, and one does so in the face of a culture where the bulwarks, so to speak, are in favor of unbelief. This is why so many Christians even feel their own hearts often to be battlegrounds, not simply between righteousness and unrighteousness but between faith and atheism.

How this change has taken place has been subject to many forms of analysis. Numerous culprits have been suggested over the years: a decadent late medieval theology; the crisis of institutional authority that flows (and keeps flowing) from the ecclesiastical disruptions at the Reformation; the rise of capitalism; the development of modern science. All have surely played their part. But at the heart of the human experience of the conflict between belief and unbelief lies the way in which individuals intuitively relate to the world around them. Their way of being in the world is central to how they understand and navigate that world.

In this book, Joseph Minich offers an account of the bulwarks of unbelief that ascribes a central role to technology. Martin Heidegger famously commented that the threat from technology to humanity did not come primarily from the ability it gave to destroy the human race through what we now call weapons of mass destruction. Rather, it came from its ability to completely dehumanize us, to transform our relationship to the world, to each other, in short to reality, in a manner that would fundamentally destroy who we are. In sum, he pointed to a basic but important fact about technology that we are all inclined to miss: technology does not simply allow us to relate to the world in faster, more efficient ways. Technology actually alters our relationship to the world in fundamental ways. Technology is, one might say, ontology.

It is that line that Dr. Minich explores with relation to the experience of belief and unbelief in the modern world. Methodologically drawing upon the tradition of phenomenology, he focuses on how the technologized environment in which we live has transformed us, not simply in the skills we have to possess but in how we intuitively imagine the world and our place within it. Simply put, the world of technology is a world where God's absence is intuitively much more plausible than it was in pre-modern society.

Yet this is neither a lament nor simply a descriptive analysis of where we are today. Dr. Minich also presses forward to positive construction. If unbelief is a problem not simply, or even primarily, of epistemology but rather of the intuitions and narratives that a technological world implicitly embodies, then the apologetic case for Christianity must be pursued in a manner that grips the whole human being.

This is an important book both in its argument and its proposals, a significant contribution to recent conversations about modernity, faith, and what it means to be human in a technological world.

CARL R. TRUEMAN,
Grove City College, PA;
Fellow, Ethics and Public Policy Center, Washington DC

INTRODUCTION

Whence Atheism? Whither God?

THE (RECENT!) PAST IS A FOREIGN COUNTRY

From 1906 to 1911, the Dutch theologian and statesman Herman
Bavinck (1854–1921) put the final revisions on his four-volume
magnum opus, *Reformed Dogmatics*. Arguably the most learned
Reformed theologian of his day, Bavinck filled his *Dogmatics* with
asides demonstrating encyclopedic knowledge of and competence
in both ancient and contemporary philosophy, law, science, and
history. What is more, his ethos throughout is one of cosmopoli-
tan generosity and poise, even while arguing positively for historic
Christian orthodoxy. It is fascinating to encounter, therefore, the
dismissiveness and brevity (only a few pages in the second volume)
with which he treats the subject of atheism. He writes:

> There is no atheistic world. There are no atheistic peo-
> ples. Nor are there atheistic persons. The world cannot be
> atheistically conceived ... There is nobody able, absolutely
> and with logical consistency, to deny God's knowability
> and hence his revelation ... A conscious theoretical athe-
> ism in an absolute sense, if it ever occurs, is rare ... But this
> [self-conscious materialism] almost never happens. Taken
> in an absolute sense, as the denial of an absolute power,

1

atheism is almost unthinkable … It therefore requires a certain effort not to believe in a personal God.[1]

Bavinck is, of course, aware of the existence of self-conscious materialists and atheists. He names several of them. He is likewise aware of all the ways in which his claims concerning the universality of a more-or-less personal notion of God could be contested by persons working in the field of religious anthropology, which had been growing since the late nineteenth century. He engages this body of scholarship. What strikes the reader about these particular statements, however, is the absolute (perceived) *implausibility* of atheism for Bavinck. While he interacts extensively with various philosophers throughout his *Dogmatics*, and while he writes frequently in his *Dogmatics* as well as in his larger corpus concerning the relationship between religion and science, the so-called problem of atheism is not treated by him as an item of significant concern.[2]

And yet, at the same time (in 1910), across the Atlantic, John Updike's fictional Reformed Presbyterian minister, Clarence Arthur Wilmot felt the last particles of his faith leave him.

The sensation was distinct—a visceral surrender, a set of dark sparkling bubbles escaping upward … Clarence's mind was like a many-legged, wingless insect that had long and tediously been struggling to climb up the walls of a slick-walled porcelain basin; and now a sudden impatient wash of water swept it down into the drain. There is no God … Life's sounds all rang with a curious lightness and flatness, as if a resonating base beneath them had been removed. They told Clarence Wilmot what he had long suspected, that the universe was utterly indifferent to his states of mind

---

1. Herman Bavinck, *Reformed Dogmatics Volume 2: God and Creation* (Grand Rapids: Baker Academic, 2004), 56–59.

2. This perhaps accounts for his loose-handed relationship to the theistic proofs. Ibid., 77–91.

and as empty of divine content as a corroded kettle. All its metaphysical content had leaked away, but for cruelty and death, which without the hypothesis of a God became unmetaphysical; they became simply facts, which oblivion would in time obliviously erase. Oblivion became a singular comforter. The clifflike riddle of predestination—how can Man have free will without impinging upon God's perfect freedom? how can God condemn Man when all acts from alpha to omega are His very own?—simply evaporated; an immense strain of justification was at a blow lifted. The former believer's habitual mental contortions decisively relaxed. And yet the depths of vacancy revealed were appalling. In the purifying sweep of atheism human beings lost all special value. The numb misery of the horse was matched by that of the farmer; the once-green ferny lives crushed into coal's fossiliferous strata were no more anonymous and obliterated than Clarence's own life would soon be, in a wink of earth's tremendous time. Without Biblical blessing the physical universe became sheerly horrible and disgusting. All fleshly acts became vile, rather than merely some. The reality of men slaying lambs and cattle, fish and fowl to sustain their own bodies took on an aspect of grisly comedy—the blood-soaked selfishness of a cosmic mayhem. The thought of eating sickened Clarence; his body felt swollen in its entirety, like an ankle after a sprain, and he scarcely dared take a step, lest he topple from an ungainly height.[3]

Here we are confronted with a curious juxtaposition. At the dawn of the twentieth century, Bavinck cannot imagine the success of atheism. Toward its close, Updike (perhaps reflecting on his own struggle) can not only haunt his reader with the felt plausibility

---

3. John Updike, *In the Beauty of the Lilies* (New York: Fawcett Columbine, 1996), 5–7.

of a purely materialist universe, but his protagonist's faith quite literally *leaves* him. Throughout the novel, Clarence wishes that he could retain his lost religion, but the former minister cannot force himself to believe what he (despite himself) no longer finds believable. What is more, Updike's protagonist has his crisis of faith in the precise decade that Bavinck declares atheism impotent in its charms.[4] And indeed, despite Bavinck's inability to imagine an atheist universe, the recent historical consensus is that it was precisely during his lifetime that the atheist option (at least in the West) became a widespread-enough temptation to marshal adherents exceeding a handful of European elites.[5] Bavinck's failure of

---

4. When this manuscript was first prepared, James Eglinton's *Bavinck: A Critical Biography* (Grand Rapids: Baker Academic, 2020) was not yet available. Eglinton shows that late Bavinck did (in fact) take atheism quite seriously as a force in European intellectual culture. Nevertheless, the above comment stands as it pertains to the *rhetorical* impact of Bavinck's treatment of atheism in *Dogmatics* (considered in itself). John Updike's own religiosity is perhaps exemplified in his 1964 story in the *The New Yorker*, "The Christian Roommates," a fictionalized account of his early encounter (as roommates) with Christopher Lasch—and in his 1960 poem, "Seven Stanzas at Easter." In the latter, he does not commit to the resurrection of Jesus Christ but criticizes compromised modern accounts of the resurrection. It begins, "Make no mistake: if He rose at all, it was as His body."

5. Relevant sources would include Michael J. Buckley, *At the Origins of Modern Atheism* (New Haven: Yale University Press, 1987) and *Denying and Disclosing God: The Ambiguous Progress of Modern Atheism* (New Haven: Yale University Press, 2004); Gavin Hyman, *A Short History of Atheism* (New York: I. B. Taurus, 2010); Alan Charles Kors, *Atheism in France 1650–1729 Volume 1: The Orthodox Sources of Unbelief* (Princeton: Princeton University Press, 1990) and *Epicureans and Atheists in France 1650–1729* (New York: Cambridge University Press, 2016); Alister McGrath, *The Twilight of Atheism: The Rise and Fall of Disbelief in the Modern World* (New York: Doubleday, 2004); and James Turner, *Without God, without Creed: The Origins of Unbelief in America* (Baltimore: Johns Hopkins University Press, 1985). James Thrower, *The Alternative Tradition: Religion and the Rejection of Religion in the Ancient World* (The Hague: Mouton Publishers, 1980), and Tim Whitmarsh, *Battling the Gods: Atheism in the Ancient World* (New York: Knopf, 2015), argue that we can find precedent for atheism in antiquity and (specifically, Thrower) in the East. Ancient (and even Western paganism) often had the gods as suspended in (sometimes impersonal) movements and forces that transcended them. This could be seen as a form of proto-atheism (i.e., the ultimate metaphysical picture) even for ancient persons who *did* believe in the gods. There are also possible parallels to the modern atheism to be found in certain non-Western contexts, such as the Hindu school of Carvaka. One must be careful, nevertheless, not to read into the sources. On the methodological challenges regarding the handling of the historical material, see Buckley, *At the Origins of Modern Atheism*, 1–36. In any case, none of this stands in tension with historical claims concerning the very specific context within which *modern* Western atheism has emerged—its distinctive character directly formed through

imagination certainly does not imply his inability to intellectually struggle with the intersection between the claims of the Christian faith and the complexities of the modern world. In fact, this struggle largely defined his youth.[6] And certainly, developments that are clear to the historian in hindsight are sometimes muddled for actual historical actors. In any case, it would seem that modern persons do not have to go very far back into history to find themselves in a foreign country.[7] What, then, constitutes this ancestral foreignness as it pertains to the plausibility of atheism? Said differently, what changed between Herman Bavinck and John Updike?

MY HYPOTHESIS

In this volume, I make two parallel arguments. My first claim is that the most illuminating point of departure for interpreting the rise of unbelief over the last century and a half is the modern sense, shared by theists and non-theists alike, of divine absence. That is, whatever one believes propositionally about the question of God, God's existence is not *felt* to be obvious in the same way that, for instance, the fact that you are reading this right now seems obvious. It is common for modern religious persons to confess doubts that render the comparative confidence of previous centuries foreign. Certainly, I do not claim that God was crudely *visible* in the past,

---

the religious discourse in relation to which it developed its identity. Nor does any of this imply that modern atheism is monolithic or that it has responded to its religious alter ego in precisely the same fashion. On this, see Peter Watson, *The Age of Atheists: How We Have Sought to Live Since the Death of God* (New York: Simon & Schuster, 2014).

6. See Willem J. de Wit, *On the Way to the Living God: A Cathartic Reading of Herman Bavinck and an Invitation to Overcome the Plausibility Crisis of Christianity* (Amsterdam: VU University Press, 2011), 16–51. Unfortunately, de Wit is beholden to a view of Bavinck in which the theologian does not resolve this conflict. His work is helpful for highlighting excellent source material that is difficult to find elsewhere, but a more compelling account of Bavinck's relationship to modernity can be found in James Eglinton, *Trinity and Organism: Toward a New Reading of Herman Bavinck's Organic Motif* (New York: Bloomsbury, 2012).

7. The phrase "The past is a foreign country" is the opening line of L. P. Hartley's famous novel, originally published in 1953, *The Go-Between* (New York: NYRB Classics, 2011). It is relevant to note that Hartley's "foreign past" (even as of half a century later) is the turn of the previous century.

but divine *invisibility* was not ordinarily perceived to be relevant to the question of God's existence as such. When did it become the case, then, that the phenomenon of divine absence pressured human persons in the direction of non-belief? If nothing else, this is a curious property of modern religious consciousness. This contextualizes my second argument. My own hypothesis is that the salient factors that explain the relationship between divine absence and modern atheism are located at the intersection of the vast proliferation of modern technoculture, the way the world *seems* or *manifests* to correspondingly alienated laborers, and the resultant loss of a sense that one belongs to, and is caught up in, a history that transcends one. I use the term "technoculture" because I am not interested in technology or its proliferation in the abstract but in its concrete historical and cultural usage and the manner in which this shapes the human's relationship with his or her self, with others, and with the world. As will be apparent, particularly important and implicit in my usage of the term is an emphasis on the nature and effects of modern labor. In any case, my argument is supported (on the one hand) by noting the rise of unbelief at the same point that these features of our modern world became most prominent. But this is more deeply explained by a phenomenological analysis (defined below) of our technological and practical condition—highlighting *how* these identified features orient us to the world in such a way that it *seems* devoid of non-projected meaning and personhood (and, therefore, of God). This is, again, *irrespective* of whether or not one happens to believe in God. I am also keen to note that this does not constitute a comprehensive moral evaluation of these phenomena. Even in using the term "alienation," I am more immediately interested in a description of our phenomenal relation to the world than I am in questions of goodness or justice.

I locate my attempted contribution here, then, at two points. First is the claim that focusing specifically on this *shared* sensibility of divine absence (as opposed to broader considerations concerning the sheer number of unbelievers) is the most useful way to illuminate the starting place from which modern persons engage the question of God. Second, I aim to highlight the *specific* manner in which our *use* of modern technology and our *experience* of modern labor cultivate a posture toward reality that reshapes our plausibility structures and our sense of reality such that God's non-obviousness is *now* felt to be an argument against His being at all.

METHODOLOGICAL CONSIDERATIONS

My method in making this argument will typically involve engaging specific questions and texts that help get into or illuminate the theme of the particular chapter considered *broadly*—and then to fill out these broader insights with *specific* examples where relevant and useful. For instance, I will fill out a more general insight concerning the philosophy of technology with a more specific insight drawn from the impact of modern film. Broadly speaking, the interlocutors I engage are influenced by the phenomenological tradition and/or its methods (usually seen as birthed in the work of Edmund Husserl).[8] Generally, this philosophical school is concerned with a fine-grained analysis of the world as it is manifested, even subconsciously or tacitly, in human experience. So, for instance, a phenomenological analysis of a building would be less interested in the process by which it was made than in how the building seems to a person consciously experiencing it. For humans, this seeming is never a bundle of separate perceptions of weight, height, color, and so forth, but a kind of whole that contains implicit interpretations, judgments, and associations. This

8. Phenomenology belongs to the broader tradition of continental philosophy. To see it mapped in the context of that broader tradition, therefore, consult Dermot Moran, *Introduction to Phenomenology* (New York: Routledge, 2000) and David West, *Continental Philosophy: An Introduction* (New York: Polity, 2010). For a contemporary manual, see Robert Sokolowski, *Introduction to Phenomenology* (New York: Cambridge University Press, 1999).

tradition is useful for my purposes because in asking the question of God in its relationship to the modern technoculture, I want to ask how the world (or reality) seems to those caught up in that technoculture—and evaluate how this might shape our approach to the question of God. To the extent that I depart from this phenomenological method (for instance, in bringing up information drawn from sociological or statistical analysis), it will be in the *service* of claims that are chiefly established through phenomenological observation of the world. My motive here is to demonstrate the consistency between the research that highlights a social or statistical correlation between, say, the parallel emergence of modern technology and unbelief and the philosophical analysis that attempts to get inside and interpret *why* this correlation takes precisely the historical shape and content that it does. In aggregate, this represents a cumulative case for my hypotheses, with phenomenological analysis taking a primary role and sociological/statistical analysis taking a confirming/secondary role.

THE LIMITS AND SCOPE OF THIS PROJECT

It should be clear, then, that this is not (as such) a work of history. What I suggest draws upon the work of historians and the analysis of philosophers to give a *theoretically* plausible account of modern belief conditions. In my judgment, the argument has a prima facie plausibility that consequently generates questions that could potentially be answered by more fine-grained historical analyses. I will try to identify these as they arise in the text.

Furthermore, this volume is *not* meant to make a case for or against atheism. In one sense, the case I make herein is deflationary for atheists who assert that the recent prevalence of atheism is obviously due to its intellectual superiority over other options. Nevertheless, it is entirely possible to be persuaded of atheism and to reject this insufficient explanation of its recent success. In the fourth chapter and in the conclusion, it will be clear that I am nevertheless writing from the position of historic Christian creedal orthodoxy (specifically in the Magisterial Protestant tradition). In these chapters, I will reflect upon the implications of the first three chapters for practitioners of Christianity within my own branch of Christendom.

My title draws upon Charles Taylor's notion of what he terms the "bulwarks of belief."[9] By this, he refers to those background features of medieval Christian culture that (both consciously and subconsciously) rendered belief in God all but inevitable. By contrast, I speak of "bulwarks of unbelief," or those features of the modern world that render unbelief as at least plausible (a "living option," in the taxonomy of William James).[10]

I execute the above argument, then, in five steps. In chapter 1, I will place my argument concerning atheism in the context of the interdisciplinary scholarly debates over the meaning of modernity, secularization, and the so-called "disenchantment of the world." Herein, I seek to identify what, in my judgment, has been insufficiently weighted in scholarly interpretations of modern unbelief—particularly as it pertains to the above-mentioned relationship between unbelief, divine absence, and modern technoculture. In chapter 2, I will attempt to make a prima facie case that there is enough of a significant correlation between the emergence of these two phenomena to warrant a phenomenological and theoretical analysis of their causal relation. In chapter 3, therefore, I will make a philosophical case for a *causal* link between them. Specifically, I will argue that modern technoculture and labor render unbelief a living option by posturing us toward reality in such a way that it seems devoid of its demonstrable immaterial dimension(s). The case having been made, I will move on in chapter 4 to consider implications—albeit from the particular vantage point of a Protestant interested in maintaining traditional creedal Christian

---

9. Charles Taylor, *A Secular Age* (Cambridge: Harvard Belknap, 2007), 25–89.

10. In classic 1896 essay, "The Will to Believe," in *Pragmatism and Other Writings* (New York: Penguin, 2000), 191–264.

orthodoxy who nevertheless cannot escape the pressures that mit-igate against it. I argue that such persons cannot orient themselves relative to modern atheism without orienting themselves relative to the forces that give rise to it. Rejecting (however) both Ludditist nostalgia and progressivist religious revolution, I will argue that the modern moment is an opportunity to render orthodox belief more substantive and mature. This is because navigating these challenges requires an integration of the mind and will in order to reattune oneself to reality in its fullness. Such mediation (between mind and will) tends to suffocate nominal and shallow mediate positions between mature faith and unbelief. I will further argue that an underappreciated dimension of modern alienation and cultural disorientation is modern humankind's felt inability to be involved with and shape the history to which it nevertheless imag-ines itself to belong. Consequently, I will argue that recognizing the divine intentionality of the larger story of which this particular moment is a part (the *civitate Dei*) helps orient us to realities from which we cannot be alienated, even in principle. It is in the repen-tance and re-habituation of the whole person that we re-inhabit the world in such a manner as to render atheism less plausible. Via a new *ordo amoris*, we learn to maturely embrace precisely *this* particular moment and our limitations and opportunities within it (the attempted transcending of which is perhaps the chief idol-atry of modernity—as well as its chief anxiety). Finally, in a brief conclusion, I will take stock of the overall argument in relation to the quandary of modern pluralism, and I will attempt to show that the public veracity of the Christian faith depends upon the persuasion of whole persons.

ONE

Atheism and Narrative

PRELIMINARIES AND BOUNDARIES

Putting atheism in historical perspective turns out to be quite tricky. Certainly, we can identify (broadly speaking) its Enlightenment emergence, its Victorian-age overhaul, and its post-1960s popularization. Interpreting the historical forces to which this story belongs, however, is the subject of enormous controversy. Narratives of atheism are, in the relevant literature, bound up with narratives of modernity, secularization, and the so-called disenchantment of the world more generally. In seeking to interpret atheism, then, it is useful to summarize interpretations of its emergence in this larger scholarly conversation and to identify where I detect a curious gap, which I aim to (at least suggestively) fill in.

First, however, it is worth addressing the most common *popular* narrative concerning modern atheism—because it is not prima facie implausible and therefore worthy of a brief retort. Its constitutive features, suspended atop a kind of historical uniformitarianism, might simplistically be identified with two plot-points: (1) There have always been atheists lying around—for example, the trope of the village atheist—but we do not hear about most of them because they have historically been afraid to speak up (on account of probable persecution) or because they *hid* their atheism in the acceptable language of Christian orthodoxy.[1] (2) Nevertheless, religion used to seem more plausible when we knew less about the inner workings and origins of the material world. The scientific method successfully exposed these inner workings as predictable in nature—lacking the agency that was projected onto nature beforehand and that supposedly revealed God's primal agency. With respect to the question of origins, developments in biology (the theory of evolution) and physics (such as quantum theory) furnished humankind with all that was needed to explain, at least in principle, cosmic and human origins.[2] God, we might say, was out of a job—our progress in knowledge directly proportionate to the narrowing gaps left for God to fill. Carried along in these cultural winds, atheism was not a positive program as much as the remainder of a cosmic hourglass that ran out of God-grains. Certainly, there were and still are attempts to carve out a space for the divine in the (allegedly immaterial) private cabinet of the human soul, but the program of modern science is a universal acid[3] whose dissolution of the cosmos does not stop at the boundary between the material and the mental. The world of *mind* is increasingly reduced to the goings on of chemistry alone.[4] Whether it be the musings of Freud or the lab of the neuroscientist,

---

1. Jonathan Israel, the learned Enlightenment scholar, fairly frequently reads historical actors as closet atheists in his corpus.

2. Two eminently readable accounts of this sort can be found in Daniel Dennett, *Darwin's Dangerous Idea: Evolution and the Meaning of Life* (New York: Simon & Schuster, 1996) and Victor Stenger, *God and the Folly of Faith: The Incompatibility of Science and Religion* (Amherst, NY: Prometheus Books, 2012).

3. I am borrowing this acid image from Dennett, *Darwin's Dangerous Idea*, who uses the image of Darwinism more specifically.

4. A significant number of modern atheists have been influenced by the claims and arguments of neuroscientists like Paul and Patricia Churchland. Two of the four so-called new atheists (Daniel Dennett and Sam Harris) have done extensive work in the field of neuroscience and/or the philosophy of mind. P. M. S. Hacker and M. R. Bennett have written a minority report as it pertains to neuroscience, *Philosophical Foundations of Neuroscience* (New York: Wiley-Blackwell, 2003), and Edward Feser has written a minority report as it pertains to philosophy of mind, *Philosophy of Mind* (Oxford, UK: OneWorld Publications, 2006).

our understanding of the soul morphs (along with any supposed immaterial scaffolding that accounts for it) into an *epiphenomenon* of the real causal features of reality—none of which require divine aid to be what and as they are.

This particular reading of the situation is perhaps the most *culturally* significant one. For those lacking historical awareness (and sometimes even those with it), it is the most plausibly intuitive telling of the tale—written into our *gut* interpretations. Indeed, for this reason, not only is the emergence of atheism of curiosity to historians, but so is the meta-history of this *reading* of its emergence. That is to ask, just how did the relationship between religion and science come to be construed in this way? It is sometimes surprising for modern persons to discover that their perception that there has been a long war between science and religion, the so-called warfare model of their relation, is all but a relic among historians.[5] By the end of chapter 3 of this work, it should be clear why this might have become a plausible historical and normative picture.

In any case, of the two above-mentioned plot points, the first is the easier to address. In actual fact, heretics who have been persecuted for their beliefs have often been open about them. Many were willing martyrs for their cause(s). It would not seem likely that there is something unique about atheists that would prevent a

5. The paradigmatic statements of the view were John William Draper's *History of the Conflict between Religion and Science* (New York: d. Appleton, 1875), and Andrew Dickson White's two-volume *A History of the Warfare of Science with Theology in Christendom* (London: Macmillan and Company, 1898). For up-to-date assessments, see John Hedley Brooke, *Science and Religion: Some Historical Perspectives* (New York: Cambridge University Press, 1991); David Lindberg and Ronald Numbers, eds., *God and Nature: Historical Essays on the Encounter between Christianity and Science* (Berkeley: University of California Press, 1986) and *When Science and Christianity Meet* (Chicago: University of Chicago Press, 2003); and Ian Barbour, *Religion and Science: Historical and Contemporary Issues* (New York: HarperOne, 1997). See especially Derrick Peterson, *Flat Earths and Fake Footnotes: The Strange Tale of How the Conflict of Science and Christianity Was Written into History* (Eugene, OR: Cascade, 2021). In it, he traces the fine-grained historical steps by which this became a popular narrative—whereas I consider my own work a *theoretical* attempt to understand why this might be a very natural and obvious reading of the situation given a particular (to be explored) relationship to the world itself.

few of them from occasional boldness in this respect.[6] And hence, in the absence of explicit counterexamples, it seems unfitting to read closet atheism into all sorts of historical actors before it is clearly an expressed option (i.e., the explicit atheism or materialism, of persons such as d'Holbach and Diderot).[7] In many instances, prominently Baruch Spinoza and Pierre Bayle, excellent scholars are in profound disagreement about their religious orientation.[8] To be clear, the issue is not whether a thinker might have hidden heterodoxy in orthodox vernacular. This can and did occur frequently. The issue is whether we have any positive reason to think that there were *atheists* (or materialists) who did so prior to the middle of the eighteenth century.

The second plot point in this popular narrative is more difficult to address. And indeed, one might say that the whole of this work constitutes an attempt to problematize it. For all the ways it might be qualified, however, it will become clear that a stubborn grain of truth remains in the popular narrative. The question becomes what this truth *implies*. Is not the import written into the tale itself? To wit: (1) God used to explain things. (2) Now science does. (3) Therefore, there is no need for the God hypothesis. What complicates this is a corresponding historical transformation concerning the very definitions of explanation and God. I herein argue that the God-explanation rejected in modern atheism is neither the God nor the explanation affirmed

---

6. On premodern unbelief, see John Arnold, *Belief and Unbelief in Medieval Europe* (New York: Oxford University Press, 2005).

7. This starting point is argued in Buckley, *At the Origins of Modern Atheism*, 34. James Thrower argues that atheism is preceded by several anticipatory elements, but "D'Holbach is probably the first unequivocally professed atheist in the Western Tradition." *A Short History of Western Atheism* (Bungay: Pemberton Books, 1971), 106. For the argument of probable atheism prior to this, see David Berman, *A History of Atheism in Britain: From Hobbes to Russell* (London: Routledge, 1990), and Michael Hunter and David Wootton, eds., *Atheism from the Reformation to the Enlightenment* (Oxford: Clarendon Press, 1992).

8. See the excellent treatment of this issue by Dominic Erdozain, "A Heavenly Poise: Radical Religion and the Making of the Enlightenment," *Intellectual History Review* 27, no. 1 (2017), 71–96.

by, for instance, Thomas Aquinas. For believers and unbelievers alike, however, those definitions underwent a shift (sometimes quite unconsciously) in the early to late modern periods. In any case, only by using the definitions woven into the fabric of our current understanding do we then project onto the past the negative photocopy of this understanding and its inevitable inversion in ourselves. Left unimagined are historically commonplace frames of reference that we have forgotten and inside of which our current situation does not appear inevitable. And so, while our story is not entirely wrong, we have inherited and been shaped by its *distortions* as well as its truths. But philosophical and historical inquiry can problematize what might otherwise seem plain, pushing us toward the *gestalt* shift required to properly modify and maintain the popular narrative.

In order to gain some understanding conducive to achieving this *gestalt* shift, it is fitting to catalogue something like "schools of interpretation" as they pertain to the question(s) of the historical emergence (and meaning) of atheism, secularization, and modernity. Admittedly, this is to traverse a jungle and to lose the specificity of trees for the clarity of the forest. This is so not only with respect to carving out schools as such (since most of the writers I will consider do not fit so neatly into any box) but also in the attempt to treat such big questions as the emergence of atheism, the phenomenon of secularity, and the interpretation of modernity together. However, such costs are warranted. Important ground-level details are lost in any useful map. In our case, while the boundaries between the interpretive trends that we will identify are fluid, they are not arbitrary. It need not be particularly controversial to state that persons who might account for many factors nevertheless do not give equal explanatory weight to all of them. Furthermore, the blending of discussions concerning atheism, secularity, and modernity is not a matter of smashing together elements that are otherwise separate. Rather, while treatments of these topics might focus upon one of these labels, the concrete discussions often treat these as mutually defining phenomena.

Nevertheless, others' habits do not automatically justify one's own. Consequently, it is worth making explicit my own motivations for my own loose-handedness with the labels. We will have occasion to speak of each (disenchantment, modernity, secularization) more specifically as the argument develops. Nevertheless, each will be treated simultaneously for the following reason. In treating the rise of atheism, I am interested in not so much the simple fact and spread of atheism but rather the condition within which atheism becomes a plausible option in the first place.[9] Framed in this manner, the question concerning the emerging and increasing *plausibility* of atheism specifically cannot be separated from the phenomenon of secularization (i.e., the rise of unbelief and the decline of belief) more generally. The debate concerning the oft-cited disenchantment of the cosmos becomes relevant precisely because of its popularity as an explanation of these twin features of the modern world. And here we encounter our final term. While certainly the most elastic of our set in its many meanings (in sociology, religion, the arts, etc.), the phenomena we seek to describe are such a constitutive feature of whatever we tend to label modernity that the latter is inconceivable apart from the former—whether it is interpreted as the cause or consequent of the other terms. What straddles my interest with each of these labels, then, is only the extent to which they collectively elucidate how a metaphysically unfurnished cosmos becomes both possible and prevalent.

9. Taylor frames the question similarly in *A Secular Age*, as does James Turner in *Without God, without Creed*.

HOW ATHEISM BECAME POSSIBLE:
SCHOOLS OF INTERPRETATION

The most basic division in the taxonomy that follows is between those scholars who emphasize intellectual versus those who identify practical causes of our religious condition.[10] We will have occasion to complicate this below. More immediately, those who emphasize predominantly intellectual factors can be further divided into those who stress broadly scientific versus specifically philosophical transformations. We have briefly alluded to the former above but will mostly focus on the latter here.

Ideological Interpretations

Standing above everyone else in this camp (certainly in energy, debatably in cogency) is the historian of the Enlightenment, Jonathan Israel, whose impressive corpus of thick volumes sets him apart not only for his matchlessly encyclopedic knowledge but also for his controversial and unabashed criticism of the postmodern tendency to reduce intellectual history to an epiphenomenon of material factors.[11] Not only do intellectual arguments demonstrably shape history (in his judgment), but they often do so precisely to the extent that they are correct. Characteristically reflecting upon Spinoza or "Spinozism," Israel writes of the latter:

> What is that position? In essence, it is the acceptance of a
> one-substance metaphysics ruling out all teleology, divine
> providence, miracles, and revelation, along with spirits sep-
> arate from bodies and immortality of the soul, and denying
> that moral values are divinely delivered (with the corol-
> lary that therefore they have to be devised by men using
> terms relative to what is good or bad for society). Logically,

10. Here I am drawing on Taylor, *A Secular Age*, 25–89, in his notion of "bulwarks of belief," which (in our era) might be called bulwarks of unbelief or at least of neutrality.

11. A spirited defense of his project can be found in Jonathan Israel, *Democratic Enlightenment: Philosophy, Revolution, and Human Rights, 1750–1790* (New York: Oxford University Press, 2012), 1–35.

"Spinozism" always went together with the idea that this man-made morality should provide the basis for legal and political legitimacy—and hence that equality is the first principle of a truly legitimate politics. Always present also is Spinoza's concomitant advocacy of freedom of thought.[12]

Israel later writes:

> Spinoza's seemingly incomparable cogency (which greatly troubled Voltaire in his last years) cannot be dismissed, as many try to, as some sort of philosophical judgment on my part. Rather it is a historical fact that in the late eighteenth century, many people believed or feared (often much to their consternation) that one-substance monism, at least to all appearances, was much the most formidably coherent philosophy obtainable.[13]

According to Israel, the success of the so-called Radical Enlightenment (emphasizing monism, democracy, and freedom of thought) over against its moderate counterpart (the Lockean variant that supported God and monarchy and emphasized mere freedom of religion specifically rather than freedom of thought more generally) was largely a matter of David defeating Goliath—the slow march of philosophical competency disintegrating philosophical compromise. The dialectical tension between these enlightenments, indeed, has birthed our world—the moderate movement a sort of cultural and historical surrogate for the eventual triumph of its radical cousin in our own time.[14]

---

12. Ibid., 11.

13. Ibid., 15.

14. The distinction between radical and moderate Enlightenments is perhaps to be traced to the pioneering work of Margaret Jacob, *The Radical Enlightenment: Pantheists, Freemasons, and Republicans* (Lafayette, LA: Cornerstone, 2006). I have taken the image of a surrogate from Jonathan Israel's lecture, "Freedom of Thought Versus Freedom of Religion: An Eighteenth-Century—And Now Also a Twenty-First-Century Dilemma" (Thomas More Lecture, Radbouduniversiteit, November 10, 2006). Israel has made this case more

Of course, one cannot do justice to Israel in this small space, but a few brief comments are in order. Most obviously, the success of an idea is not necessarily a mark of its cogency. Israel's own frustration with the reign of postmodern scholarship would seem to suggest this. What is more, in this particular case, it is demonstrably not Spinoza's greater cogency that accounts for the success of his ideas. Nevertheless, following in Israel's own footsteps, I will forego the actual demonstration.[15] More substantively, even if freedom of thought and anti-monarchical tendencies are consistent with Spinozism, they are arguably not reducible to it. Indeed, one of the chief purveyors of the former was Pierre Bayle. Perhaps because of this, Israel reads Bayle as a cryptic monist. But this is a highly contested reading. T. J. Hochstrasser has argued that not only Bayle but many French philosophers argued for the freedom of conscience (and against political coercion) on the basis of a distinctive argument rooted in natural law.[16] Dominic Erdozain has likewise competently challenged an areligious reading not only of

---

sweepingly in his *A Revolution of the Mind: Radical Enlightenment and the Intellectual Origins of Modern Democracy* (Princeton: Princeton University Press, 2010).

15. A brief summary of a critique would be that Spinoza attributes a fairly classical notion of divine simplicity to things that are irreducibly composite in nature. Importantly, however, this calls into question Spinoza as a foundation for modern atheism. What is often missed is that Spinoza's monism collapses not only mind into matter but matter into mind. Spinoza argues for not merely a singular, but a simple substance, the metaphysical pedigree of which is more medieval metaphysics than anything else. That is, Spinoza could just as easily be called a "weird monotheist" (fusing the world into the medieval picture of a simple, non-composite God) as a "proto-atheist." In propositions 12 and 13 of his posthumously (1677) published *Ethics* (New York: Penguin, 1994), he denies that even material things are composed of parts, treating both as aspects of infinity. But this is as much evaporating any classical conception of nature as it is evaporating a classical conception of God, and it accounts for why Spinoza could be appropriated by several traditions with equal plausibility. A fitting critique is to be discovered in Herman Bavinck, *Philosophy of Revelation* (London: Longmans, Green, and Co., 1908; critical edition due from Hendrickson in 2018), and W. Norris Clarke, *The One and the Many: A Contemporary Thomistic Metaphysics* (Notre Dame: University of Notre Dame Press, 2001).

16. T. J. Hochstrasser, "The Claims of Conscience: Natural Law Theory, Obligation, and Resistance in the Huguenot Diaspora," in *New Essays on the Political Thought of the Huguenots of the Refuge*, ed. J. C. Laursen (Leiden: Brill, 1995), 15–51.

Bayle but of Spinoza himself.[17] Arguments concerning Bayle's religious sentiments do not, of course, resolve whether he held ideas in tension that history resolved in the direction of a more consistent monism. Consequently, it is important to note that there are many pedigrees of modern liberalism that (1) focus on intellectual development but also (2) identify different bases than Spinozism. Eric Nelson, for instance, has argued that both republicanism and the notion of freedom of thought largely emerged from Western engagement with Jewish sources.[18] Freedom of thought, or something moving obviously in that direction, was also given an explicitly theological foundation in the systems of Christian Thomasius, Samuel Pufendorf, Johann Hamann, and Johann Herder.[19] This is not to mention the development of the doctrine of the freedom of conscience during the Reformation and its political consequences.[20] And even this is arguably grounded in tensions within Western

---

17. See Erdozain, "A Heavenly Poise." Jacob, *The Radical Enlightenment*, 135–36, concurs that Bayle's religion was genuine. Bayle's defense of freedom of thought is given explicitly theological foundation in his *A Philosophical Commentary on These Words of the Gospel, Luke 14:23, "Compel Them to Come In, That My House May Be Full,"* (Indianapolis: Liberty Fund, 2006), 82–83, 77–78, 174–84, 202–3.

18. Eric Nelson, The Hebrew Republic: Jewish Sources and the Transformation of European Political Thought (Cambridge: Harvard University Press, 2001).

19. See Christian Thomasius, Institutes of Divine Jurisprudence (Indianapolis: Liberty Fund, 2011), 148, 509; Thomas Ahnert, Religion and the Origins of the German Enlightenment: Faith and the Reform of Learning in the Thought of Christian Thomasius (Rochester: University of Rochester Press, 2006), 53–56, 126; Ian Hunter, Rival Enlightenments: Civil and Metaphysical Philosophy in Early Modern Germany (New York: Cambridge University Press, 2001), 195, and his The Secularization of the Confessional State: The Political thought of Christian Thomasius (New York: Cambridge University Press, 2007), 166–67; Samuel Pufendorf, On the Duty of Man the Citizen According to the Law of Nature (New York: Cambridge University Press, 1991), 9, 35, 152; Oswald Bayer, A Contemporary in Dissent: Johann Georg Hamann as a Radical Enlightener (Grand Rapids: Eerdmans, 2012); and Johann Herder, Philosophical Writings (New York: Cambridge University Press, 2002), 370–74.

20. See especially Barry Shain, The Myth of American Individualism: The Protestant Origins of American Political Thought (Princeton: Princeton University Press, 1996); W. Bradford Littlejohn, The Peril and Promise of Christian Liberty: Richard Hooker, the Puritans, and Protestant Political Theology (Grand Rapids: Eerdmans, 2017).

Christian thought that lay dormant until post-Reformation political realities made their relief possible.[21]

Israel might not contest these points but simply argue that Spinoza's influence had a greater causal effect. Indeed, a large portion of his scholarship is a detailed outlining of Spinoza's reception in Europe.[22] But it would be likewise quite possible to trace the pedigree of a great number of thinkers whose influence was ubiquitous in Europe and continues to this present day and whose résumés involve several claims to contributing to the emergence of modern liberalism.[23] Moreover, it is quite obviously the case that there are those who have read and who still read Spinoza, disagree with him, but nevertheless defend the modern order on grounds other than monism or rationalism.[24] As it turns out, the historical record is as messy as the contemporary reality it presumably explains. Common cause can be had with uncommon justification, cobelligerency being one of history's few constants.

Perhaps most problematic in Israel's treatment, however, is that he does not clearly treat the medieval backdrop against which early modern views (including Spinoza's) were developed. The content of what he frequently terms "scholastic Aristotelianism" is more assumed than developed, with the inevitable effect that the modern reader need only project a slightly altered version of

21. Note the varying theses of Remi Brague, *Eccentric Culture: A Theory of Western Civilization* (South Bend, IN: Saint Augustine Press, 2009); Larry Siedentop, *Inventing the Individual: The Origins of Western Liberalism* (Cambridge: Harvard Belknap, 2014); and the treatment of the modern appropriation of "covenantal" thought in Glenn Moots, *Politics Reformed: The Anglo-American Legacy of Covenant Theology* (Columbia: University of Missouri Press, 2010).

22. This theme takes up a large portion of *Israel's Radical Enlightenment: Philosophy and the Making of Modernity 1650–1750* (New York: Oxford University Press, 2001).

23. See the roles of Martin Luther, John Calvin, and Richard Hooker as discussed in Littlejohn, *The Peril and Promise of Christian Liberty.*

24. Most obvious to the author—the author. Most prominently to the reader, the recent rights-discourse in its relationship to God as a guarantor of rights. Even among unorthodox branches of the major faiths in America, such discourse is extremely common and arguably quite heartfelt. President Barack Obama is certainly an example of one for whom these moral sentiments are not ultimately extractable from his spiritual and theological beliefs.

modern sensibilities onto our ancestors to determine their views rather silly and superstitious—for example, instead of believing in forests and fairies, presumably, we now simply believe in forests. Or, instead of believing in chemicals with intrinsic mind-like directedness, now we believe in chemicals moving mindlessly and mechanistically in obedience to extrinsic laws of physics. Of course, one cannot be expected to do everything in a book (even a large one), but this is arguably an illicit oversight. Properly understanding and evaluating the historic responses to Descartes and Spinoza requires a non-trivial grasp of the quite varied scholastic tradition.[25] And for modern persons, this arguably requires a *gestalt* shift in perspective. Most relevant for our purposes, we will not be able to understand the above-mentioned transitions in the very meaning(s) of cause and God in the early modern world without considering this development. As such, we move from our discussion of Israel to consider scholarship that identifies (1) shifting concepts of causality in the early modern period and (2) the Medieval foundation that allegedly made these shifts possible.

Many historians have identified the oft-termed "mechanical philosophy" of the early modern period and its attendant denial of final causes as the original philosophical fracture that terminated in a now unfixable fault line between reason and religion.[26] Several items have been emphasized in this development. First was the paradigmatic significance of mathematics as a standard for epistemic certainty in late medieval and early modern natural philosophy.[27] As noted by Gary Deason, "The successful application of mathematics to the physical world in the seventeenth

---

25. By contrast, see Richard Muller's method in his four-volume *Post-Reformation Reformed Dogmatics* (Grand Rapids: Baker Academic, 2003), in his treatment of early modern thought.

26. On the origin and development of the mechanical philosophy in general, see Brooke, *Science and Religion*, 117–51, and Steven Shapin, *The Scientific Revolution* (Chicago: University of Chicago Press, 1996), 15–64.

27. The classic essay on this is E. A. Burtt, *The Metaphysical Foundations of Modern Science* (New York: Doubleday, 1932).

century called into question the Aristotelian conception of the world and necessitated the development of a new conception that allowed the applicability of mathematics to nature."[28] He later states, "The driving force behind the development of mechanism was the belief that recent discoveries by Kepler, Galileo, Descartes, Stevin, and others of mathematical formulae describing physical phenomena could be given conceptual foundation if nature were seen as a collection of inert material particles governed by external mathematical laws."[29] In sum, those natural philosophers who used mathematical models to understand the goings-on of the material world were *successful*, and this success suggested some underlying picture of a universe that was subject to mathematics. A fairly natural response to these intellectual pressures would be the development of a notion of the universe as mechanical and a corresponding paradigm of causality as located in sequences of material contact (i.e., corpuscularianism). What needs emphasis here, however, is that this shift was one not merely of broad intellectual paradigm but also of method. Even if the overly grandiose world-picture were rejected as speculative, what might be retained is the *method*.[30] That is, whatever has predictive power and results is useful for excavating reality. And as it turned out, philosophically inflected or not, the world yielded its secrets to this posture.[31] And this, it is important to highlight, was an impressive contrast to the seemingly endlessly debated minutiae of medieval scholasticism. Like a universal acid, the story goes, the mechanical world-picture dissolved its ideological ancestors as well as any of its ideological

28. Gary B. Deason, "Reformation Theology and the Mechanistic Conception of Nature," in Lindberg and Numbers, *God and Nature*, 168.

29. Ibid., 169.

30. That these could be separated is emphasized by Shapin, *The Scientific Revolution*, 57–64.

31. On the development of the scientific method, the most up-to-date study is Stephen Gaukroger, *The Emergence of a Scientific Culture: Science and the Shaping of Modernity, 1210–1685* (New York: Oxford University Press, 2009), which is part of a multi-volume effort.

progeny who sought to follow their grandparents in carving out a space of non-mechanical explanation and being.

Iconic in both mathematical and methodological emphases is, of course, Rene Descartes. In his famous *Discourse on Method* (1637), he recalls the moment in the development of his methodology in which he decided that he "would be borrowing all that is best in geometrical analysis and algebra, and correcting all the defects of the one by means of the other."[32] Of course, Descartes also embodied the tensions of such a view. Reducing the world to passive matter subject to mathematical laws and whatever did not fit into this material scheme to a projection of the human mind (i.e., the famous distinction between primary and secondary qualities), Descartes ultimately separated the mind, not to mention all spiritual realities, from the material world—a dualism that has occupied Western philosophy ever since.[33]

It is important to highlight, however, that in the early modern period, it was not always considered obvious that the mechanical paradigm of causality stood in any necessary tension with traditional Christian orthodoxy.[34] In point of fact, many (particularly among the Cartesians) believed that the arguments for the existence of God were better secured under it than in traditional scholastic categories.[35] What is more, much of the negotiation

---

32. Rene Descartes, *Discourse on Method and Meditations on First Philosophy* (New York: Hackett, 1999), 12.

33. Important studies can be found in Theo Verbeek, *Descartes and the Dutch: Early Reactions to Cartesian Philosophy 1637–1650* (Carbondale: Southern Illinois University Press, 1992), and Walter Ott, *Causation & Laws of Nature in Early Modern Philosophy* (New York: Oxford University Press, 2009).

34. An important study along these lines is Aza Gourdriaan, *Reformed Orthodoxy and Philosophy, 1625–1750* (Leiden: Brill, 2006), who shows that orthodox reformed theologians extensively defended the same confessional dogmas with different philosophical systems. A famous tension was that between Gisbertus Voetius (1589–1676) and Johannes Coeccius (1603–1669). Standard studies of them are to be found in J. A. van Ruler, *The Crisis of Causality: Voetius and Descartes on God, Nature, and Change* (Leiden: Brill, 1995), and Willem van Asselt, *The Federal Theology of Johannes Cocceius* (Leiden: Brill, 2001).

35. See William Ashworth Jr., "Christianity and the Mechanistic Universe," in Lindberg and Numbers, *When Science and Christianity Meet*, 61–84.

between scholastic and mechanistic conceptions of the world involved highly nuanced mediating positions at every point on the spectrum.[36] Nevertheless, it would be accurate to state that the mechanism-cum-atheism concern was an immediate and perpetual reaction to the mechanical philosophy among at least *some* European intellectuals.[37] And whatever *might* have potentially occurred, arguably the cynical prediction *actually* came to pass.[38]

However, a sufficient account would need to emphasize the progressive *abandonment* of scholasticism rather than simply the *emergence* of new ideas that, as just suggested, admitted of some variety. It would nevertheless be fair to say that to whatever extent these occurred together and in a zero-sum fashion, several consequences tended to follow. Different historians give prominence to different elements. Deason, for instance, writes, "When the mechanists rejected Aristotle's understanding of nature, they simultaneous rejected the theory of God's cooperation with nature."[39] Given the prominent role that I will later argue belongs to modern technology, Steven Shapin highlights what I consider to be a particularly important change: "The very idea of construing nature as a machine, and using understandings derived from machines to interpret the physical structure of nature, counted as a violation of one of the most basic distinctions of Aristotelian philosophy. This was the contrast between what was natural and what was contrived or artificial."[40] In a now famous study, Amos Funkenstein further argues that in the early modern period, we witness a philosophical shift wherein several of God's attributes are problematized and reexplained in ways consistent with early modern intellectual

---

36. See Ott, *Causation & Laws of Nature in Early Modern Philosophy*.

37. See, for instance, Brooke, *Science and Religion*, 139–44.

38. An important, careful, and nuanced attempt to draw some fine-grained connections can be found in David Leech, *The Hammer of the Cartesians: Henry More's Philosophy of Spirit and the Origins of Modern Atheism* (Leuven: Peeters, 2013).

39. Deason, "Reformation Theology and the Mechanistic Conception of Nature," 169.

40. Shapin, *The Scientific Revolution*, 30.

trends.[41] While these might seem like trivial concessions to modern ears, what unites each of them is an increasing collapse of God's being into the being of the world, such that the being of God and of creatures exists in a common reservoir of being-as-such. This stands in contrast to the Thomist and more traditional notion of the "analogy of being," wherein God just is Being-as-such and the being of creatures (including creaturely causal-space) is a donation of God's own radically other Being by virtue of his (ultimately singular) wisdom and will.[42]

In the above view, then, the transformation of the early modern notion of causality is arguably suspended atop (or at least attended by) an even more fundamental transformation in the understanding of God.[43] Now in a zero-sum match with creaturely being/cause, it was then important to state that the natures of the various things that furnished the cosmos did not limit God. Indeed, rather than having their own causal space, what we call their nature is not a formal reality but simply an ordinary name (hence the nomenclature of nominalism) attributed to a regularity in God's will as he effects material causes. Rather than active in nature, material items are passively moved according to laws of nature or forces that move them about (ultimately God's own will). This voluntarism, in its insistence on the relation of created things to God's will rather than to his mind, presumably laid the groundwork for the scientific method. That is, since God cannot be constrained and his will could have been otherwise, there is no necessary connection between causes and effects. Therefore, things are to be understood not through philosophical reflection upon their

---

41. Amos Funkenstein, *Theology and the Scientific Imagination from the Middle Ages to the Seventeenth Century* (Princeton: Princeton University Press, 1986).

42. See Clarke, *The One and the Many*, for a fuller explanation. This theme will also become relevant in subsequent chapters.

43. Two important treatments of the modern transformation of God are William Placher, *The Domestication of Transcendence: How Modern Thinking about God Went Wrong* (Louisville: Westminster John Knox Press, 1996), and Philip Clayton, *The Problem of God in Modern Thought* (Grand Rapids: Eerdmans, 2000).

natures and their powers but rather by the observed regularity of one thing following another. Often said to have been mediated by the Reformation, these emphases laid the groundwork for the kind of epistemic skepticism fitted to a burgeoning scientific culture.[44] Indeed, this narrative (or versions of it) has perhaps become *the* dominant account in scholarship concerning the original fracture that terminated in modern secularization.[45]

While an elegant account, it has the significant deficiency of being almost entirely wrong—at least as a historical hypothesis. Michael Horton has recently pointed out several of its flaws, including its neglect of recent scholarship on the key figure of John Duns Scotus (the alleged source of the problem) as well as the neglect of primary source evidence in the above historians' typical treatment of the Reformation.[46] Concerning the latter, Richard Muller has devastatingly argued against a Reformation rejection of the analogy of being,[47] and Peter Harrison has extensively shown that the primary sources argue against the role suggested for voluntarism by this narrative in the development of early modern science.[48] What is more, the emergence and influence of early modern

---

44. An influential account is that of Louis Dupre, *Passage to Modernity: An Essay in the Hermeneutics of Nature and Culture* (New Haven: Yale University Press, 1993).

45. Pioneered in some of its particulars by Etienne Gilson, Francis Oakley, and Louis Dupre, this story has been developed and defended more recently by historians and philosophers such as John Milbank, Michael Gillespie, and Brad Gregory. On Dupre, see ibid. On Milbank and his intellectual conversation-partners, see James K. A. Smith, *Introducing Radical Orthodoxy: Mapping a Post-Secular Theology* (Grand Rapids: Baker Academic, 2004). Gillespie's account can be found in *The Theological Origins of Modernity* (Chicago: University of Chicago Press, 2009), and Gregory's in *The Unintended Reformation: How a Religious Revolution Secularized Society* (Cambridge: Harvard Belknap, 2015). Gregory's account, as the title suggests, ropes in the typical treatment of the Protestant Reformation in this school of thought.

46. See Michael Horton, Review of Brad Gregory, *The Unintended Reformation* (The Gospel Coalition, February 15, 2016), https://www.thegospelcoalition.org/article/book-reviews-the-unintended-reformation.

47. Richard A. Muller, "Not Scotist: Understandings of Being, Univocity, and Analogy in Early-Modern Reformed Thought," *Reformation and Renaissance Review* 14, no. 2 (2012), 127–50.

48. Peter Harrison, "Voluntarism and Early Modern Science," *History of Science* 40, no. 1 (2002), 63–89.

skepticism can just as well be related to specific political and religious events (such as the spiritual turmoil caused by the Avignon papacy) as well as to the simple fact that certain ancient skeptical texts had been recently rediscovered during the Renaissance.[49] And if this were not enough, the primary hosts of these intellectual trends were actually Roman Catholic rather than Protestant. In the Catholic Counter-Reformation, it was common to use skeptical arguments to mitigate against the newer Protestant emphasis on the veracity of Scripture.[50] Granted, the early modern epistemic crisis did have a Protestant inflection because such crises were a part of much larger trends in the early modern period—covering questions ranging from soteriology to science. This was an era asking both "How can I be saved?" and "How can I know anything at all?"[51] This is not to mention the post-Reformation political contexts (such as the religious wars) that gave these intellectual trends urgent practical purchase. Stephen Toulmin has famously argued that Descartes's project makes sense largely against the frustrated efforts of European confessionalists to find common ground to resolve their differences. The development of his method, then, was an attempt to discover a way beyond such impasses.[52] In any case, there were also intellectual questions and trends for which the Protestant Reformation acted as a natural parent rather than as a

49. See Horton, Review of Gregory, *The Unintended Reformation*, for the former point, and Richard Popkin, *The History of Scepticism: From Savonarola to Bayle* (New York: Oxford University Press, 2003), for the latter point.

50. See Richard Popkin, "Skepticism and the Counter-Reformation in France," *Archive for Reformation History* 51 (1960), 58–88.

51. See Susan E. Schreiner, *Are You Alone Wise: The Search for Certainty in Early Modern Europe* (New York: Oxford University Press, 2011), as well as the important study of Henry van Leeuwen, *The Problem of Certainty in English Thought 1630–1690* (The Hague: Martinus Nijhoff, 1963). An extremely important contributor to the overall discussion of certainty (both religious and philosophical) was Richard Hooker, on whom see Littlejohn, *The Peril and Promise of Christian Liberty*.

52. See Stephen Toulmin, *Cosmopolis: The Hidden Agenda of Modernity* (Chicago: University of Chicago Press, 1990).

mere surrogate for medieval progenitors.[53] As well, it is important to reiterate that all sorts of hybrids were available. It was entirely possible in the early modern period to blend scholastic medieval philosophical sensibilities alongside a positive evaluation of early modern science and its attendant attitudes. An especially important hybrid in this respect is Leibniz.[54]

Before moving on from this view, I want to hold in reserve its explanatory use as at least having identified the *substance* of the shift between a medieval and a modern conception of being in its relationship to God and to causality. We can reasonably debate when, by whom, and for what reason(s) this transformation occurred, but not *that* it occurred. I will attempt to salvage elements of this narrative below. For the moment, let us move on to other idea-centric hypotheses concerning the pedigree of unbelief.

Of course, some stories of modernity reach far enough into antiquity to be described as epic, and some, by contrast, trace the salient moments of modernity-cum-materialism to specific occurrences after the European Enlightenment. Epic accounts usually genealogize specific features of modernity that would eventually render atheism ideologically or politically possible. Of particular importance here is the work of Hans Blumenberg, whose *The Legitimacy of the Modern Age* portrays modernity as the resolution of a tension that is as old as the Christianity-Gnosticism conflict, whose partial resolution is achieved by the time of Augustine but whose final resolution awaits the modern triumph of an ethos of curiosity as a virtue.[55] Blumenberg was, of course, responding to

---

53. Peter Harrison's revisionist efforts are key here. See especially *The Bible, Protestantism, and the Rise of Natural Science* (New York: Cambridge University Press, 1998) and *The Fall of Man and the Foundations of Science* (New York: Cambridge University Press, 2007).

54. On whom see Irena Backus, *Leibniz: Protestant Theologian* (New York: Oxford University Press, 2016) and Arnaud Pelletier, ed., *Leibniz's Experimental Philosophy* (Stuttgart: Franz Steiner Verlag, 2017). Peter Harrison, "Voluntarism in Early Modern Science," also calls into question certain often-thought anti-scholastic elements in Boyle.

55. Hans Blumenberg, *The Legitimacy of the Modern Age* (Cambridge: MIT Press, 1983).

another historical genealogy of modernity, that of Karl Löwith, whose *Meaning in History* traces our current fragmentation to the secularization of Christian eschatology in the modern science of history.[56] Moving toward more recent efforts, Charles Taylor (whose most significant contribution will be discussed below) puts the modern world against the backdrop of a history of understandings of the *self*.[57] The modern concept of the self was not intended to terminate in modernity but was necessary to ground the self/world, public/private, and faith/reason dichotomies that are definitive of the modern order. Without this fundamental dualism, the reduction of the world to passive and agentless material (with the Humean implications of a split between fact and value) would not even be possible, or perhaps even conceivable.[58] Perhaps not in content, but arguably in scope, these scholars are largely working within the genealogizing tendencies of twentieth-century continental philosophy, whose patron saint and exemplar in precisely this regard is Martin Heidegger.[59]

These tales are not usually clean linear narratives but attempt to identify the development of patterns that would eventually become

56. Karl Löwith, *Meaning in History* (Chicago: University of Chicago Press, 1949). For the Löwith/Blumenberg debate, see Stephen A. McKnight, "The Legitimacy of the Modern Age: The Löwith-Blumenberg Debate in Light of Recent Scholarship," *The Political Science Reviewer* 19 (1990), 177–95.

57. Charles Taylor, *Sources of the Self: The Making of Modern Identity* (Cambridge: Harvard University Press, 1992). Taylor's hypothesis could also be paired with Siedentop's *Inventing the Individual*.

58. I will have occasion to return to this theme in later chapters. This argument has been made in ways ranging from brilliant to bizarre by Michel Foucault, *The Order of Things* (New York: Vintage, 1970); George Steiner, *Real Presences* (Chicago: University of Chicago Press, 1989); and Owen Barfield, *Saving the Appearances: A Study in Idolatry* (Hanover, NH: Wesleyan, 1988).

59. Heidegger, of course, traces the origin of our modern dilemma all the way back to the beginning of Western dualism. See Martin Heidegger, *Early Greek Thinking: The Dawn of Western Philosophy* (San Francisco: Harper, 1985). An important conversation along these lines is in David Michael Levin, ed., *Modernity and the Hegemony of Vision* (Berkeley: University of California Press, 1993).

more prominent in Western culture.[60] Arguably, these epic developments render later outcomes a possibility rather than a necessity. Many historians tend, therefore, to interpret the modern world in light of the *recent* rather than the ancient past. Even if these more proximate events are only possible in light of more distant developments—*visible* cracks emerging from deeper fractures—it is only the latter, some argue, that render our modern belief conditions inevitable (rather than merely possible).

The chief culprits here are, of course, the European Enlightenment and the advent of Darwinian evolutionary theory. It would be difficult to read Peter Gay's elegant account of the Enlightenment without experiencing a sense of the intellectual power of the *philosophes* as well as the devastating capacity of their pen—whether it be in the critique of speculative system-building generally or their aggressive but fine-grained surgical use of the scalpel of criticism on revealed religion specifically.[61] In contrast to Israel's Enlightenment, Gay's analogue is not predominantly a philosophical movement. Indeed, Gay's *philosophes* were critical of philosophical abstraction. They were men of raw intellectual power whose chief virtue is a fierce honesty in concert with a preference for saying "I don't know" over dogmatic hubris. That is, their chief legacy was an ethos rather than a body of doctrines. Indeed, the relation between their ethos and later unbelief is sufficiently well established that even those who trace the philosophes' ethos to religious sources can nevertheless see it as the seedbed of eventual unbelief.[62]

Of course, one momentous shove in the latter direction, occurring between the era of the *philosophes* and the popularization

---

60. It is worth re-highlighting the work of Brague, *Eccentric Culture*, here. His vision is perhaps larger than anyone else's.

61. Peter Gay, *The Enlightenment: The Rise of Modern Paganism* (New York: Knopf, 1966).

62. See Dominic Erdozain, *The Soul of Doubt: The Religious Roots of Unbelief from Luther to Marx* (New York: Oxford University Press, 2016).

of unbelief in the late nineteenth century, was the publication of Charles Darwin's *On the Origin of Species* in 1859. What came to be known as "freethought" had a significant history before this.[63] But many who would later become atheists would have agreed with the recently iconic statement of Richard Dawkins that while "atheism might have been logically tenable before Darwin, Darwin made it possible to be an intellectually fulfilled atheist."[64] Nevertheless, we must be careful to avoid anachronism here. Contemporary debates over faith and science in America perhaps give the current polarities a sense of being a historically inevitable outcome.[65] This is wrong both historically and philosophically, however. Concerning the former, David Livingstone has spent a career exhaustively demonstrating the large diversity of initial and continued reactions to Darwin on several continents by persons from all over the theological and philosophical spectrum.[66] In point of fact, many orthodox theologians saw no threat even to the book of Genesis in Darwin's contentions—drawing on many ancient exegetical foundations as well as a host of related disciplines to align the content of both special and general revelation with one another (which, contrary to the popular narrative, has been the usual move when such tensions arose in ecclesiastical history).[67] This could be seen

---

63. See Edward Royle, *Victorian Infidels: The Origins of the British Secularist Movement 1791–1866* (Lanham, MD: Rowman & Littlefield, 1974), and Susan Jacoby, *Freethinkers: A History of American Secularism* (New York: Metropolitan Books, 2005). For an account of its alter ego in England (where such influences were equally common), see Timothy Larsen, *Crisis of Doubt: Honest Faith in Nineteenth Century England* (New York: Oxford University Press, 2009).

64. Richard Dawkins, *The Blind Watchmaker: Why the Evidence of Evolution Reveals a Universe Without Design* (New York: Norton, 1986), 6.

65. See Ronald Numbers, *The Creationists: From Scientific Creationism to Intelligent Design* (New York: Harvard University Press, 2006).

66. See David Livingstone, *Darwin's Forgotten Defenders: The Encounter Between Evangelical Theology and Evolutionary Thought* (Vancouver: Regent College Publishing, 1984), *Adam's Ancestors: Race, Religion, and the Politics of Human Origins* (Baltimore: Johns Hopkins University Press, 2011), and *Dealing with Darwin: Place, Politics, and Rhetoric in Religious Engagements with Evolution* (Baltimore: Johns Hopkins University Press, 2014).

67. The most thorough history of the interpretation of the most important text is Andrew J. Brown, *The Days of Creation: A History of Christian Interpretation of Genesis*

as an ad hoc adjustment of theology to science, but the response to Darwinism was not endless exegetical elasticity but also philosophical and principled.[68] Of course, the actual history played out the way that it has. It is sufficiently clear that many persons attribute their atheism to their Darwinism. But to the extent that one recognizes that there is no necessary historical or philosophical relationship between the two, one will seek deeper explanations elsewhere (as in much of the above).

Much more could be said concerning idea-centric interpretations of the rise of unbelief. I have not, for instance, touched upon Ludwig Feuerbach[69] or Friedrich Nietzsche[70]—not to mention popularizers of unbelief such as Robert Ingersoll.[71] And this is not to mention the contributions of modern existentialism or the advent of so-called postmodernity, each of which presumably offers its own distinctive possibilities for an intellectually

---

1:1–2:3 (Blandford Forum, UK: Deo Publishing, 2014). Other important studies are Jean de Fraine, *The Bible and the Origin of Man* (Staten Island: Alba House, 1967), and Mark Noll and David Livingstone, eds., *B. B. Warfield: Evolution, Science, and Scripture—Selected Writings* (Grand Rapids: Baker, 2000). Regarding the point that this sort of negotiation between religion and science is fairly traditional, see Ronald Numbers, ed., *Galileo Goes to Jail and Other Myths about Science and Religion* (Cambridge: Harvard University Press, 2009).

68. These matters are obviously still debated, but there are and always have been many attempts to conciliate between Darwin and classical metaphysics. Important studies here are Etienne Gilson, *From Aristotle to Darwin and Back Again: A Journey in Final Causality, Species, and Evolution* (San Francisco: Ignatius Press, 2009); Conor Cunningham, *Darwin's Pious Idea: Why the Ultra-Darwinists and Creationists Both Get It Wrong* (Grand Rapids: Eerdmans, 2010); and David Oderberg, *Real Essentialism* (New York: Routledge, 2007); 201–40. This is not to mention those who (via the process philosophy of A. N. Whitehead or otherwise) find in Darwinian evolution spiritual and religious inspiration. See, for instance, Frederick Turner, *Natural Religion* (New York: Routledge, 2006).

69. His work *The Essence of Christianity*, originally published in 1841, is still perhaps the greatest critique of the Christian faith ever written—and still inspires its critics. Ludwig Feuerbach, *The Essence of Christianity* (Amherst, NY: Prometheus Books, 1989).

70. On the reception of the latter in America, see Jennifer Ratner-Rosenhagen, *American Nietzsche: A History of an Icon and His Ideas* (Chicago: University of Chicago Press, 2011).

71. On whom, see Susan Jacoby, *The Great Agnostic: Robert Ingersoll and American Freethought* (New Haven: Yale University Press, 2013).

fulfilled atheism.[72] These take on an especially important role in the modern critique of the science that originally (so we are sometimes told) birthed the materialist world in the first place.[73]

Before we move on to consider schools of thought that emphasize more practical than ideological factors, a few comments are in order. In cataloging these genealogies of modernity and/or unbelief, one obvious fact is that multiple ideological features might be at play. And indeed, just as some accounts blend ideological and practical features, some blend one ideological feature with another (though each of the above has been given primacy by one account or another)—or emphasize multiple *results*. So, for instance, the mechanistic world-picture can just as well lead to intelligent design as it does to atheism. This was as true in the eighteenth century as it is today. After Darwin and twentieth-century physics, however, the latter path was far more frequently taken—with many notable exceptions.[74] Second, it is essential to remember that while some metaphors and modes of thought might become dominant in a particular era, different (and often contradictory) ways of seeing the world can always remain available options. And indeed, just as today, these contradictions are sometimes to be found incubating

72. One thinks of Jean-Paul Sartre and Albert Camus in the former category and of Richard Rorty and Jacques Derrida in the latter.

73. Philosophically influential studies along these lines are, of course, Thomas Kuhn, *The Structure of Scientific Revolutions* (Chicago: University of Chicago Press, 2012), and Paul Feyerabend, *Against Method* (New York: Verso, 2010). Exemplary historical studies that problematize naïve scientism can be found especially in Simon Schaffer and Steven Shapin, *Leviathan and the Air-Pump: Hobbes, Boyle, and the Experimental Life* (Princeton: Princeton University Press, 2011) as well as Shapin's *Never Pure: Historical Studies of Science as if It Was Produced by People with Bodies Situated in Time, Space, Culture, and Society, and Struggling for Credibility and Authority* (Baltimore: Johns Hopkins University Press, 2010).

74. Most prominently, Anthony Flew, *There Is a God: How the World's Most Notorious Atheist Changed His Mind* (New York: HarperCollins, 2009). On the other hand are those like Steven Hawking and Leonard Mlodinow, *The Grand Design* (New York: Bantam, 2010), who believe that modern physics renders the universe without any need for God. For an evaluation of this debate that transcends this way of framing the issue, see Stephen M. Barr, *Modern Physics and Ancient Faith* (Notre Dame: University of Notre Dame Press, 2003), and Robert Spitzer, *New Proofs for the Existence of God: Contributions of Contemporary Physics and Philosophy* (Grand Rapids: Eerdmans, 2010).

in a single mind. While particular instances of this are a matter of debate, it would seem that the phenomenon itself should not be particularly controversial.[75] Whatever picture of things holds us captive (whether Kuhn's "paradigm," Foucault's "*episteme*," or Taylor's "social imaginary"), it remains the case that (1) the success of a dominant idea does not occur overnight; (2) there are, therefore, eras wherein eventually successful ideas are but one possibility alongside others; (3) even after these are generally accepted, they only remain a *dominant* possibility; and (4) other dormant possibilities can be and often are resurrected.[76] All of this to preliminarily make the following somewhat commonplace point: Ideas do not cause anything as such. They are appropriated by *persons* who (apart from significant innovation) tend to be shaped by and draw from options that are readily available to interpret the world around them.

Jonathan Israel is certainly right, therefore, to criticize philosophies that reduce all ideological forces to material or social concerns. But he is wrong if he imagines that ideas have telic forces that are not themselves inflected by concrete historical actors in concrete historical situations. Steven Shapin writes, by contrast, that "if we want ultimately to understand the appeal of the mechanical metaphors in the new scientific practices ... we shall ultimately have to understand the power relations of an early modern European society whose patterns of living, producing, and political ordering were undergoing massive changes as feudalism gave way to early capitalism."[77] Indeed, in much of the above

---

75. A contemporary example might be Thomas Nagel, *Mind and Cosmos: Why the Materialist Neo-Darwinian Conception of Nature Is Almost Certainly False* (New York: Oxford University Press, 2012), who (in my judgment) incoherently combines a kind of cosmic teleology with a version of atheist naturalism. For the impossibility of this, see Clarke, *The One and the Many.*

76. We have already seen this with the early modern resurrection of skepticism. Another instance might be the modern and recent resurgence of scholasticism! Indeed, no less an authority than Toulmin, *Cosmopolis*, 11, argues that premodern thought-categories are one of the few live options in the current postmodern context.

77. Shapin, *The Scientific Revolution*, 33.

scholarship, we can already detect in these brief allusions (despite an overly neat taxonomy) the blend of concrete historical factors that are necessary to view alongside their ideological correlates to render a more complete explanatory picture.

To fully appreciate this, then, we need to consider those interpretations of modernity that emphasize practical rather than ideological factors—even those that wrongly reduce the latter to an epiphenomenon of materialist causes. If *we* cannot fully grasp the role of one without the other (even when considering ourselves), then it would seem that the same was true our ancestors.[78] A few preliminary caveats and clarifications are in order, however. First, it is important to state that ideas have *tacit* as well as *overt* force. That is, to speak of an idea as available does not necessarily imply that the negotiation between an idea and a historical actor is *only* one of conscious decision. Rather, a picture can "hold us captive."[79] For this reason, I am not entirely persuaded that one has refuted the significance of voluntarism in early modern thought, for instance, if a scholar merely notes its frequent rejection. Even those who consciously reject it might, in hindsight, be quite obviously shaped by it in their thought patterns, categories, problems, and emphases. It is clear that the human relationship to thought, language, and interpretation is not entirely conscious.[80] Second,

---

78. Admittedly, this contention implicitly depends upon some concept of human nature. One might suggest many tomes on this massive subject, but because the general is best approached through the specific, one could not do better than to engage with Richard Sennett, *The Craftsman* (New Haven: Yale University Press, 2008), who captures an instance of what might plausibly be called "the universal" (the primal human drive toward engagement in a project). On historical method in particular, one could again address this directly, but one who wisely engages a philosophy of history with a sophisticated anthropology is Jose Ortega y Gasset, *History as a System: And Other Essays Toward a Philosophy of History* (New York: Norton, 1941), on whom see Julian Marias, *History of Philosophy* (New York: Dover, 1967), 442–68.

79. I take this phrase from Hubert Dreyfus and Charles Taylor, *Retrieving Realism* (Cambridge: Harvard University Press, 2015)—both of whose work is also relevant for the contention in the previous footnote.

80. See ibid. for an intelligent account of this. Taylor's fullest engagement of this topic can be found in his recent *The Language Animal: The Full Shape of Human Linguistic Capacity* (Cambridge: Harvard Belknap, 2016).

however, this does not afford any license to speculate about the impact of the unconscious apart from evidence. Nor should we be cynical that a human *can* take a posture of excavation toward the self and the world.[81] And while this posture is perhaps more the exception than the rule, a portion of those who take it can nevertheless become influential in subsequent generations.[82] Finally, then, it is important not to treat each generation or intellectual as some combination of their predecessors. Humans do cultivate, but they also create—and even human cultivation is ultimately an activity of re-creating (consciously or not).[83] Such a caveat, as we shall see, is not merely a philosophical aside but also a caution that helps us to be careful in interpreting the historical data, while also helping us to more insightfully interpret ourselves.

Practical (Circumstantial) Interpretations

It is a rare convenience that one of the pioneering critics of idealism, Karl Marx, is also a crucial interpreter of modernity itself. The German philosopher famously described the modern order as one in which "all that is solid melts into air, all that is holy is profaned, and man is at last compelled to face with sober senses his

---

81. In all of these reflections, I am particularly influenced by the cultural liturgies project of James K. A. Smith in its treatment of the manner in which humans are formed through liturgized desires. See his *Desiring the Kingdom: Worship, Worldview, and Cultural Formation* (Grand Rapids: Baker Academic, 2009) and *Imagining the Kingdom: How Worship Works* (Grand Rapids: Baker Academic, 2013). I criticize his work, nevertheless, for failing to account sufficiently for the role of the critical faculties in human formation. See my appreciative critique of his overall corpus (by the date of publication), Joseph Minich, "Class(ic) ifying Jamie Smith," Calvinist International, May 27, 2013, https://calvinistinternational. com/2013/05/27/classicifying-jamie-smith/.

82. Here I am particularly thinking of James Hunter's contention that it is fundamentally elites who tend to change culture via what he calls "centers of cultural capital." See James Davison Hunter, *To Change the World: The Irony, Tragedy, and Possibility of Christianity in the Late Modern World* (New York: Oxford University Press, 2010).

83. On this, see Robert Pogue Harrison, *Juvenescence: A Cultural History of Our Age* (Chicago: University of Chicago Press, 2014), and Andy Crouch, *Culture Making: Recovering our Creative Calling* (Downers Grove, IL: InterVarsity Press, 2013).

real conditions of life and his relations with his kind."[84] Humanity's real conditions are, of course, the epoch-making rise of the bourgeois class alongside its social implicates in the constantly shifting modes of production. Not to be missed, however, is that it is at last that human beings are compelled to face their condition. Capitalism does not invent this condition but rather expands and globalizes it while (and because) it has the capacity to either consume or absorb those institutions (to the extent that they do or do not interfere with the end of increased capital) that have traditionally provided orientation for humans.[85] One of these was, of course, religion. Indeed, Marx directly compares the alienation of humanity from their labor with humanity's investment in God. He writes, "The more man puts into God, the less he retains in himself. The worker puts his life into the object; but now his life no longer belongs to him but to the object."[86] Similarly, the critique of idealism is an attempt to unmask the manner in which social arrangements are often only perpetuated and justified rather than being *grounded* in and emerging from ideas as such. Humankind will fail to develop the class consciousness necessary for improving his state if it fails to recognize that its condition is not the necessary result of an ideal agent. Rather, it is the person-person relation that must be exposed. Humans make history, and their ideas arise from and are often *for* justifying and perpetuating concrete social conditions.[87]

While we might modify Marx, we would be remiss if we did not recognize how much he (as he did with Hegel) turns interpreters of modernity on their heads. That is, modernity is just as

---

84. Karl Marx, *Economic and Philosophic Manuscripts of 1844* and the *Communist Manifesto* (Amherst, NY: Prometheus Books, 1988), 212. This particular section is from The Communist Manifesto.

85. See ibid., 212–13, wherein Marx provides an early discussion of the globalizing effects of capitalism.

86. Ibid., 72. This is from his fragment on estranged labor in *Economic and Philosophic Manuscripts of 1844*.

87. See Marx's critique of Hegel in ibid., 141–68.

easily rendered a concrete, material, and lived condition—as it is an intellectual one. Indeed, it is very possibly more the former than the latter. Particularly in his analysis of the alienation of individuals from the objects of their labor, from themselves, and from their fellow human beings, Marx provides analytical tools without which (I will argue) we cannot understand our current condition.[88]

Two other seminal readers of modernity, of course, are Max Weber and Sigmund Freud—both of whom seek to excavate the *noumena* behind the *phenomena* of the modern West. The former's "disenchantment of the world" is more often cited than understood. As well, it is important to focus on the ways in which disenchantment is a posture that is carried along as much in our labor as in our habits of mind.[89] For our immediate purposes, we may treat it (as it has been often *understood*—true to Weber or not) as that condition wherein modern people, even those who believe in God, no longer tacitly perceive the world as agentic. Rather than seeming suffused with inner potencies of mind, all of reality at least *feels* reducible to predictable and (what is more) manipulable matter. Freud, on the other hand, quite literally diagnoses modernity as a condition in which people have traded some of their needs (freedom—especially of the sex drive) for others (security). The result is a sort of civilizational neurosis and anxiety—an experienced unsettledness of a person in herself—the reasons for which the human remains ignorant of.[90]

It would not be overstating the matter to say that most twentieth-century interpreters of modernity simply mix and match

88. Marx is a difficult thinker, and it is important to criticize any tradition that attempts to conflate him with Marxism, or that interprets the latter as any singular school. In fact, there are are many schools of Marxist thought. For Marx himself, see Alex Callinicos, *The Revolutionary Ideas of Karl Marx* (Chicago: Haymarket Books, 2012), and Amy Wendling, *Karl Marx on Technology and Alienation* (New York: Palgrave Macmillan, 2009). For Marxism, see David McLellan, *Marxism after Marx* (New York: Palgrave Macmillan, 2007).

89. On Weber's controversial notion of enchantment, see Jason A. Josephson-Storm, *The Myth of Disenchantment: Magic, Modernity, and the Birth of the Human Sciences* (Chicago: University of Chicago Press, 2017), 269–301.

90. Sigmund Freud, *Civilization and Its Discontents* (New York: Norton, 2010).

these motifs. Modern urbanization, for instance, is often tied to restricted uses of rural land (i.e., the oft-cited enclosure of what used to be the commons)—the result of which was a condition of wage slavery, since persons moving to cities were removed from access to resources that enabled economic independence.[91] And, arguably, it was in this *lived* context that many of the philosophical trends described above gained their most important influence. This is because humans make theoretical sense of the world by means of their primal and prior contact with it. Intellectual movements are ordinarily birthed in the contact between concrete life and reflective discourse. The separation between mind and world and the increased mechanization of the latter do not therefore cause modernity but are available ideas which are repurposed to explain the experience of it.[92] It becomes apparent, in this context, that the salient emphasis is not merely urbanism as such but the mode of life in modern cities that will find its *telos* in late modern industrialism. It is particularly in the latter context that these trends are intensified. Of major importance here is the progressive shift away from local and immediately personal networks of trust and dependence (the family and local community) to trust/dependence on quasi-abstract systems that can even transcend the control of states.[93] This connection is rendered even

---

91. On enclosure and urbanization, see Joseph Rykwert, *The Seduction of Place: The History and Future of Cities* (New York: Vintage, 2002), 21–42. For a more theoretical analysis, see Anthony Giddens, *The Consequences of Modernity* (Stanford: Stanford University Press, 1990), 60: "Industrialism becomes the main axis of the interaction of human beings with nature in conditions of modernity. In most pre-modern cultures, even in the large civilizations, humans mostly saw themselves as continuous with nature."

92. I will speak more of this in later sections—attempting to give a retooled phenomenological analysis of late techno-capitalism. Important studies that similarly highlight the ephemeral quality of modern life are Marshall Berman, *All That Is Solid Melts into Air: The Experience of Modernity* (New York: Penguin, 1988), and Zygmund Bauman, *Liquid Modernity* (New York: Polity, 2012).

93. This is a major emphasis of Giddens, *The Consequences of Modernity*, and Jerrold Seigel, *Modernity and Bourgeois Life: Society, Politics, and Culture in England, France, and Germany Since 1750* (New York: Cambridge University Press, 2012). Once again, I will try to address this matter phenomenologically in later sections. For current purposes, see also Joel Mokyr, *The Enlightened Economy: An Economic History of Britain 1700–1850* (New Haven:

more plausible by noting the temporal proximity of the Industrial Revolution with the aforementioned rise of explicit atheism. The former is often seen as climaxing in the middle of the nineteenth century.[94] The latter comes to prominence in the second half of the same century. This trend curiously inverts the God/city relation that existed in most of human history. For most of our ancestors, the city was perceived to be that location wherein God's presence and activity was most prominent. In the experience of modernity, divinity has moved to the country.[95] Once again, we will reflect on this in later sections.

Other circumstantial factors have been pointed to as relevant for understanding the popularity of unbelief. While the medium is often the perpetuation of explicit ideas, the latter nevertheless depend upon a material architecture without which the ideas would not disseminate and *with* which their influence is relatively predictable. Along these lines, one might point to those sources that highlight a relatively significant correlation between material comfort and the decline of religion—the former presumably rendering moot some of the traditional motivations for being invested in the latter.[96] Also relevant would be studies that claim a significant relationship between religion and particular sorts of family structures.[97] Historically contextual factors can also be highlighted,

Yale University Press, 2012), and Stuart Blumin, *The Emergence of the Middle Class: Social Experience in the American City, 1760–1900* (New York: Cambridge University Press, 1989).

94. See Robert Allen, *The Industrial Revolution: A Very Short Introduction* (New York: Oxford University Press, 2017).

95. The classic study of the ancient city is Lewis Mumford, *The City in History: Its Origins, Its Transformations, and Its Prospects* (Orlando: Mariner Books, 1968). For an account of the transition, see Keith Thomas, *Man and the Natural World: Changing Attitudes in England 1500–1800* (New York: Oxford University Press, 1996).

96. See Phil Zuckerman, "Atheism, Secularity, and Well-Being: How the Findings of Social Science Counter Negative Stereotypes and Assumptions," *Sociology Compass* 3, no. 6 (2009), 949–71.

97. Most relevant along these lines is Mary Eberstadt, *How the West Really Lost God* (West Conshohocken, PA: Templeton Press, 2013), and Christian Smith's "National Studies of Youth and Religion," Association of Religion Data Archives, http://www.thearda.com/Archive/NSYR.asp. Perhaps more speculatively, psychologist Paul Vitz has claimed a

such as the decisive manner in which questions of theodicy have been intensified since World War I.[98] Indeed, the mere fact that one might be put on the defensive with respect to one's faith commitments necessarily cultivates a different and reflexive relationship to them. And so the very fact of freethought, of God's proclaimed death, makes unbelief possible not just as an idea but as a new *circumstance* in which one finds one's own dogmas relativized.[99] Historically, this was accomplished not just by explicit atheism but by the culturally cross-pollinating effects of an emerging globalism, which increased the exposure of the West to radical others and played no small part in the development of religious studies, the dogma-relativizing effects of which must not be understated.[100] Religious communities have, of course, attempted to cope with and/or respond to these situations—but with perhaps counterintuitive results. What has often motivated unbelief has actually not been other positive unbelief but rather the felt need to respond to such unbelief in the first place. In the West, basic theism was obvious until the moment it was actually on the defensive. And it was the explicit defense that was found by many to be either wanting or (by the mere fact of its need) disturbing.[101]

---

correlation between the early perpetuators of atheism and the phenomenon of fatherlessness. See his *Faith of the Fatherless: The Psychology of Atheism* (Dallas: Spence Publishing Company, 2000). While I have not developed this argument in the book, I think this is a significant explanation of atheism's plausibility and is highly correlated to conditions of modern technoculture that have had a drastic impact on the nuclear family. In short, it is possible (indeed, likely) that earthly paternal absence tends to render one numb to any notion of divine paternal presence/being as the ground of reality.

98. For information rather than interpretation, see Charles O'Connor, "The Great War and the Death of God: Postwar Breakdown of Western Culture, Retreat from Reason, and the Rise of Scientific Materialism" (PhD diss., Georgetown University, 2012).

99. Taylor, *A Secular Age*, makes much of this. I will discuss his work below.

100. See especially Hans Kippenberg, *Discovering Religious History in the Modern Age* (Princeton: Princeton University Press, 2001). An important work on the Christian reaction to this phenomenon can be found in Timothy Larsen, *The Slain God: Anthropologists and the Christian Faith* (New York: Oxford University Press, 2014).

101. This is emphasized by Buckley, *At the Origins of Modern Atheism*; Hyman, *A Short History of Atheism*; Kors, *Atheism in France*; Thrower, *A Short History of Western Atheism*; and James Turner, *Without God, without Creed*.

Of course, one might argue that these are all but epiphenomena of Marx's alienation or Freud's civilization-wide pathology. However, even *these themselves* (on another reading) are epiphenomena of the very tools that make them possible in the first place. Consequently, we have to consider the inescapable phenomenon of modern technology in all its culture-shaping effects.[102] Many intellectuals have linked the experience of modernity to its technologies.[103] And here we must not think merely in terms of "industrialism." Especially in recent decades, we have to consider the manner in which we attempt to overcome our communal disintegration through communications technology. In some ways, the human race is as non-isolated as it has ever been.[104] Many authors have highlighted, however, the manner in which our technical relationship to the world shapes us to perceive the world as the *kind of object* to which tools relate, that is, a machine. Here the mechanical philosophy is not so much a matter of philosophical arguments as a *posture* toward reality that is perceived to be warranted simply because reality actually seems to continually yield to it.[105] This would account, presumably, for why the scholastic tradition was not so much *refuted* as *discarded*. To the extent that scholasticism's frame of reference did not resonate with the manner in which the world instinctively *seems* to those who are related to it as to a machine—scholasticism was and is dismissible.[106] And indeed,

---

102. The chief theorist of this phenomenon remains Jacques Ellul, *The Technological Society* (New York: Vintage, 1964).

103. See, for instance, Gilbert G. Germain, *A Discourse on Disenchantment: Reflections on Politics and Technology* (Albany: State University of New York Press, 1993).

104. See Manuel Castells, *Communication Power* (New York: Oxford University Press, 2013).

105. See Martin Heidegger, "The Question Concerning Technology," in *Basic Writings*, ed. David Farrell Krell (New York: Harper, 1993), 307–42. See Also Gilbert G. Germain, *Spirits in the Material World: The Challenge of Technology* (Plymouth: Lexington Books, 2009), and *Thinking about Technology: How the Technological Mind Misreads Reality* (Plymouth, MA: Lexington Books, 2017).

106. On the theme of "invisibility," see Neil Postman, *Technopoly: The Surrender of Culture to Technology* (New York: Knopf, 1992), 48.

the history of early modern science is replete with projects abandoned more for covert philosophical than for empirical reasons.[107]

The Ideological and the Practical as Reciprocal Influences

Having moved from the ideological to the practical, one soon gets the impression that we cannot linger long upon the practical without moving to the ideological. Indeed, many of the studies listed above could arguably be placed in either category, though I have *tried* to place them in those places where their emphasis is most prominent. The most persuasive accounts in each are those that attempt to think through both. Nevertheless, to merely state that both are important is not the same thing as clarifying their relation. To this end, a few comments are in order. While I have preliminarily mentioned some of these points in the previous section, now that we have summarized practical interpretations of modernity, we are in a place to take larger methodological and philosophical stock.

First, ideas can function as background options or even as generally accepted truths that are nevertheless not particularly prominent in a system of thought—or held in tension with other equally or more prominent aspects of that system of thought. Material conditions can drastically change this to the extent that they reshape both the explicit and subconscious experience of the world that is being intellectually engaged. Certain metaphors or constructions might gain prominence to the extent that they map on to historically shifting precognitive human experience. This new equilibrium can then reshape the ideological world, which then has further ideological influence, via humans, on the material realm. This can take the form of shaping an entire populace or of shaping key elites whose ideological influence is necessarily wider than others'. For this reason, the relationship between material and

---

107. See the fascinating work of Hasok Chang, *Is Water H$_2$O? Evidence, Realism, and Pluralism* (Cambridge: Springer, 2014).

mental influences is analogous to the famous "chicken and the egg" conundrum. We fail to capture a whole picture unless we capture the relation as a nonhierarchical negotiation that is seamlessly experienced in human consciousness.[108]

Second, when we refer to ideas, we need not necessarily think in terms of explicit or consciously articulated beliefs. Nor need we think of an individual worldview as a kind of extractable and self-contained *system* through which humans filter all their conscious experiences. Not only do humans characteristically fail to be fully consistent with themselves, but their most deeply held intuitions are often carried along in a social fabric and social practices that are difficult to recognize objectively from the inside. This is perhaps something like Jameson's "political unconscious" or Foucault's "*episteme*," but what is apparent in each is that the individual is appropriated within a social fabric. And indeed, the just-mentioned tensions might be located more properly in these larger fabrics than in the individual mind as such.[109] While these structures can be consciously engaged with great effort, and while I would contend for a universal *base* inflected in a cultural and particular *superstructure* (to misuse Marx), I would nevertheless maintain that just as we know form through matter, we know the universal through the particular.[110]

Third, reemphasizing what was stated earlier, ideas can be operative for individuals even when they are explicitly rejected. So, again reiterating the above, it will not entirely do simply to state that Reformed theologians rejected nominalism or voluntarism as such. To the extent that these drastically shaped a culture's intellectual habits, it is quite possible to reject them in principle or

---

108. For a philosophy of human nature along these lines, see Julian Marias, *Metaphysical Anthropology: The Empirical Structure of Human Life* (University Park: Pennsylvania State University Press, 1971).

109. See Fredric Jameson, *The Political Unconscious: Narrative as a Socially Symbolic Act* (Ithaca: Cornell University Press, 1982), and Foucault, *The Order of Things*.

110. Here I am echoing the tradition of Michael Polanyi, *Personal Knowledge: Towards a Post-Critical Philosophy* (Chicago: University of Chicago Press, 1974).

in theology but to be instinctively shaped by their categories of thought and to tacitly accept them in, say, politics. It is possible, in other words, to become the *accidental* surrogate of secularizing potential that is, nevertheless, only actualized in a later concrete historical context. I am not, however, making that particular case here (concerning the Reformation and voluntarism) and doubt very much that it could be made persuasively. Moreover, if such a case were made, it would need to be *shown* more than merely asserted, but this *in principle* possibility is necessary to make explicit in order to outline what a fully persuasive account would contain.[111]

Fourth, and perhaps most importantly, we need to be sufficiently conscious of the extent to which any historical reconstruction is of concern to us only because it enables us to comprehend our own contemporary experience. One recipe for myth involves isolating singular features of our current experience, tracing their pedigree, and then telling linear narratives from their natal stage to their maturation.[112] Historians likewise can reify some aspect of our culture, search for its historical seed form, and then connect the dots from point A to point B without sufficient attention to just how embedded point A is in its own context.[113] This means that discussing the continuous development of one thing inevitably involves discussing the *discontinuous* development of other things. Indeed, there are typically many *possible* outcomes

111. A contemporary example might be found in the scientific dimension of the so-called culture wars. On the one hand, one side is constantly critical of materialism. And yet, on the other, this same side often takes certain post-metaphysical assumptions for granted while trying to carve out a place for religion. The "God question," then, becomes one of finding evidence for a designer or lack thereof rather than its more primal placement in relation to the question of being in general. For analysis along these lines, see Cunningham, *Darwin's Pious Idea*.

112. Here I am referring to myth not in contrast to truth but in its aspect as a sort of self-projection that isolates some bits of reality, silences others, and, therefore, makes sense out of the world from very particular vantage points—but frames them as though they were natural and obvious. See Roland Barthes, *Mythologies* (New York: Hill and Wang, 2013).

113. On this, see Nathan Perl-Rosenthal's short essay, "Modern Times," *The New Republic*, May 5, 2010, https://newrepublic.com/article/74617/modern-times.

from any historical period looking forward, but only one *actual* one. And explaining the actual one requires consideration of the points listed above. We might all feel like the inevitable outcome of our grandparents, but from our grandparents' perspective, there are as many obvious outcomes as there are actual grandchildren. The importance of this point increases as the timeline under consideration does. The import of this is that the essential moments that gave us our contemporary experiences might very well have been much more recent than we are prone to think. And for this very reason, many scholars consider the very notions of modernity, disenchantment, and secularism to be mythologies. We now turn briefly to these interpretations.

Contrarian Hybrid Interpretations

Of first importance for contrarian interpretations of modernity is the simple observation that almost all of the behaviors that are associated with being secular or disenchanted do not obviously describe most persons who are presumably modern.[114] There is still (stubbornly) widespread religion, so much so that many persons have argued for a religious *gene* to explain its near ubiquity.[115] There is still widespread interest in angels and miracles.[116] Analogously, Robert Allen has stated of early modernity that "enthusiasm for science may have been a film floating on a lake of superstition."[117] This can possibly be accounted for by class and education divisions, but in at least some non-Western contexts, these are less predictive of religion or its lack.[118] Perhaps this is due to idiosyncratic social

---

114. On this debate, see Steven Bruce, ed., *Religion and Modernization: Sociologists and Historians Debate the Secularization Thesis* (New York: Clarendon, 1992).

115. Most prominently, Dean Hamer, *The God Gene: How Faith Is Hardwired into Our Genes* (New York: Random House, 2005).

116. See William J. Birnes and Joel Martin, *The Haunting of Twenty-First Century America: From the Millennium to the New Age* (New York: Forge, 2014).

117. Allen, *The Industrial Revolution*, 14.

118. On their intersection with Western secularization, see Talal Asad, *Formations of the Secular: Christianity, Islam, Modernity* (Stanford: Stanford University Press, 2003).

or institutional features of religion in our civilization that do not have an analogue in many other contexts.[119]

But here, many theorists would argue that the concepts of magic and enchantment have not so much disappeared as shifted. Not a few observers have noted that modern technology can function as modern magic, science as modern religion, and scientists as modern priests.[120] While it might be correct to say that this is founded in the success of its methods, it is nevertheless demonstrably the case that modern persons tend to trust the conclusions of whatever can be labeled as science without critical reflection—even in cases in which what has been given the imprimatur of science has turned out to have it wrong.[121] As one of C.S. Lewis's memorable characters puts it cynically in *That Hideous Strength*, "It's the educated reader who can be gulled. All our difficulty comes with the others. When did you meet a workman who believes the papers? He takes it for granted that they're all propaganda ... But the educated public, the people who read the highbrow weeklies ... They'll believe anything."[122] Putting these points together, arguably the paradigmatic experiment (or *sacrament!*) that sustains faith in this myth is located wherever we consume the fruits of *Science*'s obvious and apparent effect on the world. That is, science is mediated to us by technology in general and by technologies in particular.[123] These are modern sacraments, participation in which

119. See Saba Mahmood, *Religious Difference in a Secular Age: A Minority Report* (Princeton: Princeton University Press, 2015).

120. See Richard Stivers, *Technology as Magic: The Triumph of the Irrational* (New York: The Continuum Publishing Company, 1999).

121. While I do not agree with many of his conclusions, this particular point is well made by Feyerabend in his now classic, *Against Method*.

122. C. S. Lewis, *That Hideous Strength* (New York: Scribner's Sons, 1996), 99–100. See also his essay, "The Inner Ring," In *The Weight of Glory* (New York: HarperOne, 2001) 116–40, which captures this phenomenon more broadly and brilliantly.

123. See David Channell, *A History of Technoscience: Erasing the Boundaries between Science and Technology* (New York: Routledge, 2017); Srdjan Lelas, "Science as Technology," *The British Journal for the Philosophy of Science* 44, no. 3 (1993), 423–42; and Lewis Mumford, "Science as Technology," *Proceedings of the American Philosophical Society* 105, no. 5 (1961), 506–11. I am taking the notion of the paradigmatic experiment, of course, from Kuhn, *The*

is the most immediate and personal manifestation (i.e., payoff) of science considered abstractly. This participation shapes the imagination to transubstantiate Science's obvious competence in respect of some things specifically to a competence in respect of all things generally.[124] The myth of this omnicompetence is encoded in its own hagiography and religious history,[125] complete with mythic literature in the form of science fiction,[126] and devotional literature clearly manifested in titles such as *The Greatest Show on Earth*.[127]

But this is only to speak of the contemporary scene. In point of fact, it is questionable whether disenchantment (for instance) is an apt description of post-Reformation Europe. In many cases, the progress of the sciences was accompanied not only by a rise in religious fervor but by interest in subjects that we would not think of as scientific by modern standards. The field of magic studies has significantly complicated our historical picture in this respect.[128]

More to the point, however, there are those scholars who argue that both modernity and disenchantment are myths that illuminate the *modern* sense of self rather than the realities of the past. In his *We Have Never Been Modern*, Bruno Latour argues that when we identify the sorts of behaviors against which we contrast modern sensibilities and then compare these with our own behavior, we discover that we behave very much like our ancestors and very little like our supposed selves. That is to say, the practices we

Structure of Scientific Revolutions, who is a good complement to Feyerabend, mentioned above.

124. Not a week goes by when one does not find articles in prominent news outlets claiming that science shows something that is rather obvious apart from it.

125. See Jacoby, *Freethinkers*.

126. See James Herrick, *Scientific Mythologies: How Science and Science Fiction Forge New Religious Beliefs* (Downers Grove, IL: InterVarsity Press, 2008).

127. Richard Dawkins, *The Greatest Show on Earth: The Evidence for Evolution* (New York: Free Press, 2010).

128. Most importantly, see Keith Thomas, *Religion and the Decline of Magic* (New York: Scribner's Sons, 1971).

associated with modernity are not even true of us, and modernity winds up being a discourse projected *upon* ourselves *by* ourselves. We become modern at the very moment we began to imagine ourselves as modern. For Latour, the content of this projection is that we *believe* that we distinguish between nature and culture (in contrast to participating in the nature/culture hybrids of our ancestors).[129] Quite similarly, Jason Josephson-Storm has recently argued that disenchantment is also a modern myth. He writes that "the myth of disenchantment … results in the simultaneous private embrace and public rejection of enchantment."[130] His questions, therefore, are, "Why did European societies come to think of themselves as disenchanted? How did Europe come to imagine—even to the extent of taking it as a central feature of its civilization—that it did not believe in spirits, despite persistent evidence to the contrary?"[131] Josephson-Storm traces this discourse from its inception among nineteenth-century German intellectuals to its modern ubiquity (despite, in his judgment, obvious evidence to the contrary). That is, the story of disenchantment is a story about how and why we began to *think of ourselves* as disenchanted. Concerning secularization, as the above might suggest, there is manifold doubt about whether we are or ever have been secular. Ian Hunter has recently written that "rather than beginning with any kind of process … a history of secularization must begin with the array of nineteenth-and-twentieth-century theological and philosophical programs in which a variously characterized process of secularization was advanced for rival cultural-political purposes."[132] Just as in the case of disenchantment discourse,

---

129. Bruno Latour, *We Have Never Been Modern* (Cambridge: Harvard University Press, 1991), 1–12, 114–16. Later in his career, Latour has reconsidered some of the formulations in this work. See also Robert Pippin, *Modernism as a Philosophical Problem* (Malden, MA: Blackwell, 1999), who considers modernity discourse in its nineteenth century context.

130. Josephson-Storm, *The Myth of Disenchantment*, 18.

131. Ibid., 17.

132. Ian Hunter, "Secularization: Process, Program, and Historiography," *Intellectual History Review* 27, no. 1 (2017), 8.

secularization discourse possibly says more about how we began to think of ourselves as secular rather than anything else.

In the following, it will be made clear that I am largely sympathetic with the perspectives offered by these scholars. Nevertheless, I will here attempt to caveat them. To wit, even if there is a mythology involved in the typical attempts to speak about medieval and modern religion(s) and the path that gets us from one to the other, it would seem that we have to grapple with the plain fact (whether it has been well interpreted or not) that there is some massive difference between the two of them. One problem with being overly aware of all the details and exceptions is that we can very well miss the forest for the trees, and there are some basic things about the big picture that will stubbornly resist dismissal. Similarly, in one recent study that expresses skepticism about disenchantment narratives, Alexandra Walsham nevertheless concludes, "We still have to acknowledge, even if we cannot completely explain, the accumulation of individual transformations that have made many aspects of the past seem like a foreign country."[133]

The categories identified in the two previous sections are useful here. To wit, the transformations need not be articulated in terms of explicit belief but can just as well be articulated in practical postures, cultural background noises, or, most basically, the world as experienced and felt. For persons in the Middle Ages and throughout much of the early modern period, arguments for final causality were not just a matter of rational inference from empirical observation. They were a matter of an immediate *sense* of the phenomena being described as such. Teleology was quite literally observed.[134] Later, one might still make a philosophical case for teleological causes, but that same person might nevertheless *experience* the world as mechanistic or materialistic.[135] This phenomenon and

---

133. Alexandra Walsham, "The Reformation and 'The Disenchantment of the World' Reassessed," *The Historical Journal* 51, no. 2 (2008), 528.

134. See Foucault, *The Order of Things*, 17–45.

135. See ibid., 46–77.

the cognitive dissonance it creates will be much discussed later in this work—as will what I take to be the chief material conditions that partially sired this situation.

Moreover, modern analogues of ancient magic and enchantment have significant discontinuities with the latter. It is true that there are still many readers of horoscopes, but those who take them half-seriously also tend to take them with a grain of salt. Technological enchantment can only ever be an impersonal proximate to tacitly experiencing reality as fundamentally agentic. Even if not personally understood, it is felt to be something that I could understand if I wanted. Consequently, technology is explicitly *felt* to be an instance of human meaning-making suspended in a more fundamentally impersonal reality.[136]

In any case, isolating the phenomena in this manner and with these caveats, the labels of modernity or secularization or disenchantment can possibly be recycled as still useful in a chastened fashion. However, we are self-conscious in starting with a *present* sense of things—and one not reducible to a set of ideas. As such, the goal is reframed as an attempt to identify not when ideas changed but when a more basic and general experience of the world was, by our standards, foreign, and what changes have moved us from just *those* ancestors to just *these* descendants.

However, pinning these labels to our experience of the world and asking at which point we find our ancestors foreign needs two attendant qualifications. First, there need be nothing in the shape of the question itself that either overly laments or celebrates the contrast between now and then. Most agree that we cannot recover the past, but they nevertheless regard it with sentiment

---

136. As it turns out, this sense that I could know if I wanted to is probably closer to what Weber originally meant by disenchantment. See Josephson-Storm, *The Myth of Disenchantment*, 269–301. Cixin Liu's *The Three Body* trilogy, initiated in *The Three Body Problem* (New York: TOR Books, 2016), is an interesting example of this. It is common for the characters therein to find the universe quite beautiful and to wish that they were not atheists—suggesting a conscious cosmic bedrock of impersonality behind their sentiments.

or cynicism and evaluate our prospects for the future with varying degrees of nostalgic despair or progressivist hope.[137] In part of what follows, I hope to make a case for a sort of sober hope concerning our historical location. Second, stating the problem in this manner might have the result that we find ourselves in a foreign country (in just the relevant senses) far more recently than we might expect. Indeed, in what follows, I will be arguing that there are good reasons to suspect that the metaphysical furniture of the cosmos and our basic/tacit sense of things probably changed less (at least in the West) between 750 and 1750 than it did between 1850 and 1950.[138] One of the reasons we are obsessed with these narratives is precisely because we are still in the middle of this epochal shift—a shift that is very difficult to see objectively from the inside. That is, narratives of modernity, secularization, and disenchantment are often therapeutic attempts to come to grips with the felt fact that the world has *recently* changed and that it will continue to do so in fundamental ways for the foreseeable future while we are carried along for the ride.

But we must not get ahead of ourselves. Before leaving the taxonomy of interpretations of modernity, I have saved the most important recent intellectual, Charles Taylor, for last. I will consider his proposal in more detail, not least because he approaches the matter, in my judgment, in a way that factors in the kinds of reciprocally interacting forces that I alluded to above. For this reason, he does not neatly fit into the above taxonomy—even in emphasis. After situating and summarizing his narrative, I will suggest wherein I think there are important gaps in Taylor's explanation and propose how those gaps might be filled in.

---

137. Mark Lilla considers each respectively in *The Shipwrecked Mind: On Political Reaction* (New York: The New York Review of Books, 2016), and *The Once and Future Liberal: After Identity Politics* (New York: Harper, 2017).

138. See David Edgerton, *The Shock of the Old: Technology and Global History Since 1900* (New York: Oxford University Press, 2007).

CHARLES TAYLOR AND
THE PROBLEM OF MODERNITY

It is important to see Charles Taylor's 2007 work *A Secular Age* as a climax to several decades of reflection on related themes.[139] His *Sources of the Self* and *Modern Social Imaginaries*[140] are attempts to grapple with unique aspects of modern identity in a way that blends historical narrative and philosophical reflection. Said differently, Taylor's philosophical anthropology significantly informs what sorts of historical explanations he finds plausible.[141] And while this is to the ire of some of his critics, it is precisely what motivates me to situate my own labors in relation to his.

And so what is Taylor's distinctive contribution? Rather than framing the question of secularity (including the possibility of modern atheism) in terms of mere belief trends, Taylor focuses rather on the conditions of belief. That is, whether one is an orthodox believer, an atheist, or anything in between, "what is it like" to believe in a particular context?[142] He writes,

> Belief in God isn't quite the same thing in 1500 and 2000 … Even in regard to identical creedal propositions, there is an important difference … The difference … is one of the whole background framework in which one believes or refuses to believe in God. The frameworks of yesterday and today are related as "naïve" and "reflective."[143]

For Taylor, what has changed between 1500 and 2000 is the *pistic* background noise within which Western persons form their beliefs. In 1500, as argued above, it was certainly possible to question

---

139. For a helpful summary of this volume by someone who is conversant with his entire project, see James K. A. Smith, *How (Not) To Be Secular: Reading Charles Taylor* (Grand Rapids: Eerdmans, 2014).

140. Charles Taylor, *Modern Social Imaginaries* (Durham, NC: Duke University Press, 2003).

141. This is made explicit at several points in *A Secular Age*.

142. Taylor develops this question in ibid., 1–89.

143. Ibid., 13.

elements of creedal orthodoxy, but disbelief in a basic metaphysical picture that included God or something vaguely transcendent was nearly inconceivable. Said differently, it was not *plausible*. In the modern world, however, our conditions of belief are such that even the most fervent orthodox believer *experiences* their belief as one option among many options. Even the most apparently confident believers often confess periods of intellectual (which is somewhat different than spiritual) doubt about very basic pieces of their cosmic picture.[144] We can already see that Taylor's method involves capturing the transition in its *lived* dimensions, which necessarily involves attention to individual, social, ideological, and material transitions.[145]

How did this transition occur? In its most basic outline, "(1) There had to develop a culture that marks a clear division between the 'natural' and the 'supernatural,' and (2) it had to come to seem possible to live entirely within the natural. Point 1 was something striven for, but point 2 came about at first quite inadvertently."[146] As it pertains to the former, Taylor largely (but certainly not entirely) glosses the scholarship that I have discussed above under the ideological heading. But it is the second point that constitutes the bulk of his narrative and distinctive contribution. Indeed, he contrasts what he terms the "Intellectual Deviation" (he has in mind John Milbank, in particular, here) story of modern secularism from what he terms his own "Reform Master Narrative."[147] While the former is important, it is the latter that tells the main story, in his judgment.

---

144. See ibid., 10–11.

145. Taylor's most robust defense of this method of analysis, particularly in relation to *A Secular Age*, is "Afterword: Apologia pro Libro suo" in Craig Calhoun, Michael Warner, and Jonathan VanAntwerpen, eds., *Varieties of Secularism in a Secular Age* (Cambridge: Harvard University Press, 2010), 300–21.

146. Ibid., 304.

147. Taylor, *A Secular Age*, 774.

And so what is this narrative? Taylor's work defies elegant summary, but several points can be made. (1) Resolving spiritual tensions that have their pedigree in the Hebrew prophets' critique of idolatry, late medieval pre-Protestant Reform movements began to critique any notion of two-track spirituality wherein there was a different standard for clergy and for laity. Rather, all Christians were expected to live according to the radical teachings of Jesus Christ.[148] (2) In the early modern period, partially as a result of the Reformation's "affirmation of the ordinary life,"[149] this Reform mentality began to have its terminus not merely in otherworldly ends that are often associated with the spiritual calling but rather in the earthly callings of marriage, society, and neighbor. That is, it was the so-called immanent order of things that was the locus of spiritual effort.[150] (3) Combined with the early modern (and Reformation) critique of folk superstition, as well as the ideological factors mentioned above, this rendered possible the progressive separation of natural from supernatural realms/ends—and rendered the latter progressively superfluous—as modes of the moral life were increasingly reduced and explained entirely in terms of the immanent order (societies organized around notions of mutual benefit and individual rights).[151] (4) The decisive transition occurs at the point when the supernatural or dogmas associated with it actually come to be seen as a threat to our participation in the immanent order.[152] (5) And while there are many reactions and counterreactions (Taylor's "nova effect"),[153] what we begin to see is the rise of exclusive humanism and what Taylor terms the

148. See ibid., 90–145.

149. This particular phrase comes from Taylor, *Sources of the Self*, 211–302.

150. See Taylor, *A Secular Age*, 90–211.

151. See ibid., 221–69.

152. See ibid., 270–95.

153. See ibid., 299–419. One might think of Romanticism, organicism, and even Nietzsche here.

"immanent frame," or the possibility of persons making practical and moral sense of their lives without reference to God.[154]

Again, this is not predominantly an intellectual "making sense of" but rather the simple possibility that modern Western humans do, in fact, instinctually move around in a tacitly (not intellectually) coherent cosmic and moral world which does not require constant conscious reference to the divine. That is, we can go about our day, talk about the planets, have experiences of how I *ought* to be polite (etc.), without a conscious thought of God. He might be invoked as a *sense-maker* of these phenomena, but we often make sense of each without immediate reference to the divine. In that sense, the divine can be experienced as a sort of *addition* (perhaps a necessary one) to our conscious default settings—a fact to be remembered. In any case, it is within this experienced situation that *our* beliefs are cultivated.

Several items are worthy of note here. First, Taylor's story is not what he calls a "subtraction story."[155] That is, the modern conditions of belief generally (or unbelief specifically) are not the result of the subtraction of one belief after another (from medieval orthodoxy, to its Reformation modifications, its Enlightenment overhaul, and finally its impending death in modern times). Modern unbelief is suspended atop its own positive proposals and orthodoxies. We have moved not from dogma to its absence but from dogma to dogma. Second, modern dogma is irreducibly historical in character. Said differently, it belongs to a historical consciousness of "having overcome a previous condition."[156] This is why, Taylor argues, it is not sufficient to simply describe belief in 1500 and in 2000 and note the differences. We cannot finally understand what it is like to believe in 2000 without understanding the twenty-first-century person's self-conscious sense of "what

---

154. See ibid., 242–69, 539–93.

155. Ibid., 26–29.

156. Ibid., 28.

has happened" since 1500 as a definitive element of the modern belief-formation. To *imagine* ourselves as scientific and modern automatically *imagines* a non-scientific and premodern mode of life against which I make sense of my own. Third, it is important to note that Taylor's phenomenology of our conditions of belief is not general but fine-grained. If the reception of his work is any indicator, it is quite likely that his description produces an "I have never thought of it that way before" sort of sensation for his readers that is nevertheless felt to illuminate the familiar. And it is that not-previously-obvious and insightful description from which he seeks to redescribe the difference between the premodern and the modern. There is perhaps some speculation in his work, but it is not random (or even general). He is attempting to capture the genealogy of precisely *this* lived condition in a more fine-grained way than most.[157]

In the remaining portion of this book, I will use Taylor as a springboard for my own proposal. Once again, I think Taylor gets at the question in just the right way, but some of his particular claims are problematic, and some of his arguments warrant significant supplementation. A series of observations is in order.

First, there are some historical problems with Taylor's account. Of particular importance, as Michael Horton argues, is that the Reformation was more an interruption than a catalyst for many of the salient features of so-called secularization. What is more,

---

157. Here I find Ian Hunter's criticism misguided when he argues that "Taylor's account takes place in a discursive space where it cannot be shown to be historically true, or thence false." "Secularization: Process, Program, Historiography," 17. Taylor's project is capable of generating many more fine-grained historical research programs, and his focus, if he has accurately grasped what humans are and how they operate, is non-arbitrary. Arguably, any history that actually attempts to be interesting cannot avoid the cross-pollinating relationship with legitimation that seems to be the object of Hunter's critique. Nevertheless, such cross-pollination does not necessitate intellectual or historical dishonesty. In fact, it actually takes Taylor on several historical detours that are often not factored into the discussion (and that help synthesize a vast number of phenomena—suggesting that he is onto something).

the post-Protestant reform impulses were just as often formed by anti-Protestant theology as by Protestant theology.[158]

Second, the primacy of the Reform Master Narrative is rendered plausible largely in relation to Taylor's own tendency to treat religion in its relation to what he terms "fullness," and the latter to the aesthetic and moral dimensions of human life.[159] And yet, if rendered historically relevant, this runs the risk of treating dimensions that are only isolated in *modern* consciousness as extractable in our treatment of historical actors in *their* world. But this would seem to be in tension with Taylor's own attempt to hold these irreducible dimensions of human existence together. And if so, this also suggests that other equally plausible stories of Taylor's sort could be told—as each dimension of human existence is mutually implicated in the others. Nevertheless, my point is not that Taylor's selection is arbitrary. On the contrary, it seems to me that it is rooted in his own sentiments concerning the human relation to the religious dimension as such. And yet it also seems to me that his treatment of this subject is itself modern—with its own contingent (not to mention intellectually problematic) pedigree.[160] What is required for more persuasive *historical* analysis, then, is an enhanced phenomenology of religion as such. That is, an enriched religious phenomenology would likewise enrich our historical understanding. In particular, it seems to me that transitions in our cosmic picture are at least as important as moral

---

158. See Michael Horton, "The Enduring Power of the Christian Story: Reformation Theology for a Secular Age," in *Our Secular Age*, ed. Collin Hansen (Deerfield, IL: The Gospel Coalition, 2017), 32–38. Taylor also makes much of the secularizing import of reaction to certain tenets of Reformed theology. Horton argues, however, that none of the doctrines that Taylor points out were uncommon in the medieval period. As such, this historical reaction requires a more precise explanation.

159. Horton, ibid., 24–32, surmises (with some evidence) Taylor's own apparent appreciation for folk over dogmatic religion.

160. See the similar critique of Matthew Rose, "Tayloring Christianity: Charles Taylor Is a Theologian of the Secular Status Quo," *First Things*, December 2014. On the very notion of "religion" as a modern phenomenon, see Brent Nongbri, *Before Religion: A History of a Modern Concept* (New Haven: Yale University Press, 2013), and Peter Harrison, *The Territories of Science and Religion* (Chicago: University of Chicago Press, 2015).

transitions. To be sure, Taylor does not neglect what he terms the "cosmic imaginary." But he seems to treat the fundamental transitions as located in our moral rather than in our cosmic imaginary. In my judgment, it is not philosophically or historically obvious that this prioritization is warranted. Possibly, my difference with Taylor here reflects a deeper philosophical divide about the nature of humans in general.

Third, even in *combination*, however, it is unclear how the modern moral, social, and cosmic imaginaries *specifically work* to get us to the actual emergence of the full-fledged materialism that is felt to be plausible for modern persons. Granting that moral fullness might be associated entirely with temporal ends, that we tend to move around within the immanent frame, that organized religion might be seen as stifling, and so forth, we have only narrowed the gap toward the possibility of atheism. The closest Taylor comes to filling it in is in his claim that irreligion became plausible at the moment when religion could be seen as a threat to the imminent moral order. It is nevertheless unclear why this would warrant atheism generally rather than anticlericalism specifically (which still permits religion as such). Can this gap, then, be more specifically filled in? Certainly, we can locate *when* it arises, but *why* (more specifically) does it rise when it does—especially given the fact that different responses to all of these phenomena are possible? For those (like myself) who consider the philosophical arguments decidedly in favor of the older scholastic metaphysical system, the questions become, then: (1) How did inferior theories become successful? (2) How did our felt sense of things shift away from what the mind might otherwise know to be reality? That is, how did a godless cosmic imaginary become a (*felt*) plausible reading of the world with which modern persons must negotiate— perhaps even despite what they otherwise consciously believe? Below, I will suggest that it is actually the answer to question 2 that explains the answer to question 1. And if we can identify this decisive shift, we might arrive at a plausible account of how several intellectual, moral, and social trends (including those identified by Taylor) were combined to make explicit philosophical sense out of a more basic lived experience of the world (a tacit sense of being).

Fourth, putting the previous two points together, an interesting tension in Taylor's project comes to the fore. While Taylor's historical problematic takes its point of departure from the historical consciousness of modern persons, the sense of "having overcome" previous arrangements, this modern historical consciousness is an implicit "subtraction story." This is not *necessarily* a problem, but there is perhaps a conflation of discourses. On the one hand, Taylor justifies his own historical focus in relation to this subtraction story-esque modern historical consciousness. But on the other, he treats the subtraction story itself mostly as a theory to be critiqued rather than as a significant piece of the plausibility structures he attempts to explain. He is successful at the former, but I would argue that his narrative nevertheless leaves unclear how it is that the subtraction story seems so historically plausible in the first place. This is tied up with my second question above. The felt plausibility of the subtraction story is part and parcel of the felt possibility of atheism. How, then, might we supplement Taylor's project?

SUMMARY OF THE REMAINING QUESTIONS

The question before us (variously stated), then, is, "How did atheism become a *felt* possibility?" "How did the subtraction story come to seem right?" "Sans hypothesizing superior arguments (a la Jonathan Israel), how did these arguments nevertheless win?" "How did it become the case that God's existence was not *felt* to be viscerally obvious?" This last way of putting it, in my judgment, is the most helpful way of getting at all of the others. Said differently, all of these things became possible the moment God seemed absent. Before the modern period, by contrast (and really this was not common until quite late within it), the universe was commonly perceived to be suffused with agency "all the way down."

And here I am referring not to the theoretical articulation of this but to the basic pre-articulated *experience* of the world.[161] Later, divine absence stands in contrast to the felt *clarity* and *obviousness* of the material world. While tacitly perceived to be passive, inert, and devoid of agency, it nevertheless has an immediate facticity that lends its attendant discourse (i.e., science) an ambiance of felt clarity in contrast to which engaging classical metaphysical questions seem abstract, circuitous, and elusive. Whether true *in fact* or not, scientific discourse *purports* to be about the sorts of phenomena which could not be disbelieved if actually observed— even if one wanted to disbelieve them. Religious discourse, on the other hand, appears to be about the sorts of phenomena that cannot be observed and therefore that easily eludes even those willing to believe.[162] This contextualizes the modern phrase "loss of faith." Lost faith captures an element of modern belief that is often overlooked. To wit, even if rooted in arguments and felt to be rational, faith is often experienced as something held *onto*, such that to cease gripping would be to lose its content.[163] By contrast, we feel no such active quality in our belief that the sun is in the sky, for instance.

In my judgment, then, we need to understand the *modern* phenomenon of divine absence. To be sure, divine absence has always been discussed as it relates to theodicy, but it is distinctively

---

161. Once again, Foucault's *The Order of Things* is key here, alongside Taylor's discussion of "bulwarks of belief" in *A Secular Age*, 25–89.

162. This perhaps accounts for the pop-impression that religious beliefs are entirely mediated by choice. "Why would you believe in a God who … " and so forth. This is reinforced by the fact that a lot of modern religious belief is precisely this. The relationship between the will and belief is classically engaged by William James in "The Will to Believe," in *William James: Pragmatism and Other Writings*, ed. Giles Gunn (New York: Penguin, 2000), 198–218.

163. Two recent (and excellent) film portrayals of this tension can be found in *Higher Ground*, directed by Vera Farmiga (Sony Pictures Classics, 2011), and *The Grey*, directed by Joe Carnahan (Open Road Films, 2012).

modern to discuss it in debates concerning the *being* of God at all.[164] And so, for those who believe that there are persuasive arguments for fairly classical metaphysics but who nevertheless find themselves feeling that the world inferred from these arguments remains psychologically distant, it is necessary to ask how this gap came about. Taylor has focused on the modern moral order and the rise of exclusive humanism. This is a part of the story. But, for the reasons stated above, I would argue that he only *shrinks* rather than *closes* the explanatory gap.

Several threads, therefore, must be woven together. If the plausibility of modern unbelief is what we are trying to explain, and it was in the middle of the nineteenth century that atheism became a live option in America and Europe for a significant portion of the population, we have to ask what was distinctive of this particular historical moment. Most immediately and obviously, this was the height of those items which are classically associated with the secularizing and modernizing process: industrialism, the urban movement, the rise of the middle class, and so forth.[165] It hardly seems likely that this is a coincidence. And importantly, as noted above, it was during this time that European intellectuals initiated the various discourses of secularity, disenchantment, and modernization, as ways of distinguishing their (then) historical present from their past. That is, the rise of unbelief and the reflexive and felt sense that this world is modern occur simultaneously. It would seem a prudent research program, then, to develop an enhanced phenomenology of the lived experience of late capitalism, urbanization,

---

164. The objection could be stated as, "If God wants people to believe, couldn't he be far more obvious? Perhaps the fact that he's not suggests there is no God." See Daniel Howard-Snyder and Paul Moser, eds., *Divine Hiddenness: New Essays* (New York: Cambridge University Press, 2002); Paul Moser, *The Elusive God: Reorienting Religious Epistemology* (New York: Cambridge University Press, 2008); and J. L. Schellenberg, *The Hiddenness Argument: Philosophy's New Challenge to Belief in God* (New York: Oxford University Press, 2015).

165. See Steven Bruce, *Secularization: In Defense of an Unfashionable Theory* (New York: Oxford University Press, 2011). But see the alternative perspective of Jose Casanova, "The Secular and Secularisms," *Social Research* 76, no. 4 (2009), 1049–66.

64

CHAPTER ONE

and modern technology. I propose to do this by focusing on the modern experience of divine absence as a segue into these larger questions.

SUMMARY OF MY ANSWER AND ARGUMENT

A. While Taylor's modern moral order and the development of modern science[166] played key roles in the making of modern conditions of belief, these were not commonly attached to, combined, and used to explain the world as devoid of agency until a very particular period. They had this latent possibility, and organized religion or divine revelation was even sometimes seen as a threat to genuine morality and science, but it took a more basic catalyst for the world to seem devoid of agency in a *general* sense (rather than simply in terms of moral experience).

B. An important and often discussed aspect of this transition is, of course, the incredible story of modern technology. To the extent that the world manifests as manipulable and ceases to be a force around which I must learn to navigate, it ceases to be experienced as a quasi-agent in relation to my agency. However, this relation to the cosmos is only rendered likely and tempting, not necessary, by the world-mediating impact of modern technology's ubiquitous proliferation.

C. Of course, modern technology and its attendant urbanization involved not just humankind's control of nature but also some people's control of other people. This period, then, is notably also a highpoint in the development of modern wage slavery and the alienation of humans from their labor.[167] Alienated labor is labor

---

166. Perhaps the most important recent argument on this front is from Peter Harrison, "Science and Secularization," *Intellectual History Review* 27, no. 1 (2017), 47–70.

167. An important evaluation of this can be found in Owen Chadwick, *The Secularization of the European Mind in the 19th Century* (New York: Cambridge University Press, 1975).

that tends to disenable the human person from relating to the world as full of meaning. This is because it is through labor that humans have historically had a primal contact with the world—in which the world was experienced as a site of innate meaning that humans cultivate, channel, and respond to. The privation of this contact, then, is the privation of a primal sense of cosmic agency.

D. The previous two points can be put together if we ask the following question: Inasmuch as it obscures the agency of the world *and* of humankind, what does the modern techno-capitalist lived world suggest to us (both subliminally and explicitly) concerning what it means for a thing to be *real*? What are humans in such an environment shaped to imagine concerning reality as such? My argument is that this lived world shapes us to perceive reality according to the projected counterpart/image of the technology-as-used (both on the world and on men) itself. That is, we experience the world and reality as such to be fundamentally a realm of manipulable material, meaninglessly arranged until the human mind imposes meaning on it. As the old adage has it, "To a man with a hammer, everything looks like a nail."

E. Finally, it needs to be insisted that this is a shared experience of the world. What I am describing here is not atheist consciousness but the common Western consciousness within which we form our beliefs. Against this background, belief is possible, but only by fighting against what the world *seems like* in very fundamental respects—or by constant reminder. Unbelief is easily experienced as the default option, and many philosophical and scientific hypotheses are then read in such a way as to make the modern sensibility inevitable. What is hidden in this is the radical historical contingency of this arrangement, which I intend to address in what follows.

In the next two chapters, then, I make the above argument in two steps. In chapter 2, I will highlight the *correlations* between a modern sense of divine absence, the rise of unbelief, and the technological developments that warrant the phenomenological analysis just summarized. In chapter 3, I will make a philosophical and phenomenological argument that technological and labor developments are prima facie the most probable *explanations* for the predictable emergence of these plausibility structures.

TWO

Modern Atheism as a Technocultural Phenomenon I: Correlation

REFINING THE QUESTION

The invisibility (or absence) of God has historically been a matter of anxiety for human beings. Throughout the ancient Near East, the inactivity of God (or the gods) in lieu of human suffering was a point of expressed anguish.[1] One also frequently encounters the theme in classic Jewish, Christian, and Muslim writings.[2] It is given a particularly elegant expression in Luther's *deus absconditus*.[3] But it was not until recently—around the middle of the nineteenth century or so—that the absence of God was frequently seen to be a problem associated with the question of his existence. It is perhaps first theoretically treated in relation to atheism in Pascal's analysis of the "hidden God."[4] But in our own era, it is commonplace— often treated explicitly in philosophy and in cinema.[5]

---

1. See Joel S. Burnett, *Where Is God? Divine Absence in the Hebrew Bible* (Minneapolis: Fortress Press, 2010).

2. See Adam Greene and Eleonore Stump, eds., *Hidden Divinity and Religious Belief: New Perspectives* (New York: Cambridge University Press, 2016), 155–226.

3. On which, see B. A. Gerrish, "'To the Unknown God': Luther and Calvin on the Hiddenness of God," *The Journal of Religion* 53, no. 3 (1973), 263–92.

4. See Schellenberg, *The Hiddenness Argument*, 24–25.

5. See, for instance, Moser, *The Elusive God*.

Traditionally, the problem of divine absence has been a matter related to the question of theodicy. That is, how can God be good if he does not show up to defeat evil? Yet the famous trio of options surrounding the problem of evil (how can both evil and God exist if God is all powerful and all good) has historically been resolved by either a denial of the reality of evil, a denial of divine sovereignty, or a fearful pondering concerning whether God is good after all.[6] The option of God's nonexistence has been, for the most part, considered wildly implausible. God's existence *as such* has not typically been considered an epistemic problem except in the banalest sense (i.e., going through the motions of establishing how we know God exists even though we cannot see him).[7] But in the late modern period, divine absence came to be an argument against divine existence from both angles. That God does not show up when humans suffer demonstrates that he does not exist. And that God is invisible and unavailable to the senses—even though (if he existed) he might presumably demonstrate his being beyond the shadow of a doubt to all persons—is likewise a prima facie case against his being at all.

The problem of evil would be frequently resolved in the direction of God's nonexistence in the middle of the nineteenth century, and this trend would only continue after World War I and the Holocaust. The narrative voice has been a particularly effective tool to communicate this. Carolyn Briggs's memoir of her own loss of faith and recent films like *The Grey* (directed by Joe Carnahan, 2012) narrate atheism in its relationship to God's unavailability in crisis.[8] And, of course, this theme is reversed in all sorts of directions in stories like Shusaku Endo's 1966 novel *Silence* and in Majid Majidi's 1999 film *The Color of Paradise*. The theistic alter ego of

---

6. On such trends, see Henri Blocher, *Evil and the Cross: An Analytical Look at the Problem of Pain* (Grand Rapids: Kregel Academic, 2005).

7. This is a commonplace interpretation of what is going on in Anselm and Aquinas.

8. See Carolyn Briggs, *This Dark World: A Memoir of Salvation Found and Lost* (New York: Bloomsbury, 2002).

this argument has been the modern version of the argument for God from morality. Classically, the argument from morality took public or common moral reality for granted and concluded that human moral experience (and its object) must be grounded in God. In its modern variant, there is an attempt to stoke the fear that if you do not have what is often cited as an "objective basis for morality," you cannot ground your own objection to World War I or the Holocaust. This is a significant rhetorical shift—involving not a little implicit skepticism.[9]

Even more unique, however, is the *epistemic* problem as it relates to divine absence. On the one hand, this might seem to be a problem for reasons related to "god of the gaps"-style arguments. That is, to the extent that the evidence for God was seen to be the world itself, and to the extent that this world was progressively seen to be explained by natural causes, to that extent God was seen to be out of a job. As scientific explanation moved forward, God (in a zero-sum competition with a natural explanation) was perceived to be an unnecessary proposition—lacking any positive evidence for his being that is not explained by other things. As Bertrand Russell was purported to have said when asked how he would account for his unbelief if he encountered God after death—"Not enough evidence."[10] But this does not quite get at the epistemic problem. Presumably, even if all these other bits are explained by science, God still has recourse to miracles and to divine revelation. The perceived absence of any publicly verifiable and irrefutable versions of these, however, can become a crisis when all the chips are in this basket.[11] Most importantly, though,

---

9. C. S. Lewis is a modern exemplar of the classical approach. See Joe Puckett, *The Apologetics of Joy: A Case for the Existence of God from C. S. Lewis's Argument from Desire* (Eugene, OR: Wipf & Stock, 2012).

10. As recounted in Schellenberg, *The Hiddenness Argument*, 27.

11. I recall listening to a young woman on National Public Radio several years ago who was attending a summer camp for agnostics. Given the opportunity to present one of her skeptical missiles, she asked why God did not simply intrude through the clouds every day at 3:00 p.m. for a very brief visit. Presumably, even if he did nothing else, this

even if one thinks that all of this begs the question, and even if one thinks that there are metaphysically demonstrative reasons to believe in God (no matter the science), it is still quite possible to struggle with believing in him for precisely the reason that we cannot see him.[12] That is, this question is not merely whether we have an answer to this epistemic problem. Rather, the question is why we can (1) believe that we have an answer to it and (2) still worry that our answer is wrong and that God does not, after all, exist. I will argue in the next chapter that the reason for this has to do with our tacit and existential comportment to reality in the first place. But for the time being, it is sufficient to give the problem mere utterance. It is evidenced in a recent conversation in the philosophical community concerning the problem of divine absence.[13] The chief philosopher who argues that this argument constitutes a decisive case against God nevertheless argues that the argument is fairly new and does not reach sufficient clarity and popularity until quite late in the modern period.[14] And like the question of theodicy, the epistemic variant of the problem of divine absence admits to all sorts of hybrids—from those emphasizing the virtue of having both faith and doubt, to those who locate religious certainty in a private psychological sphere (putting in refrain the distinctive role that the "argument for religious experience" takes on in the late modern period), and so forth.[15] Added to both of these,

---

frequent visitation would get rid of atheism overnight. And given this, it seems possible that divine absence implies a divine vacuum (at least if God is presumably interested in persons believing in him). In any case, for the curious, the literature on the epistemology and metaphysics of miracles is vast. Significant treatments can be found in C. S. Lewis, *Miracles* (New York: HarperOne, 2015); Colin Brown, *Miracles and the Critical Mind* (Grand Rapids: Eerdmans, 1984); and Craig Keener, *Miracles: The Credibility of the New Testament Accounts* (Grand Rapids: Baker Academic, 2011).

12. I have treated this issue at length in Joseph Minich, *Enduring Divine Absence: The Challenge of Modern Atheism* (Landrum, SC: The Davenant Trust, 2018).

13. See Howard-Snyder and Moser, *Divine Hiddenness*.

14. Schellenberg, *The Hiddenness Argument*, 23–34.

15. See Paul Moser, *Understanding Religious Experience* (New York: Cambridge University Press, 2019).

as we will see below, is philosophical discourse on the themes of presence and absence more broadly—a dialectic that haunts many more conversations than this one.

For these reasons, in this chapter, I will develop the argument that there is a significant correlation between a well-recognized spread of atheism from about the middle of the nineteenth until the middle of the twentieth century and a developing divine absence discourse in the same period that is the most illuminating point of departure for understanding the forces at play in the spread of atheism *as such*. Furthermore, there is an even more significant correlation between both of these and the then-emerging discourses of modernity, disenchantment, and secularization. Finally, these trends and forms of discourse are highly and non-arbitrarily to be correlated with the advent of a distinctive arrangement of technology, urbanity, and labor—the lived world of modern technoculture.[16] By the lived world of modern technoculture, I name the collection of realities that we take for granted—that become tacit background noise for us—but that (in aggregate) so integrate technology with ordinary life that they are difficult to distinguish except in the abstract. Of course, such a lived world could be correlated with all sorts of developing and well-studied phenomena in this period.[17] Here I discuss only the problem of belief in God. Finally, it is to be admitted that correlation is not the same thing as causation. The next chapter will be taken up with establishing a plausible causal connection between this lived experience of modernity and the development of atheism in the same period.

---

16. On this quasi-Heideggerian notion of "worldhood," see Dreyfus and Taylor, *Retrieving Realism*.

17. Indeed, one popular text of the period (by Jurgen Osterhammel) is consequently titled *The Transformation of the World: A Global History of the Nineteenth Century* (Princeton: Princeton University Press, 2015). One might mention gender in this connection, or even religion. The nineteenth century also saw the Second Great Awakening, the religiously subjectivizing tendencies of which represent a religious inflection of the influences I highlight throughout this essay. See especially Nathan Hatch, *The Democratization of American Christianity* (New Haven: Yale University Press, 1991).

THE DEVELOPMENT OF WESTERN ATHEISM

Charles Taylor's *A Secular Age* is predicated on the near-impossibility of atheism in the late medieval period and its apparent availability as a belief option in our late modern context. At what point do we actually see atheists in these periods? Not surprisingly, there is debate about various figures (Baruch Spinoza, David Hume), and so we will concentrate on those whose atheist pedigree is considered less controversial. Also not surprising is that the development of atheism is punctuated by a representative figure here and there for several centuries. By the end of the nineteenth century, it is not an uncommon position among cultural elites and certain sections of the working class, but it is not until the middle of the twentieth century that it has significant representatives among persons in all walks of life. Let us briefly detail these claims.

Quite possibly the first atheist in early modern Europe was a German named Matthias Knutzen (1646–1674), whose work is not very well known.[18] More commonly known is the French atheist John Meslier (1664–1729), whose atheist writing was discovered after his death.[19] We possibly find an instance of early English atheism in the figure of Anthony Collins (1676–1729).[20] More popular and influential were the writings of Denis Diderot (1713–1784) and Baron d'Holbach (1723–1789), and later of Percy Shelley (1792–1822) in England and Bruno Bauer in Germany (1809–1882).[21] In many (perhaps most) of these early examples, however, we find not an atheism that was ordinarily felt to be plausible but one that stood at the end of a significant intellectual journey—the

18. He is mentioned as such in the very helpful annotated bibliography, "Unbelief: A Historical Bibliography" (2011), by Dr. J. Gordon Melton of the Department of Religious Studies at San Diego State University.

19. On Meslier, see Buckley, *At the Origins of Modern Atheism*, 268–72, and Kors, *Atheism in France*, 4–6.

20. On whom, see David Berman, *A History of Atheism in Britain*, 70–92.

21. Another important text (perhaps the first example of "avowed atheism" in England) was the anonymous *Answer to Dr. Priestly's Letters to a Philosophical Unbeliever* (1782), on which see David Berman, *A History of Atheism in Britain*, 110–33.

conclusion of a long series of inferences. It is significant to note, on this point, that three of the most significant historians of atheism in our day (Michael Buckley, Alan Charles Kors, and James Turner) have as one of their central theses that European atheism developed out of early modern Christian apologetics—the dependence upon particular (especially post-Cartesian) philosophical trends to shore up proof for the articles of their faith. But this dependence upon such philosophy was a double-edged sword. In any case, until figures like the aforementioned Shelley and Bauer in the early nineteenth century, atheism is a drastically extreme position—even among the European intelligentsia. By the early nineteenth century, it receives its first push beyond a mere handful of adherents. It is in the middle of the nineteenth century, however, that we discover something of a turning point in European atheism.

Perhaps the best study of belief and religious practices in Europe in the relevant period is Hugh McLeod's *Secularisation in Western Europe 1848–1914*. McLeod argues that the alliance of socialist and atheist philosophy—perhaps the former helping to account for the latter—really started to pick up in the 1860s to 1880s.[22] This period corresponds to an even more significant decline in the public exercise of religion (such as church attendance) in England, France, and Germany, but this is not to be conflated with becoming an atheist. It is rather to be associated with a decline in ecclesiastical influence and the availability of other religious options and hybrids.[23] Across the Atlantic, the situation was similar in America. While one can find an occasional atheist

---

22. Hugh McLeod, *Secularisation in Western Europe 1848–1914* (New York: Palgrave Macmillan, 2000), 120–21. Certainly European atheism begins to grow in the first half of the nineteenth century. One need only think of Feuerbach and Marx in Germany, and a not-insignificant group of cultural agitators in England, on whom see Royle, *Victorian Infidels*. But the point about the more significant flourishing in the second half of the nineteenth century is captured by the title of Royle's follow-up volume, *Radicals, Secularists, and Republicans: Popular Freethought in Britain, 1866–1915* (Lanham, MD: Rowman & Littlefield, 1980). In the latter half of the nineteenth century, freethought became "popular."

23. See McLeod, *Secularisation in Western Europe 1848–1914*, 147–215.

before the latter half of the nineteenth century, according to historian James Turner, it is only after the 1860s that it becomes a plausible option for more than an eccentric handful.[24]

However this is explained, it seems clear that there was a fairly consistent transatlantic trend in the development of atheism in the latter half of the nineteenth century. The continuity of this trend into the twentieth century is, of course, complicated. Hugh McLeod has persuasively argued that a "fine balance" of the forces of religion and secularism was achieved in the early twentieth century in western Europe but that the scales tipped decisively in the secular direction after the 1960s.[25] And while we cannot discount the role that World War 1 and Auschwitz played on belief in God, it would seem nevertheless that a fragile equilibrium survived their impact but was nevertheless resolved in the direction of a far more prominent rate of unbelief after the 1960s in both Europe and America. Since then, trends in unbelief have been remarkable.[26]

There does seem to be some relative consensus, then, on the significance of (circa) 1860 and (circa) 1960. Where consensus breaks down is on the interpretation of the causes for these trends. The most obvious candidates for interpreting the significance of the earlier date are the rising influence of biblical criticism, the impact of Darwin's theory of evolution, and the forging of nonorthodox philosophies. Certainly, this accounts for some of the trend. Early nineteenth-century British atheism does show signs of having appropriated intellectual currents from the German universities of the time.[27] Nevertheless, several of these trends could

---

24. See James Turner, *Without God, without Creed.* Another significant recent study is Leigh Eric Schmidt, *Village Atheists: How America's Unbelievers Made Their Way in a Godly Nation* (Princeton: Princeton University Press, 2016).

25. See Hugh McLeod, *The Religious Crisis of the 1960s* (New York: Oxford University Press, 2007), 17.

26. See the analysis of Bruce, *Secularization.*

27. See Martin Priestman, *Romantic Atheism: Poetry and Freethought* (Cambridge: Cambridge University Press, 1999). Elisabeth Hurth, *Between Faith and Unbelief: American Transcendentalists and the Challenge of Atheism* (Leiden: Brill, 2007), shows the influence of

simply result in a form of deism, and there is evidence that con-version to atheism based upon the ideas of Darwin, for example, was relatively rare. Susan Budd, in cataloging 150 instances of the loss of faith in the Victorian era, found only three instances in which scientific hypotheses played a role in newfound unbelief.[28] A more persuasive account might attempt to ask *who* accounts for the spread of atheism in the period(s) in question. In the 1860s, it would appear to be members of the urban working class. Peter Royle's two-volume work on Victorian freethought paints a por-trait of the British secularist movement as deriving support mostly from this group, through the comparatively more curious and edu-cated sorts within it.[29] In the 1960s and after, it would appear that unbelief had adherents across the social spectrum—but rose par-ticularly among the comfortable upper middle class (during its proverbial heyday—at least in America).[30] Extensive research has been done on the conditions that give rise to *recent* nonbelief in Western and non-Western countries, and conditions associated with middle-class values and life are often seen as the defining predictors. One recent study argues that secularization tends to come into being with an openness to diversity, with economic security, with personal freedom, and with education.[31] There is

German scholarship in America during this time as well, though perhaps without the same degree of tendency toward explicit atheism. Important general treatments of Romantic-era secularization can be found in Colin Jager's two books, *The Book of God: Secularism and Design in the Romantic Era* (Philadelphia: University of Pennsylvania Press, 2006), and *Unquiet Things: Secularism in the Romantic Age* (Philadelphia: University of Pennsylvania Press, 2014).

28. As summarized in Erdozain, *The Soul of Doubt*, 194.

29. See Royle, *Victorian Infidels*, 1, 237–40, and *Radicals, Secularists, and Republicans*, 126–28.

30. On the rise of the working class in America and its impact on communal life, see Allan Carlson, *From Cottage to Work Station: The Family's Search for Social Harmony in the Industrial Age* (San Francisco: Ignatius Press, 1993) and Blumin, *The Emergence of the Middle Class*. For the trends immediately before, during, and after the mid-twentieth century (in both American and Europe), see Thomas Piketty, *Capital in the Twenty-First Century* (Cambridge: Harvard Belknap, 2014).

31. See the summary of this research program in Sigal Samuel, "Artificial Intelligence Shows Why Atheism is Unpopular," *The Atlantic*, July 23, 2018, https://www.theatlantic.com/

perhaps a significant difference between 1860 and 1960 here. In the former, unbelief was liable to be a more conscious option. By 1960, there is the possibility that you are raised in such a nominally religious context that nonbelief is experienced as either a default or a not particularly large step from the religious environment in which one was raised.

This is a helpful starting point, but it narrows rather than erases the question. This is because, of course, all of these conditions might be mediating rather than direct causes. McLeod highlights evidence that nineteenth-century radical politics, for instance, was a significant force among the working classes and was itself often the cause (rather than the effect) of deconversion.[32] And so we need to be careful not to immediately associate belief conditions with class as such. *Rather, the point is to ask what the ordinary experience of being a member of a particular class was, and how this might help explain behavioral and belief tendencies.* And, indeed, though we shall fill out this picture more below, the attraction to radical politics and the urban context need to be carefully weighed—not least because both gained influence among the middle classes a century later. In any case, political devotion was often felt to be morally fulfilling and purpose-giving—requiring courage rather than cowardly faith.[33] What, however, rendered the "having of a cause" an attractive possession? If radical politics was the scratch, what constituted the itch? Again, we shall address these matters below, but preliminarily it is worth highlighting the connection between economic dependence in urban environments and the functional slavery to other men that so often attended late nineteenth-century wage earning. Possibly the attraction of radical politics was its vision of the non-dependence of one person on another and the

---

international/archive/2018/07/artificial-intelligence-religion-atheism/565076/. See also the remarkable write-up of Phil Zuckerman et al., "Atheism: Contemporary Rates and Patterns," https://pdfs.semanticscholar.org/f379/ed99e57782aca6391ef5f666da7ba41f1333.pdf.

32. McLeod, *Secularisation in Western Europe 1848–1914*, 121.

33. Royle, *Victorian Infidels*, 200. See also Taylor, *A Secular Age*, 539–93.

corresponding possession of one's own agency and destiny. With respect to the 1960s, on the other hand, both Charles Taylor and Steven Bruce, who are on opposite ends of the debate concerning secularization, nevertheless correlate modern secularization with increased religious agency—the availability of religious options as well as well as the felt freedom to choose among them.[34] This, of course, was simply the religious manifestation of such increased agency in general (mobilization, food, career, lifestyle, gender norms and expression, etc.). Whatever the case, if unbelief from the 1860s through the 1960s can be correlated with the dynamics of urban economic life, it is worth seeking to understand the latter more fully in an attempt to discern whether it accounts for, is accounted for, or suspended atop a common causal force as the development of unbelief. Moving toward an attempt at a plausible interpretation, let us briefly consider some distinctive features of technology, urbanity, and labor in this context.

It is worth reiterating that while we are obviously describing an increase in the number of unbelievers or atheists, this is taken as a thumbprint of the more basic phenomenon of the increased *plausibility* of atheism as such. The latter is manifest not merely in the number of positive atheists but in the number of persons who struggled with atheism as a matter to be reckoned with. In Victorian literature, this struggle is a commonplace.[35] Similarly, the modern pedigree of atheism as a plausible option is measured far more by persons engaging with and struggling against it in our day than by counting the number of atheists after the 1960s as such.

---

34. This is a central argument of Taylor, *A Secular Age*, and Bruce, *Secularization*.

35. Two relevant studies are Lance St. John Butler, *Victorian Doubt: Literary and Culture Discourses* (New York: Harvester, 1990), and A. N. Wilson, *God's Funeral: The Decline of Faith in Western Civilization* (New York: Norton, 1999).

TECHNOLOGY, ECONOMY, URBANITY, AND LABOR
AS MUTUAL FORCES

What forces were at play in the century (or so) under discussion?
What common forces exerted themselves upon western European
and American cities, as well as the economy more generally? To get
at these, we shall briefly highlight relevant developments in technology, urbanity, economy, and, finally, labor (which is arguably
a practical sight of their combination)—as well as some relevant
overt responses to each during the period. We shall, in the next
chapter, attempt to synthesize such responses phenomenologically
and theoretically.

Concerning developments in technology, the Industrial
Revolution reached its climax toward the middle the of the nineteenth century.[36] While we might be tempted to think of the most
significant inventions in this era as those of the steam engine or
some such, it is worth noting that the most immediate changes
for working-class persons were in the method and availability of
work. After the progressive enclosure of the commons (especially
in England), and in light of improved agricultural techniques, the
availability and type of labor tended to push the European population toward urban centers.[37] These technological-cum-economic
transformations were a settled feature of European life before the
middle of the nineteenth century. Important to highlight, then,
is that the climax of the push toward the city was a generation
prior to the popularity of unbelief. The increased plausibility of
unbelief is to be associated not (therefore) just with the city as
such but with *having been formed in* the late modern western city.
This trend continues for the other significant date of the 1960s.
Especially in America, a generation of workers' rights movements
in conjunction with a postwar economy (suspended atop massive

---

36. See Allen, *The Industrial Revolution*.
37. See Rykwert, *The Seduction of Place*, 3–42.

technological development)[38] created what historians have often referred to as the golden age of the middle class—defined in terms of relative material comfort. And it was largely persons *formed* in this background who account for the increasing rise of unbelief in the Western world (starting around the 1960s).

Now, this does not prove that this economic and urban life *caused* the rise of unbelief. At most, it might constitute that without which unbelief would have been a lesser trend. But the link could be a mediating one. Mary Eberstadt and Christian Smith, as pointed out in the previous chapter, have both demonstrated the link between family practices/dynamics and the continuity of religion in parents and children. And it is possible that the well-studied effects of modern urban and economic life, including the delocalization of networks of trust and the privatization of the family as the site of economic activity, inevitably make it such that the bonds that have historically and naturally reinforced religious continuity have evaporated. Charles Taylor likewise notes the sustaining effects of a certain form of parish religion that tended to evaporate in the cities.[39]

Another possibility, however, is that something in the nature of technological urban experience *as such* helped to render unbelief plausible. To get at the latter, it is important to come to grips with the existential and psychological response to the developing technological world—whether it be William Blake's "Satanic Mills" or Henry Adams's response to the dynamo.[40] And so we must focus not on technology in the abstract but on technology as concretely *experienced*. What did the average urban citizen of Europe or America experience when they looked out their window? How did they instinctively respond to what Leo Marx has termed the

---

38. See Edgerton, *The Shock of the Old.*

39. Taylor, *A Secular Age,* 443.

40. On the latter, see Henry Adams, *The Education of Henry Adams* (New York: The Modern Library, 1999), 379–90.

"machine's increasing dominance of the visible world"?[41] How did the urban scene and its technological motions affect them? We will posit a theoretical answer to this in the next chapter, but we can establish a few key points here.

On the one hand, technological anxiety is a well-studied phenomenon, especially in its relationship to economic development.[42] But this does not quite capture the affective dimension of our ordinary relationship to the technology that mediates our relationship to the world. What sort of world do we feel ourselves to inhabit when we walk outside and move around on sidewalks, pick up newspapers, and so forth? How do we instinctively or perhaps subconsciously respond to the architecture that ubiquitously populates our ordinary field of vision? There is a growing literature engaging these questions, particularly as it pertains to Victorian culture, though there is little that addresses the impact concerning religious development as such.[43] One exception is James Turner, whose work focuses on American unbelief. He insightfully ponders:

> As divinely created nature receded before the work of human hands, God's daily presence did not disappear, but

---

41. Leo Marx, *The Machine in the Garden: Technology and the Pastoral Ideal in America* (New York: Oxford University Press, 1964), 364.

42. See Joel Mokyr, Chris Vickers, and Nicholas L. Ziebarth, "The History of Technological Anxiety and the Future of Economic Growth," *Journal of Economic Perspectives* 28, no. 3 (2015), 31–50.

43. See Colette Colligan and Margaret Linley, eds., *Media, Technology, and Literature in the Nineteenth Century: Image, Sound, Touch* (Burlington, VT: Ashgate, 2011); Charles A. Fenton, "The Bell Tower: Melville and Technology," *American Literature* 23, no. 2 (1951), 219–32; Tamara S. Ketabgian, *The Lives of Machines: The Industrial Imaginary in Victorian Literature and Culture* (Ann Arbor: University of Michigan Press, 2011); Scott McQuire, *The Media City: Media, Architecture, and Urban Space* (Los Angeles: Sage Publications, 2008); Adam Miller, "Enframing and Enlightenment: A Phenomenological History of Eighteenth-Century British Science, Technology, and Literature" (PhD diss., Vanderbilt University, 2014); Ben Moore, "Invisible Architecture: Ideologies of Space in the Nineteenth-Century City" (PhD diss., University of Manchester, 2014); David Spurr, *Architecture and Modern Literature* (Ann Arbor: University of Michigan Press, 2012); Herbert L. Sussman, *Victorians and the Machine: The Literary Response to Technology* (Cambridge: Harvard University Press, 1968).

it became somewhat less tangible. The effects came mostly below the level of consciousness, where poets speak more clearly than historians. ... Before the eighteenth century (the mid-nineteenth in most places), virtually the only structures that overtopped the trees were church steeples. The terrain filled the eye with God's presumed handiwork, and churches alone of man's creations towered over nature. Did this make divine presence more manifest? Did God then more naturally flow into the background of consciousness? And did blocking out the panorama of divine creation with commercial buildings and factories diminish God's pervasion of the mental image of the world that undergirded conscious thought? ... The effect cannot possibly be demonstrated, much less measured, but it needs to be pointed to. Insulation from nature ultimately had much the same consequence as the growing sense of control over nature. And both reinforced the encroachment, at more articulated levels of thought, of natural causes on divine activity, pushing God's direct presence farther from everyday experience into an intangible spiritual realm ... Capitalist organization, technological change, and urbanization had subtly dissociated God from ordinary verities. And this subliminal disjunction more often pushed belief in God up from the dim layer of unexamined assumptions that form the background of thought into the full light of consciousness. There God lay exposed to reflection and questioning.[44]

Though Turner suggests that this hypothesis cannot be demonstrated or measured, my own argument is that a plausible and probable connection can and should be made. What is more, it would seem that research programs could be developed that look for evidence in literary, poetic, and private writings that highlight

---

44. James Turner, *Without God, without Creed*, 118–19.

the subconscious engagement of the phenomena that Turner points to. Of particular interest is that Turner speaks of the problem in terms of divine presence and absence rather than in terms of personal belief. As I will develop below, this motif seems to take on a particularly prominent role in late modernity—and provides a key access-point (I have argued) in seeking to understand it.

In my judgment, however, a piece is still missing. In the above, Turner highlights the active quality of nature and technology in its impact on humans—the manner in which backgrounds impose themselves on us. But we must also seek to understand the human's tacit relationship to these things as constituted by *human* activity. Human beings relate to their backgrounds both passively and actively. To be sure, Turner has highlighted the extremely important dimension of human control over nature, but not the corresponding shift in the human being's *relation* to its own doings.[45] For concomitant with this shift in background was a shift in the foreground of one's relationship to the world in human labor. And here we must not reduce the matter to something like the monotony of factory work. It is rather to highlight how the background and foreground give a whole picture—a change in one implying some change in the other. Perhaps it is possible that (for example) big buildings could exist without a corresponding sense of divine absence. That we might associate these perhaps leaves unnamed a corresponding shift in humanity's active relation to the world. And so what we have is not just a change of scenery. It is a matter not just of nature versus technology but of the manner in which technology is *used* to divorce people's daily labor from that background and from their immediate lives (and therefore both from immediate meaning—even if monotonous).[46] This emphasis puts human choices and the corresponding system of economic dependencies

---

45. A bit earlier, Turner himself notes the relation between social change and the growth of capitalist economic structures. Ibid., 115

46. This is, of course, Marx's great insight in his *Economic and Philosophical Manuscripts of 1844* (Amherst, NY: Prometheus, 1988), which I shall return to in the next chapter.

in the forefront—themes to which I will return in chapter 4. In any case, then, considering the psychological impact of technology cannot be divorced from considering the psychological impact of the active labor that is organically connected to it. And before and after the 1960s, this is a subject of great anxiety as we see, for instance, in Kurt Vonnegut's 1952 novel *Player Piano* or in the film *The Graduate* (directed by Mike Nichols, 1967). This technological and labor disorientation only increase thereafter.[47]

Finally, the evidence I have just mentioned helps us clarify why atheism is largely associated with the working class around the 1860s and comes to be associated with the middle class around the 1960s. On the one hand, this is just the spread of unbelief to include more people and classes. But there are some important differences. Victorian unbelief, for instance, is almost always attended by the push-factor of anticlericalism. But mid-twentieth-century unbelief is far more characterized by religion simply having little pull factor.[48] On the other hand, the middle class was partially insulated from the social fragmentation of late capitalism until the postwar economy both drew many of the working class into the middle class and gradually disintegrated formerly middle class community and labor patterns into the structures that have been so famously associated with Europe and American in the 1950s.[49] And as Herbert Marcuse famously argued, the compensation to both groups (often via the mediating influence of labor movements) for being sucked into the gravitational force of the modern economy was the anesthesia of the material well-being with its concomitant concerns and (now) sans many of the

47. See Peter Berger, Brigitte Berger, and Hansfried Kellner's important work, *The Homeless Mind: Modernization and Consciousness* (New York: Vintage, 1973), and Richard Sennett, *The Corrosion of Character: The Personal Consequences of Work in the New Capitalism* (New York: Norton, 2000).

48. This is a key point in Steven Pinker, *The Better Angels of Our Nature: Why Violence Has Declined* (New York: Penguin Books, 2012).

49. See Seigel, *Modernity and Bourgeois Life*.

structures that sustained investment in (at least traditional) religion.[50] For many of the working class in the 1860s, religion seemed like a distraction from real-world injustice. For the middle class of the 1960s *and afterward*, religion was progressively seen as less a nuisance than a nonentity.[51] The latter, however, does not imply that previous motivations for irreligion did not continue to exist and exert significant influence. It is rather that new reasons for irreligion emerged alongside the old ones.

Taking stock of my argument thus far, I have noted the correlation of key moments in the trajectory of Western unbelief initially with the rise of the urban working class and, eventually, with the height of the middle class. Both of these are suspended atop periods of astounding technological development, and both involve an adjustment of labor patterns to this technology-as-used. I have tried to use the term "technoculture" to capture the inter-relational dynamic among these dimensions of life (religious, technological, economic, etc.). But, of course, I am not interested in these in the abstract. Rather, I am interested in how they constitute and shape a lived world as a complex nexus of factors within it. And it is here that the language of presence and absence becomes significant. However explained (I will theorize concerning this in the next chapter), this language becomes extremely important when speaking about religious matters in this period. That is, correlated with all of the above is not merely the rise of unbelief and the decline of religion but the rise of a discourse concerning divine absence, an intense struggle to maintain faith, and so forth. In my judgment, as I have argued throughout, this is the most concrete and helpful jumping-off point by which we might arrive at a refined reading of the modern world as well as its self-conscious sense of being modern, secular, and disenchanted.

---

50. Herbert Marcuse, *One-Dimensional Man: Studies in the Ideology of Advanced Industrial Society* (New York: Beacon Press, 1991).

51. See Terry Eagleton, *Culture and the Death of God* (New Haven: Yale University Press, 2015).

THE EMERGENCE OF PRESENCE AND
ABSENCE DISCOURSE

As we have already pointed out, divine absence discourse has typically been associated with questions of God's goodness and interest in humans. In our period, it becomes quite popular to speak of divine presence and absence in terms of God's being or not being at all. What we must notice, however, is that urban life as such elicits similar metaphors. Summarizing the former theme in Victorian literature, Butler writes, "God's absence from the world is not only something lamented by Hardy or, more ambiguously, Carlyle; it is present in, for instance, Charlotte Bronte's use of the theme of the orphan in Jane Eyre and Villette where it becomes 'the symbol of man's metaphysical homelessness.' "[52] Butler also notes the theme of divine absence in Blake's "dark Satanic mills."[53] Of course, Blake's Satan is God's opposite. But urban space *as such* is described in similar terms in Dickens's depiction of *stillness*:

> The street-lamps burn amidst the baleful glooms
> Amidst the soundless solitudes immense
> Or ranged mansions dark and still as tombs.
> The silence which benumbs or strains the sense
> Fulfils with awe the soul's despair unweeping:
> Myriads of habitants are ever sleeping,
> Or dead, or fled from nameless pestilence.[54]

The metaphors of stillness and silence are, then, used of both God and urban space.[55] And there is a symbiotic relationship between this and cosmic isolation.[56] F. W. H. Myers once had a conversation with George Eliot after which he described the effect of her conversation: "And when we stood at length and parted, amid

---

52. Butler, *Victorian Doubt*, 13.

53. Ibid., 30.

54. Quoted in ibid., 49. See also the discussion of church architecture in ibid., 76–77.

55. There is a possible resonance here with Carlyle's "false modern world" in ibid., 35.

56. See ibid., 43.

the columnar circuit of the forest-trees, beneath the last twilight of starless skies, I seemed to be gazing, like Titus at Jerusalem, on vacant seats and empty halls—on a sanctuary with no Presence to hallow it, and heaven left lonely of a God."[57] One could also add the example of Hardy's freethinking urbanite, Sue Bridehead, whose non-religion contrasts with the naive faith of her country lover, Jude.[58]

Across the Atlantic in America, divine absence is arguably a theme in the poetry of Emily Dickinson in the middle of the nineteenth century.[59] A silent cosmos in the face of such realities as death is also an important metaphor in Jack London's 1901 short story *The Law of Life*[60] and in the poetry of Robert Service.[61] And then there is the moving deconversion story of Langston Hughes, which is articulated in the theme of his childhood inability to *see* Jesus.[62]

This discourse becomes especially prominent in the literature and culture that was produced by World War I. In his 1920 novel *This Side of Paradise*, F. Scott Fitzgerald famously described the postwar generation as one "grown up to find all Gods dead, all wars fought, all faiths in man shaken."[63] The postwar period provides several examples of unbelief in the style of lamentation for the killed gods,[64] though there is also significant evidence that the war had an impact in a more general sense on the trend toward

---

57. Cited in A. N. Wilson, *God's Funeral*, 152.

58. Thomas Hardy, *Jude the Obscure* (New York: Penguin, 1998).

59. See Donald W. Dow, "Internal Differences: Secularism, Religion, and Poetic Form" (PhD diss., Rutgers University, 2008), 262–70.

60. Jack London, *The Law of Life* (Providence: Jamestown Publishers, 1976).

61. See his "Reptiles and Roses" in *Freethought on the American Frontier*, ed. Fred Whitehead and Verle Muhrer (Amherst, NY: Prometheus Books, 1992), 205.

62. Ibid., 289–90.

63. F. Scott Fitzgerald, *This Side of Paradise* (New York: Dover, 1996), 213.

64. See, for instance, Walter Lippmann's 1929 book, *A Preface to Morals* (Piscataway: Transaction Publishers, 1982), and Joseph Wood Krutch's book of the same year, *The Modern Temper* (San Diego: Harvest Books, 1957).

unbelief.[65] In any case, divine absence rhetoric is frequent in the war's poetry. One example reads,

> Whose silver cool remakes the dead,
> And lays no blame on any head
> For all the havoc, fire, and lead,
> That fell upon us suddenly,
> When all we came to know as good
> Gave way to Evil's fiery flood,
> And monstrous myths of iron and blood
> Seem to obscure God's clarity.[66]

And another,

> These, in the day when heaven was falling,
> The hour when earth's foundations fled,
> Followed their mercenary calling
> And took their wages and are dead.
> Their shoulders held the sky suspended;
> They stood, and earth's foundations stay;
> What God abandoned, these defended,
> And saved the sum of things for pay.[67]

It is worth pointing out, of course, that divine discourse need not come from atheists as such. It is rather that it was, in the case of some doubters, associated even with *fears* that God was not to be found at all.[68] In a 1951 poem, Anne Ridler gives utterance to this feeling:

---

65. See O'Connor, "The Great War and the Death of God." On a countertrend toward wartime "re-enchantment," see Philip Jenkins, *The Great and Holy War: How World War I Became a Religious Crusade* (New York: Harper One, 2014), 120–24.

66. Osbert Sitwell, "Therefore is the name of it called Babel," in *The Penguin Book of First World War Poetry*, ed. George Walter (New York: Penguin, 2006), 76–77.

67. A. E. Housman, "Epitaph on an Army of Mercenaries," in ibid., 246.

68. See Butler, *Victorian Doubt*, 19–20.

Yet it is a long pursuit,
Carrying the junk and treasure of an ancient creed,
To a love who keeps faith by seeming mute
And deaf, and dead indeed.[69]

Other responses include a sense of loss, a motif that has particular resonance in a larger Victorian discourse.[70] Of particular importance would be responses that motivated unbelief by appeal to bravery and courage (for instance, Carlyle).[71] Or divine absence could be the object of a religious taunt in the style of Elijah before the prophet of Baal (as in the case of Algernon Charles Swinburne):

Cry aloud; for your God is a God and a Savior;
    cry, make yourselves lean;
Is he drunk or asleep, that the rod of wrath is
    unfelt or unseen?
Is the fire of his old loving-kindness gone out,
    that his pyres are acold?
Hath he gazed on himself unto blindness, who made
    men blind to behold?[72]

The diversity of responses to this commonly felt phenomenon approximates what Charles Taylor labels the "nova effect" of this era.[73]

The theme continues, of course, into our own time. The theme is ubiquitous enough in modern film and literature, as some examples provided at the beginning of this chapter indicate, as to barely need mention.[74] A fascinating example can be found in John Lennon's famous secular hymn, "Imagine," released in 1971. It

---

69. Quoted in A. N. Wilson, *God's Funeral*, 15.

70. Butler, *Victorian Doubt*, 21.

71. See A. N. Wilson, *God's Funeral*, 66–67.

72. Ibid., 229.

73. Taylor, *A Secular Age*, 299–422.

74. For a brief treatment, see Ralph Wood's helpful article, "Everything, Something, Nothing: The Modern Novel and the Departure of God," ABC Religion & Ethics, November 26, 2015, http://www.abc.net.au/religion/articles/2015/11/26/4360472.htm.

begins, "Imagine there's no heaven. It's easy if you try." The striking line is the second rather than the first. It is that such unbelief is easy that renders the song a modern one. The theme of God's absence (or potential presence) is also fairly common in modern dystopian and science fiction.[75] And, of course, it continues in modern philosophy.[76]

In order to fully appreciate divine absence language and metaphors, we must try to see them in the context of a distinctively modern discourse related to presence and absence as such.[77] Martin Heidegger and Jacques Derrida both speak of a "metaphysics of presence" that has dominated Western thought since Plato. However, the language of presence and absence—used almost in the abstract—takes on a major role in the writings of Jacques Ellul, Walter Ong, and George Steiner (whose *Real Presences* is an influential book-length critique of the divorce of words from their participation in the world's meaning). I will argue in the next chapter that this trend is something like a negative photocopy of our modern comportment to the world. In any case, for our present purposes, it is worthy of note that metaphors of presence and absence have larger purchase and resonance than their pertinence to the present question. This is possibly to be correlated, as we will see, with the rise of particular sorts of communications technologies that render the larger question of presence and absence prominent in our ordinary lives. Before we move on to this, however, it is worth highlighting one more essential correlation between the rise of divine absence discourse and modern atheism. And this is the rise of discourse concerning the disenchantment of the world,

75. See especially W. Warren Wagar, "World's End: Secular Eschatologies in Modern Fiction," in *The Secular Mind* (New York: Holmes & Meier, 1982), 220–38, particularly his reflections on Alfred Bester, "Adam and No Eve," *Astounding Science Fiction*, September 1941, and J. G. Ballard's disaster novels. Also relevant is Herrick, *Scientific Mythologies*.

76. In addition to Schellenberg himself, he gives several examples in *The Hiddenness Argument*, 27–28.

77. On the prevalence of this dialectic in early to late modern religion, see Robert Orsi, *History and Presence* (Cambridge: Harvard Belknap, 2016).

modernity, and secularism. It would appear that all three of these descriptors gain influence at precisely the time that divine absence discourse does.

THE EMERGENCE OF DISENCHANTMENT, MODERNITY, AND SECULARIZATION DISCOURSE(S)

As suggested by the previous chapter, debates over the causes and meaning of the world's supposed disenchantment, the nature of modernity, and the trend toward secularization are enormously complicated and variously interpreted. However one interprets these things, though, it is worth noting that all of these descriptors arise in the same generation as divine absence discourse—to which they are integrally related. And as with divine absence discourse, these terms possibly say more about their original contexts than they do about the history in terms of which they define themselves. It has been demonstrated that the intellectual pedigree of each dates to the middle of the nineteenth century.[78]

To speak of modernity is, of course, to assume the existence of an epoch over against which one measures oneself. And not surprisingly, we are not the first humans to think of ourselves as modern in this sense.[79] And even within that period that we consider properly modern versus medieval, modernity occupies an ambiguous location.[80] Often identified as the first modern use of the term (that is, modernity) is Charles Baudelaire's 1863 essay "The Painter of Modern Life," wherein he famously defines modernity as "the ephemeral, the contingent, the half of art whose other half is eternal and immutable."[81] Many thinkers would soon opine

---

78. On modernity and disenchantment, see Josephson-Storm, *The Myth of Disenchantment*. On secularization, see Ian Hunter, "Secularization: Process, Program, and Historiography."

79. See Robert Pogue Harrison's interesting discussion, *Juvenescence*, which interrogates many ancient thinkers concerning the question of the cultural age of the human race.

80. See the periodization in Marshall Berman, *All That Is Solid Melts into Air*, 15–36.

81. Quoted in ibid., 133.

concerning the sense that they belonged to a modern world. Here, I want to isolate the figure of Max Weber (1864–1920), whose contribution to discussions of what was/is unique about recent Western life set the terms of the debate, in many respects, for discussions that succeeded him. In what follows, I will draw from his late-in-life lecture "Science as a Vocation," which was delivered at Munich University in 1917—and which represents his mature thought (he died just a few years later).[82]

In this lecture, Weber addresses a group of university students—many of whom, presumably, were scientists in training—and he asks, "What are the conditions of science as a vocation in the material sense of the term?"[83] After informing the students that they must expect to endure the mediocrity of many colleagues, he goes on to consider the internal situation pertinent to the scientific vocation.[84] Concerning this he writes that "science has entered a phase of specialization previously unknown and that this will forever remain the case. Not only externally, but inwardly, matters stand at a point where the individual can acquire the sure consciousness of achieving something truly perfect in the field of science only in the case he is a strict specialist."[85] He goes on to relate such specialization to the smallest bits of progress that are associated with the scientific vocation.

This specialization and its attendant progress, a measure of the scientific spirit, becomes Weber's springboard to discussing science in a larger historical context. Indeed, the recent advance of science is part of a much larger history. And here we must quote Weber at length:

82. I have found the treatment of Josephson-Storm, *The Myth of Disenchantment*, 269–301, particularly helpful in its treatment of Weber's thought.

83. Max Weber, "Science as a Vocation," in *Essays in Sociology* (New York: Oxford University Press, 1946), 129–56.

84. Ibid., 4.

85. Ibid.

Scientific progress is a fraction, the most important fraction, of the process of intellectualization which we have been undergoing for thousands of years and which nowadays is usually judged in such an extremely negative way. Let us first clarify what this intellectualist rationalization, created by science and by scientifically oriented technology means practically. Does it mean that we today, for instance, everyone sitting in this hall, have a greater knowledge of the conditions of life under which we exist than has an American Indian or Hottentot? Hardly. Unless he is a physicist, one who rides on the streetcar has no idea how the car happened to get into motion. And he does not need to know. He is satisfied that he may 'count' on the behavior of the streetcar, and he orients his conduct according to this expectation; but he knows nothing about what it takes to produce such a car so that it can move. The savage knows incomparably more about his tools. ... The increasing intellectualization and rationalization do not, therefore, indicate an increased and general knowledge of the conditions under which one lives. It means something else, namely, the knowledge or belief that if one but wished one could learn it at any time. Hence, it means that principally there are no mysterious incalculable forces that come into play, but rather that one can, in principle, master all things by calculation. This means that the world is disenchanted. One need no longer have recourse to magical means in order to master or implore the spirits, as did the savage, for whom such mysterious powers existed. Technical means and calculations perform the service. This above all is what intellectualization means.[86]

---

86. Ibid., 6–7.

Several items are worthy of note here. First, Weber (perhaps a bit surprisingly) belongs to that group of thinkers who see modern life as having its seminal pedigree in trends that are quite ancient—particularly early Greek philosophy.[87] And here we meet a mature use of the term disenchantment. For Weber, disenchantment does not (as it is often thought) imply the eradication of religion as such. It is important to note, in this respect, that he sees disenchantment as having taken place in a quite religious age.[88] Nor does it imply, as is more explicit in the above quote, that the average human knows more about the world than previous humans. Rather, what is in view is a kind of epistemic posture or instinct—a sense that the world is such that I could understand any dimension of it that I wanted to or if I tried—a sense that the objects to be known are entirely reducible to and will yield to the categories of my intellectual inquiry. What this eradicates is not the divine as such, then, but rather any tacit sense of the unpredictability and incalculability of the divine (which Weber would have tied to the development of rigid doctrine) *as well as*, consequently, unpredictable folk magic and spirits. A key point to note, on this score, is that Weber's account of disenchantment suggests that for modern persons, divine and mechanical agency have a zero-sum relationship to one another. That is, to whatever extent a thing is calculable, it is not magical or moved by spirits. This will become an important point in what follows.

Concerning the notion of disenchantment, Weber later continues:

Now, this process of disenchantment, which has continued to exist in Occidental culture for millennia, and, in general, this "progress," to which science belongs as a link and motive force, do they have any meanings that go beyond

87. See also the treatment of Kippenberg, *Discovering Religious History in the Modern Age*, 155–74.

88. See also the important discussion of Ivan Strenski, *Thinking about Religion*, 198–232.

the purely practical and technical? You will find this question raised in the most principled form in the works of Leo Tolstoi. He came to raise the question in a peculiar way. All his broodings increasingly revolved around the problem of whether or not death is a meaningful phenomenon. And his answer was: for civilized man death has no meaning. It has none because the individual life of civilized man, placed into an infinite "progress," according to its own imminent meaning should never come to an end; for there is always a further step ahead of one who stands in the march of progress. And no man who comes to die stands upon the peak which lies in infinity.[89]

Weber considers this, of course, an urgent question for his audience. Belonging, as these students intend, to a discipline that progressively disenchants the world—it is natural to raise the question of meaning. He again asks, "Has 'progress' as such a recognizable meaning that goes beyond the technical, so that to serve it is a meaningful vocation?"[90] And here we encounter a dialectical aspect of Weber's thought. On the one hand, the drive for progress is rooted in a framework of meaning. On the other, the progress itself has given us a glance into a cosmos that is not obviously meaningful. Weber writes that "the fate of our times is characterized by rationalization and intellectualization and, above all, by the 'disenchantment of the world.' Precisely the ultimate and most sublime values have retreated from public life either into the transcendental realm of the mystic life or into the brotherliness of direct and personal human relations."[91] For Weber, the modern quest for meaning cannot be found in public religion, which is no

---

89. Weber, "Science as a Vocation," 7.

90. Ibid.

91. Ibid., 12. There is a parallel between this and his argument in *The Protestant Ethic and the Spirit of Capitalism* (New York: Scribner's Sons, 1976) that the original religious underpinnings of the modern economy gave way, as a kind of scaffolding, to a self-sustained cultural order out of step with its original ethic of self-denial.

longer viable. Rather, one can take the path of mysticism or find meaning in immediate brotherly relations. If one is interested in traditional religion, Weber continues,

> To the person who cannot bear the fate of the times like a man, one must say: may he rather return silently, without the usual publicity build-up of renegades, but simply and plainly. The arms of the old churches are opened widely and compassionately for him ... One way or another he has to bring his "intellectual sacrifice"—that is inevitable ... Such an intellectual sacrifice in favor of an unconditional religious devotion is ethically quite a different matter from the evasion of the plain duty of intellectual integrity, which sets in if one lacks the courage to clarify one's own ultimate standpoint.[92]

It is not, therefore, that Weber does not consider orthodox religion a fitting option for the modern individual. It is rather that this (1) cannot be public and (2) cannot be reconciled with the spirit of inquiry that has disenchanted the world. The options are to find ultimate meaning through an intellectual sacrifice or to find contingent and particular meaning in private experience or personal relationships.[93] And this highlights an important dimension to Weber's treatment of secularization. While scientific and technical progress do not immediately eradicate religion, they progressively privatize it, change it (mysticism), and render it intellectually costly. This is not to mention the impact of technical progress in reshaping the world to be more safe, easy, pleasurable, and entertaining—the opposite of which often fueled invocation of the divine for aid and relief.[94]

92. Ibid.

93. On this point, I have been helped by David L. Swartz, "Review of Michael Symonds, *Max Weber's Theory of Modernity: The Endless Pursuit of Meaning," Contemporary Sociology* 46, no. 2 (2017), 221–23.

94. Weber is, of course, exhorting persons who have taken up the sciences as a vocation, and so there is an attempt to dignify this calling therein. In some ways, he portrays those who can do this well as particularly mature (i.e., the one who can bear the fate of the

It is important to highlight, furthermore, how allied technological and scientific progress are for Weber. As he understands it,
the disenchantment of the world happens directly in proportion
to our ability to manipulate, control, and harness it (obscuring any
sense of its prior agency). Particularly because we would be right
to query whether these might be accounted for by contemporane-
ous developments in anthropology, biblical criticism, and religious
studies, it is fascinating to note that Weber (who was involved in
these projects as well)[95] locates the fracture precisely where he
does. This is likely because these developments were seen as the
conclusions of science more broadly considered.

Nevertheless, to the extent that Weber's science was and can
be resolved in a direction other than his own, it is worth asking
why he (alongside many contemporaries) was persuaded that they
meant cosmic disenchantment.[96] And it is this question, it seems
to me, that highlights the potential fruitfulness of our theme of
divine absence as an existential phenomenal sensibility that is
discursively elaborated in terms of secularization, modernity, and
disenchantment. That is, getting inside divine absence discourse,
and the corresponding development of the plausibility of atheism might provide a fruitful line of inquiry for interpreting why
Weber's particular intellectual project (and those like it) were so
prevalent and plausible in the nineteenth century until today. This
is because such discourse seems to imply and attempt to articulate
a more primal experience of the so-called modern world that is
then explained in these other terms. Suggestive in this direction is

times "like a man"). This person perhaps sacrifices certain sorts of transcendental meaning
to invest in the immediate needs of a society for the sake of others. That is, one might read
them as sacrificing a certain aspect of their own spiritual fulfillment in order to cultivate
a society that preserves these benefits for others. They must work without guides or clear
metaphysical vantage point.

95. See Weber, *The Sociology of Religion* (New York: Beacon Press, 1993), and Strenski,
Thinking about Religion, 198–232.

96. On "other" resolutions, see Timothy Larsen's two books, *Crisis of Doubt* and *The
Slain God*.

that each term is resonant with absence (or even loss) discourse because there is an implied negation in each (at least as used). Disenchantment is the negation of an agentic cosmos. The secular is the absence of the religious—in whatever sphere. Even modernity is very often defined in terms of the disintegration of classical social structures and belief patterns rather than any singular new ones. What I am suggesting here is that—rather than the terms explaining the experience of divine absence—perhaps the experience of divine absence explains why the terms themselves, and their implicit narratives (even when they turn out to be wrong), become plausible. Making this case requires the theoretical and phenomenological analysis in the next chapter.

THE ARGUMENT SO FAR

In this chapter, I have *not* argued that post-industrial technology and labor structures caused atheism to be a living option for Europeans. Rather, I have argued that we can at least detect a significant correlation between these phenomena. Specifically, the European migration to the cities and the corresponding swell of lower-class industrial workers began to occur a generation prior to the moment we began to see significant growth in unbelief in Europe. The middle class of the twentieth century is constituted by now more stable former members of the working class (after the efforts of many labor movements) as well as former members of the middle class whose economic fate and social life nevertheless depended on adjusting to the new industrial economy.[97] Within a generation of the golden age of this middle class, we see another swell in unbelief. Moreover, what we see is not merely the rise of the plausibility of unbelief but the development of the sensibility

---

97. See the helpful summary of Jeffrey Helgeson, "American Labor and Working-Class History, 1900–1945," *Oxford Research Encyclopedia of American History*, http://americanhistory.oxfordre.com/view/10.1093/acrefore/9780199329175.001.0001/acrefore-9780199329175-e-330, and Jurgen Kocka, "The European Middle Classes," *The Journal of Modern History* 67, no. 4 (1995), 783–806.

that divine absence or invisibility is a relevant consideration in respect of God's existence at all. This is all to be further correlated with the origins of our still ongoing discussions concerning modernity, secularization, and disenchantment—each of which (as used) name either a loss or (minimally) an absentiality.

Nevertheless, these correlations warrant an analysis of the causal relationships between these associated phenomena (even if they do not explain each other but are rather explained by another common cause). But what sort of analysis do I mean? On the one hand, one could pile up mountains of empirical evidence from the literature and private archives of the period in question. But even if the causal direction of such associations were made explicit in such material, they would remain interpretive. What is more, a good interpretation of human behavior is not necessarily whatever is closest to humans' own interpretation of themselves. That is, even if the causal links are not made explicit by persons undergoing the changes in question (and I am not claiming they were not), this does not automatically constitute an argument against any particular reading. Human beings often give more primitive utterance to what is later brought into the discursive realm by others.[98] The sense in which I seek to offer an interpretation, then, is in trying to creatively imagine and articulate a theoretical and phenomenological account of "what it is like" to dwell in the conditions associated with the rising plausibility of unbelief, to imagine (by contrast) "what it is like" to be otherwise, and (most importantly) *how* it is that the lived world(s) that we are analyzing gives rise to one or the other.

And it is here that I seek to supplement Charles Taylor's account. He focuses on the moment in European consciousness when it was possible to live entirely within what he terms the "immanent frame" and (more importantly) when religion became a threat to

---

98. One need not necessarily think of Freud here, but rather of Martin Heidegger or Julian Marias.

a fulfilled moral life in that dimension.[99] I stated in the previous chapter, however, that this isolates morality from a sense of larger worldhood in a way that speaks (perhaps) to Taylor's own religious instincts rather than human religious behavior as such.[100] Because the question could be pushed back a level. Why did it become possible to live entirely within the immanent frame? What transitions made this possible? In asking this, I do not think Taylor's account is so much wrong as incomplete. Much of nineteenth-century unbelief was *consciously* motivated by moral revulsion to Christianity or to the church. But the plausibility of atheism in relation to such moral critique could be suspended atop an already experienced world where God's being was felt to be a necessarily ineradicable feature. To dispense with God, then, God has to *seem* dispensable as a theoretical and practical concept in the first place. And it is a shift in that latter structure that I seek to illuminate.

The plausibility of my argument will depend upon several preconditions in my reader. First, my account may or may not resonate as an explanation of the reader's own sense of what reality is like. Admittedly, the strength or weakness of my account will hinge upon this. Second, and to a lesser extent, the plausibility of my account cannot be divorced from what one thinks of the normative issues implicit in the discussion. That is, if one believes that God's existence is rationally necessary (as I do), then the question is really a matter of how inferior ideas had so much influence, how our felt sense of things shifted away from what our mind knows to be reality, how a godless cosmic imaginary became a (*felt*) plausible reading of the world with which modern persons must negotiate—perhaps even despite what they otherwise consciously believe. However, the more important point of connection with the reader is the first one.

---

99. See Taylor, *A Secular Age*, 270–95.

100. See Horton, "The Enduring Power of the Christian Story: Reformation Theology for A Secular Age," 23–38.

My own proposal is that the transition from belief to unbelief was not a transition from belief (say) in Aquinas's five proofs and Aristotle's four causes to belief in materialism and modern science. Rather, each of these brings a more primal world relation into discourse. And it is that primal world-relation, then, that renders these discourses *not* right or wrong, but *plausible* or *implausible*. Preindustrial life need not be sentimentalized, but for most persons it involved navigating the world alongside persons who were immediate to oneself. That is, humans (whether they liked one another or not) ordinarily lived a life in which one's network of trust was personal. Furthermore, the world itself, co-navigated with immediate persons, was felt to have the character of an agent *not* because of the projection of some theory but because (like persons) it *insisted itself* upon a local community. One's life involved a negotiation with the structures of the world and a navigation around them through trial and ordeal. In each of these dimensions, then, reality was experienced as having the characteristics (practically) of the personal and the agentic. It is not surprising in such a lived context that God-discourse was a natural way of speaking about reality as such.

What shifts with enclosure and the movement to cities is, first, the character of one's relationship to one's own labor and therefore one's relationship to the world (the meaning of which I will unpack in the next chapter). Concomitant with this is the progressive eradication of immediate networks of trust to (as briefly noted in the previous chapter) networks of dependence that function at a distance. Humans began to depend on systems guaranteed by unseen experts. The progressive erosion of communal immediacy and dependence corresponded to the furniture of one's lived world as well. Increasingly, the house is not built by "dad" and the meal is not prepared by "mom," but rather the furniture of the world (increasingly mediated by artifice) is mass product for mass humanity, which products act as compensation for the chasm now fixed between one's life and one's labor. To the extent that the world reinforced itself upon men, nevertheless, it was still possible for religion to be a sort of lifeline in a crisis, the so-called opiate of the masses.[101] However, as technological artifice is perfected, as worker's movements turn working-class persons into middle-class persons, and as formerly middle-class persons adjust to the impact of industrialism in their relationship to the modern economy, the active relationship between humanity and world shifts. And so in addition to the foreclosure of one's primal and active meaning-making activity in the world, not only is the passive reinforcement (in the face of other persons) of cosmic agency erased but so is the agency of the world itself. Tailored as it increasingly becomes to human taste and convenience as compensation for involvement in the market, the world itself is progressively reduced to passivity as the world is progressively mediated almost entirely by artifice. And it is likely for this reason, in my judgment, that we see a second swell of unbelief in the 1960s, representing the psychological comportment of a generation that had been raised entirely within the lived worldhood of the golden era of the middle class (with both its material comforts and existential ennui—the common soil of that generation's various responses to their condition).

Divine absence discourse is (then) a way of naming the erasure of God from our conscious reflexive instincts about the world. Once again, this does not make unbelief inevitable, but it renders it plausible. And finally, my account is not intended to subtly pine for the preindustrial condition over the modern one. As I will further argue in chapter 4, this is misguided. But first, let us turn to the above case.

---

101. Possibly the appeal of twentieth-century pared-down liberal theologies, crisis theologies, or existential theologies can be accounted for in this vein. The best account is James Livingston and Francis Schussler Fiorenza, *Modern Christian Thought: The Twentieth Century* (Minneapolis: Fortress Press, 2006).

THREE

Modern Atheism as a Technocultural Phenomenon II: Causation

SUMMARY OF REMAINING ARGUMENT

In this chapter, I propose a theory of the relationship between modern technoculture and the emergence (as well as the expansion) of modern atheism's prevalence and *plausibility*. At the broadest level, I seek to accomplish this by asking and answering the following question: What does modern technoculture—in our practical involvements with it—explicitly and tacitly suggest to us concerning what it means for a thing (in its broadest possible sense) to be real? I argue that this attunes us to interpret the world in terms of materiality and manipulability. Said negatively, this attunes us toward the world in such a way that it manifests as devoid of *inherent* meaning or *internal* agency (which are rather felt to be projections onto it). God is perceived to be absent from the world, then, to the extent that the features of the world that have classically reinforced him are rendered mute.

This attunement is not merely a matter of technoculture acting upon a passive human subject. The very mention of culture implies that this attunement also includes men's *active* engagement as well. This means that we must consider the ordinary means of men's contact with the world, which, in a modern context, means we must consider the world-making impact of modern human labor. In much modern labor, I will argue, the world becomes the unconscious projection of the human—but of an *impersonal* rather than agentic self.

My argument plausibly explains *why*, then, divine absence discourse and atheism become prevalent in the 1860s. It is (plausibly) because alienated urban laborers experienced their involvement in the world as scripted and mechanical—the resultant perception being that a world adequated to such labor must be material and manipulable. But the urban lower classes still had some remaining local community life and the hardship of the world itself to reinforce (in the polar confrontations of such things as love and death) the active and agentic nature of the world as *passively* experienced by the human. But as the lower classes were progressively transformed into the middle class, and as they (along with previous members of that class) were compensated for their increasing alienation by the reality-suspending comforts of modern technology (which comforts define the class itself), even this *active* dimension of the world was increasingly obscured, mechanized, and scripted. Shaped by people for people, and especially in requiring the gradual outsourcing of formerly overlapping networks of trust, the agency of the world tended to be covered over. It is for this reason that the second major moment in the rise of unbelief corresponds to the golden era of the middle class, as well as to the birth of its existential crisis. In short, in the above question and in this reply concerning modern technocultural worldhood, we discover *how* modern technoculture actually *accounts for* the phenomenon of divine absence in its modern form.

It is important to highlight, additionally, that our contemporary cosmic imaginary cannot be adequately described without unimagining it. This is because, as Charles Taylor argues, our identity as modern implies the self-perception of "having overcome a previous condition."[1] We must immediately caveat that the past is not the negative photocopy of the present. As well, we will have

---

1. Taylor, *A Secular Age*, 28.

occasion in the next chapter to suggest that modern persons often nevertheless feel themselves to be alienated from *involvement* in the history in which they believe their era is caught up. But we want to creatively imagine, rather than dialectically and negatively define, the previous order.

My aims in *this* chapter, then, are four-fold. First, I will orient my inquiry in relation to several theorists of technology and labor whose insights illuminate the relationship between modern humanity, modern technology and labor, and the human's resultant experience of reality. Taking their theses for granted, I seek to integrate and fill out their arguments in relation to my own particular inquiry. In order to do this, I will, second, attempt to unimagine the current order of things in order to hypothesize the relationship between labor, urbanity, and the felt presence of the divine in much of human history until the European Industrial Revolution. This will then ground my brief attempt to describe how these relationships were rearranged in the modern order. Third, with these general plot points in place, I will then seek to supplement the insights of the aforementioned theorists with a refined phenomenology of the lived worldhood of our modern order in its active and passive dimensions (labor and technology—constituting modern technoculture). Though my general argument will be clear by this point, I will, fourth and finally, come full circle (from a broader to a more specific argument) to interrogate the modern dialectic of presence and absence in relation to our modern culture's prioritization of seeing versus hearing as a model for what it means that a thing is real or present. This being accomplished, I will have set the stage for some evaluative reflections in the next and final chapter.

TOOLS FROM THE PHILOSOPHY OF TECHNOLOGY AND LABOR

In theorizing the relationship between modern technology, labor, and the human perception of reality, I am, of course, (if I am wise) standing on the shoulders of giants. Consequently, in this section, I gather several insights from some of the most important theorists of modern technology and labor in order to integrate and supplement their insights in the rest of this chapter. I start with two philosophers of technology (Jacques Ellul and Martin Heidegger) and then move on to two philosophers of labor (Karl Marx and Herbert Marcuse).

Jacques Ellul on Technique

Jacques Ellul's *The Technological Society* is an impressive and complex book. For Ellul, previous philosophers of technology had missed the central feature of modern technological culture because they had focused upon "the machine" rather than what he calls "technique." He uses the concept many times and defines it in several ways. He writes, for instance:

> Let the machine have its head, and it topples everything that cannot support its enormous weight. Thus everything had to be reconsidered in terms of the machine. And that is precisely the role that technique plays. In all fields it made an inventory of what it could use, of everything that could be brought into line with the machine. The machine could not integrate itself into nineteenth-century society; technique integrated it ... But when technique enters into every area of life, including the human, it ceases to be external to man and becomes his very substance. It is no longer face to face with man but is integrated with him, and it progressively absorbs him. In this respect, technique is radically different from the machine. This transformation, so obvious in modern society, is the result of the fact that technique has become autonomous.[2]

---

2. Ellul, *The Technological Society*, 5–6. Ellul goes on, "We can even say that technique is characteristic of precisely that realm in which the machine itself can play no role." Ibid., 7.

One can sense the ghost of Marx in the notion that technique becomes humanity's very substance. We become what we do. But, for Ellul, the agent is not just man, but autonomous technique itself. Again defining technological culture, Ellul writes:

> The twofold intervention of reason and consciousness in the technical world, which produces the technical phenomenon, can be described as the quest of the one best means in every field. And this "one best means" is, in fact, the technical means. It is the aggregate of those means that produces technical civilization. It is ... the specialist who chooses the means.[3]

Jacob Van Vleet's recent analysis of Ellul's thought helpfully summarizes two aspects of Ellul's notion of technique. "First, it refers to the modern mindset guided by a desire for greater efficiency, instrumentality, and control. Second, technique refers to the technological milieu of contemporary industrial society. Overall, technique is the pernicious force underlying modern forms of capitalism, socialism, and other economic systems."[4] As reflected here, two themes constantly emerge. Technique has taken on a systemic life of its own, and it affects whatever it touches. This flattens our world. Writes Van Vleet:

> For Ellul, technique is first and foremost a mindset—a worldview driven by an unfettered desire to efficiency and control. Technique has also become a "totality of methods rationally arrived at and having absolute efficiency ... in every field of human activity." As a worldview and a methodology, technique inevitably becomes linked with science, technology, politics, the military, education, and nearly every other sphere of modern society. Technique, which

---

3. Ibid., 21.

4. Jacob Van Vleet, *Dialectical Theology and Jacques Ellul: An Introductory Exposition* (Minneapolis: Fortress Press, 2013), 13.

is characterized by rationality and artificiality, leads to an overemphasis on logic and science over arts and the humanities. It also leads to a loss of personal psychological and spiritual development as well as a devaluating of creativity. As Ellul puts it, technique leaves us living in a "logical dimension alone." By providing an artificial environment in which humans live, technique also strips us of our relationship with the natural world. As a result of this artificiality, we begin seeing the world as an alien object.[5]

That last sentence is particularly important. The artificiality of technique, when proliferated to a large enough extent, makes the world feel quite different. We are alienated from nature, but nature does not seem like reality. It seems foreign. Ellul writes that "technique is the translation into action of man's concern to master things by means of reason, to account for what is subconscious, make quantitative what is qualitative, make clear and precise the outlines of nature, take hold of chaos and put order into it."[6] And again, "In technique, whatever its aspect or the domain in which it is applied, a rational process is present which tends to bring mechanics to bear on all that is spontaneous and irrational."[7]

The independence of this process and its tendency to shape whatever it touches are related phenomena. Ellul writes:

The new factor is that the multiplicity of these techniques has caused them literally to change their character. Certainly, they derive from old principles and appear to be the fruit of normal and logical evolution. However, they no longer represent the same phenomenon. In fact, technique has taken substance, has become a reality in itself. It is no longer

---

5. Ibid., 214–15.

6. Ellul, *The Technological Society*, 43.

7. Ibid., 78–79.

merely a means and an intermediary. It is an object in itself, an independent reality with which we must reckon.[8]

One can already detect that Ellul hints at how it is that technological society influences our beliefs about the sacred and the transcendental. Humans have often interpreted the realm of the divine and the transcendental to be free and undetermined. God, it is often said, cannot be put in a box. His ways are mysterious. We cannot reduce the divine to rational calculation nor the echoes of the divine in human experience to a formula. But in a world wherein it is difficult to cognitively separate the mentality of technique from the objects it dominates (the now alien world), these things can either be reduced to what they are not or seem invisible altogether. With respect to the former, Ellul writes that the phenomenon of self-augmentation gives technique a strangely harsh aspect. It resembles nothing other than itself. Whatever the domain to which it is applied, man or God, technique simply *is*; it undergoes no modifications in the movement which is its being and essence. It is the only locus where form and being are identical. It is only a form, but everything conforms to it. Here technique assumes the peculiar characteristics which make it a thing apart. A precisely and well-defined boundary surrounds it: there is that which is technique and there is everything else, which is not. Whatever passes this boundary and enters into technique is constrained to adopt its characteristics.[9]

With respect to the latter, technique can hide the divine by itself becoming an object of veneration.

> Man cannot live without the sacred. He therefore transfers
> his sense of the sacred to the very thing which has destroyed
> its former object: to technique itself. In the world in which
> we live, technique has become the essential mystery, taking

---

8. Ibid., 63.
9. Ibid., 94.

widely diverse forms according to place and race. Those who have preserved some of the notions of magic both admire and fear technique. Radio presents itself an inexplicable mystery, an obvious and recurrent miracle. It is no less astonishing than the highest manifestations of magic once were, and it is worshipped as an idol would have been worshipped, with the same simplicity and fear.[10]

Nevertheless, despite technique's tendency to hide or reduce reality, it cannot *ultimately* accomplish this. Van Vleet argues that *The Technological Society* must be read in the whole of Ellul's corpus, and in that context, he reads Ellul as a philosopher of hope.[11] He writes, "Technique envelops the human sphere and is constantly changing, but ultimately humans exist as contraries to technique. Their essence is not efficiency, like that of technique, but something qualitatively different, and thus they remain fundamentally unsynthesizable aspects within technique."[12] Again, "Technique's ultimate goal is to reconcile all of nature and humanity into itself. This may happen to a large extent, but in the end, according to Ellul, this is impossible."[13]

Human beings look for freedom in new forms of technology, consumerism, and television, according to Ellul. Within this sphere of technique, however, freedom cannot be found. Only through the spiritual can one escape the realm of necessity. But how can one connect to the spiritual? Ellul maintains that the dialectical link between the closed and the open realms is *hope*.[14]

Talking stock of Ellul's theory, then, the key to the impact of modern technological society on religious beliefs is something like not the contrast between the visible machine versus the invisible

10. Ibid., 143.
11. See Van Vleet, *Dialectical Theology and Jacques Ellul*, 160–70.
12. Ibid., 152.
13. Ibid., 153.
14. Ibid., 39, emphasis in original.

110

CHAPTER THREE

God but rather the contrast between the visibility of results versus any aspect of reality that cannot be so reduced.[15] It is, in other words, our increased inability to imagine a reality that fundamentally and essentially has features that are more like persons (i.e., agents) than things or blind processes.

Martin Heidegger on the Destining of Revealing

Heidegger's essay "The Question Concerning Technology" is difficult, and grasping its point will require more extended analysis. Heidegger speaks of a free relationship to technology, which can only occur "if it opens our human existence to the essence of technology."[16] However, "technology is not equivalent to the essence of technology."[17] Indeed, "the essence of technology is by no means anything technological. Thus we shall never experience our relationship to the essence of technology so long as we merely represent and pursue the technological, put up with it, or evade it."[18]

And so, what is the essence of technology? It is defined often as a means to an end and as a human activity. For Heidegger, this is the "merely correct" but "not yet the true. Only the true brings us into a free relationship."[19] What these definitions of the essence of technology do not get at is an answer to the question, "What is the instrumental itself?"[20] Heidegger begins to unpack the meaning of the instrumental with a brief discussion of Aristotle's fourfold causality. "The four causes are the ways, all belonging to each other, of being responsible for something else."[21] They are "ways of bringing something into appearance. They let it come forth into

---

15. Ellul is interested in questions concerning the mode of God's presence—the word versus the modern emphasis on vision. See Ibid., 64–97.

16. Heidegger, "The Question Concerning Technology," 311.

17. Ibid.

18. Ibid., 311.

19. Ibid., 313.

20. Ibid.

21. Ibid., 314.

presencing."[22] The language of presencing (which I discuss below) is worth highlighting.

Similarly, modern technology is a "revealing."[23] "And yet, the revealing that holds sway throughout modern technology does not unfold into a bringing-forth in the sense of *poiesis*. The revealing that rules in modern technology is a challenging, which puts to nature the unreasonable demand that it supply energy which can be extracted and stored as such."[24] The contrast to *poiesis* is that the latter has the "irruption belonging to bringing-forth, e.g., the bursting of a blossom into bloom, *in* itself."[25] So, for instance, "the work of the peasant does not challenge the soil of the field. In sowing grain it places seed in the keeping of the forces of growth and watches over its increase."[26] What is made present in modern technology is not made manifest in such a manner as to honor the nature of the object that is engaged, but what is challenged upon is demanded to reveal itself *as* and for something other than what belongs to its inner momentum (perhaps even against it). This is a "setting-upon, in the sense of a challenging-forth."[27] Modern technology demands that all things reveal themselves as for it. As we will see, this means that what might otherwise be revealed in things and in the world is concealed by means of our active imposition and comportment.

For modern technology, then, *as* what do all things reveal themselves? "What kind of unconcealment is it, then, that is peculiar to that which results from this setting-upon that challenges?"[28] All things are revealed as standing-reserve,[29] as potentially useful

---

22. Ibid., 316.
23. Ibid., 320.
24. Ibid., 320.
25. Ibid., 317, emphasis mine.
26. Ibid., 320.
27. Ibid., 321.
28. Ibid., 322.
29. Ibid.

means to ends determined outside and irrespective of a things inner momentum. "Whatever stands by in the sense of standing-reserve no longer stands over against us as an object."[30] One might think of an airliner as an object, for instance. And certainly, "we can represent the machine so. But then it conceals itself as to what and how it is. Revealed, it stands on the taxi strip only as a standing-reserve, inasmuch as it is ordered to ensure the possibility of transportation."[31] An airliner, truthfully understood, reveals itself as potential transport over against the merely correct description of its structure.

Heidegger then naturally queries, "Who accomplishes the challenging setting-upon through which what we call the actual is revealed as standing-reserve? Obviously, man."[32] But humanity is "already challenged to exploit the energies of nature," and so humanity itself belongs "more originally than nature within the standing-reserve."[33] And yet, precisely because human beings are more original, they are not "merely standing reserve."[34]

Individuals' activity in technology is moved by something prior to their acts. How is the world revealed to humanity in such a way that they see and use the world in the way that they do? "Wherever man opens his eyes and ears, unlocks his heart, and gives himself over to meditating and striving, shaping and working, entreating and thanking, he finds himself everywhere already brought into the unconcealed."[35] Heidegger goes on:

> Thus when man, investigating, observing, pursues nature as an area of his own conceiving, he has already been claimed by a way of revealing that challenges him to approach nature

30. Ibid.
31. Ibid.
32. Ibid., 323.
33. Ibid.
34. Ibid.
35. Ibid., 324.

as an object of research, until even the object disappears into the objectlessness of standing-reserve. Modern technology, as a revealing that orders, is thus no mere human doing. Therefore we must take the challenging that sets upon man to order the actual as standing-reserve in accordance with the way it shows itself. That challenging gathers man into ordering. This gathering concentrates man upon ordering the actual as standing-reserve ... We now name the challenging claim that gathers man with a view to ordering the self-revealing as standing-reserve: enframing.[36]

The concept of enframing, for Heidegger, is crucial. "Enframing means the gathering together of the setting-upon that sets upon man, i.e., challenges him forth, to reveal the actual, in the mode of ordering, as standing-reserve. Enframing means the way of revealing that holds sway in the essence of modern technology and that is itself nothing technological."[37] Enframing, which is a way of revealing, shapes the way in which reality automatically appears to us. In a modern technological society, the world is enframed as standing-reserve such that it appears naturally to us as an object for use. Perhaps Heidegger's central claim, then, is that "the essence of modern technology starts man upon the way of that revealing through which the actual everywhere, more or less distinctly, becomes standing-reserve."[38] Worthy of note is that, for Heidegger, we have already been started on the way of seeing everything in this manner.

In starting us in a particular way, enframing "sends into a way of revealing. "[39] This sending into revealing is a "destining of revealing."[40] Unpacking this, what may be revealed to us in the

36. Ibid.
37. Ibid., 325.
38. Ibid., 329.
39. Ibid., 330.
40. Ibid.

enframing of modern technology has been predetermined by the enframing (which is a way) itself. What can be revealed to us has been destined by the path we have been set upon. And what is then revealed may be some aspect of a thing's potential being, but the very questions we ask of reality may bracket out other (more truthful) dimensions of its existence. Hence, we may "misconstrue the unconcealed and misinterpret it."[41] Heidegger goes on, "In a similar way the unconcealment in accordance with which nature presents itself as a calculable complex of the effects of forces can indeed permit correct determinations; but precisely through these successes the danger may remain that in the midst of all that is correct the true will withdraw."[42]

The danger of this concealment is that "as a destining, it banishes man into the kind of revealing that is an ordering. Where this ordering holds sway, it drives out every other possibility of revealing."[43] In short, "The rule of enframing threatens man with the possibility that it could be denied to him to enter into a more original revealing and hence to experience the call of a more primal truth."[44] Heidegger goes on to argue that precisely what makes the essence of modern technology dangerous is itself a granting which, if we are aware of the essence of technology, can herald the possibility of other grantings that do not enframe all things as standing-reserve.[45]

As I will briefly consider in the next chapter, while Heidegger does speak of technology in ways that are reminiscent of Ellul (i.e., taking on a life of its own as it challenges the individual), for Heidegger it is nevertheless *human beings* who wield technology, and human beings who can redirect it. For Ellul, by contrast, there is no solution to the problem of modern technology as such, and

---

41. Ibid., 331.
42. Ibid.
43. Ibid., 332.
44. Ibid., 333.
45. Ibid., 333–41.

certainly not by a different use of technology. The two thinkers differ, therefore, concerning the relationship between humanity, technology, and hope. Nevertheless, contained in this disagreement is an implicit characterization of humanity's active involvement in the world. And it is to the theorization of this that we now turn.

Karl Marx on Labor and Estrangement

So far, we have focused upon what may be called the *active* dimension of modern technoculture. But even if technology takes on a life of its own (see chapter 4), it is a life that is parasitical on *human* activity. And if we grant that the human imaginary is carried along in humanity's practical life, then it is necessary to consider (in particular) modern labor in its relationship to our perception of reality. Labor is a major site of reality's mediation to us.

Few thinkers addressed this aspect of our quandary more famously and originally than Karl Marx.[46] Of chief importance in Marx's theoretical apparatus is the concept of alienation. For Marx, human beings are essentially laborers who make things. To labor and to make something out of the world is to live a meaningful human existence. But in the system we know as capitalism, human beings are alienated from their own labor and consequently from their own nature. This is because labor is divorced from one's own self-possessed agency but is, rather, of practical necessity, sold to another for wages.

Developed predominantly in his *Economic and Philosophic Manuscripts of 1844*, there are many aspects of Marx's doctrine of the human's estrangement from his own labor. Of first importance and often overlooked is Marx's grounding of his doctrine in

---

46. Marx is, of course, drawing (even in his theory of labor) upon the prior work of Hegel in the latter's *Phenomenology of Spirit*. See G. F. W. Hegel, *The Phenomenology of Spirit*, trans. Michael Baur (New York: Cambridge University Press, 2018).

a theory of human nature, or what he terms humanity's "species being." Marx writes:

> The animal is immediately identical with its life-activity. It does not distinguish itself from it. It is its life-activity. Man makes his life-activity itself the object of his will and of his consciousness. He has conscious life-activity. It is not a determination with which he directly merges. Conscious life-activity directly distinguishes man from animal life-activity. It is just because of this that he is a species being. Or it is only because he is a species being that he is a Conscious Being, i.e., that his own life is an object for him. Only because of that is his activity free activity. Estranged labor reverses this relationship, so that it is just because man is a conscious being that he makes his life-activity, his essential being, a mere means of his existence.[47]

For Marx, human beings are alienated not only from their labor and from their fellow humans via estranged labor but from their own nature as such. What is distinctive about humanity is that they, as a species, have a distinctively conscious and free relation to their own lives (i.e., life is an object for them). To the extent that the latter, however, is reduced to the status of a mere *means* for his animal survival, humanity has inverted the more primal relationship between survival and life. And this is precisely how it is reduced when people are estranged from their own labor— when their conscious engagement with the world is reduced to a means of surviving. This is inevitable, for Marx, in modern labor systems. Marx writes:

> What, then, constitutes the alienation of labor? First, the fact that labor is external to the worker, i.e., it does not belong to his essential being; that in his work, therefore,

---

47. Marx, *Economic and Philosophic Manuscripts of 1844*, 76.

he does not affirm himself but denies himself, does not feel content but unhappy, does not develop freely his physical and mental energy but mortifies his body and ruins his mind. The worker therefore only feels himself outside his work, and in his work feels outside himself.[48]

Putting these two passages together, Marx argues that in order for labor to "belong to the essential being" of the laborer, it is required that work be an object of engagement and involvement for the worker—that is, that it be a matter of people's conscious and free life.[49] But to the extent that an individual's labor belongs to another, Marx goes on, "Man (the worker) no longer feels himself to be freely active in any but his animal functions—eating, drinking, procreating, or at most in his dwelling and in dressing-up, etc.; and in his human functions he no longer feels himself to be anything but an animal. What is animal becomes human and what is human becomes animal."[50]

This alienation is cultivated, then, to the extent that humanity is prevented (via stolen access to the means of production) from making in the world with which he is always already involved. To the extent that people's access to this world is not free and is mediated by other individuals, "the more he deprives himself of means of life in the double respect: first, that the sensuous external world more and more ceases to be an object belonging to his labor—to be his labor's means of life; and secondly, that it more and more ceases to be means of life in the immediate sense, means for the physical subsistence of the worker."[51] Essential to Marx's notion of freedom, then, is an individual's free relation to their own labor (and therefore, a free relation to other men). Finally, the above quote makes it clear that Marx sees a free relation to one's own way

48. Ibid., 74.

49. On "engagement," see Sennett, *The Craftsman*.

50. Marx, *Economic and Philosophical Manuscripts of 1844*, 74.

51. Ibid., 72.

of making subsistence as essentially tied up with a free relation to the labor that is for life more generally. Perhaps labor blends the two (as when a craftsman does what he loves and makes a living at the same time). This sort of arrangement is cultivated to the extent that people are free in relation to their labor *and* mode of subsisting (which are not the same thing!) more generally.

It should be clear, then, that alienation here has reference to something more specific than a sense of general ennui or general spiritual disorientation. It rather highlights a specific (and historically contingent!) relationship to one's labor, which is larger than—but also includes—one's relationship to the means of physical subsistence. Amy Wendling helpfully summarizes, "The worker is alienated (1) from the objects produced, (2) from the means of production (i.e. the tools and instruments through which production is carried out), and (3) from the process of objectification itself, because he or she finds that his or her practical life activity stunts, abuses, and undermines itself."[52]

An original theorist of labor, Marx was also a theorist of early industrial technology. While alienation from one's own labor is partly a function of the fact that one does not possess one's own agency but rather sells it to another, it is also due (for Marx) to the feature of industrial machine society wherein one has very little actual expertise in or understanding of what one actually does. As Wendling continues:

> In capitalism, workers neither own nor understand the means of production, or the tools and instruments with which they work. Increasingly in the capitalist era, sophisticated and complicated machines are introduced. These

---

52. Wendling, *Karl Marx on Technology and Alienation*, 17. Callinicos, *The Revolutionary Ideas of Karl Marx*, 76, similarly writes, "What should be 'life activity', through which he affirms his humanity, of 'species being', becomes a mere means to an end. And because he has thus become alienated from his own human nature, the worker is also alienated from nature, for it is through labor that he transforms nature, and thus humanizes it, and he is also alienated from other human beings."

absorb the worker's functionality and, Marx will claim, deprive the human activity of production in labor of all interest. This leads to what I call the theme of "technological alienation" in Marx's work. Technological alienation is a situation in which the practical life activity of the vast majority of human beings is undertaken as labor on machines that they neither own nor understand. Such labor is characterized by the reduction of the worker to an extremely partial use of his or her faculties.[53]

This alienation from one's own agency, as well as the process and products of one's labor, means that people try to find their identity elsewhere. And in a capitalist society, it is often through what Marx calls "commodity fetishism," a sort of worship of things that embody human essence (i.e., labor). Again, Wendling writes, "Fetishism is a kind of idolatry of the human essence, implanted by human objectification. In alienated capitalist production, this objectification is misunderstood. Human essence is seen as a property belonging to the commodity rather than to its creator."[54] The maker of these products, the machine, takes the place of God.[55] Given that machines are a projection of human labor, it is not difficult to see why Marx also sees God as a projection of humans.

For Marx, then, modern technology shapes us in much the same way that we shape one another, through direct agency. This is because technological agency is alienated human agency—an objectified surrogate of real human life that must ultimately collapse under its own artifice. Commodities and things are the payoff meant to distract us from the loss of our own essence. Marx's

---

53. Ibid., 56.

54. Ibid., 54.

55. Ibid., 57. Freud develops a similar line of thought in his discussion of modern technology in the third chapter of *Civilization and its Discontents*. For Freud, advanced technology ultimately makes humanity god-like.

solution, of course, is the development of a class consciousness that nourishes resentment and anger toward the system.[56]

In sum, technology shapes human thought by shaping human labor (which is our essence). One's relationship to one's own agency has everything to do with one's relationship to one's neighbor and to the world in general. Consequently, Marxist thought has always related ideologies to certain modes of production. Labor is not a derivative of something like religion, then. Rather, religion (or the lack thereof) derives from a mode of labor and the thought patterns that are tacitly carried along with it.[57]

Marx, nevertheless, is not entirely cynical about the machine. As Wendling writes, "Modern Industry has both capitalist and communist components. Both periods had the same means of production as their foundation: machines."[58] Machines quickly become obsolete and are driven by greater and greater efficiency. But they "have the potential to revolutionize what for Marx is the most important division of labor: the polarizing division between two classes. Because of this ... machines themselves are key elements of developing revolutionary consciousness as well as the material foundations for the communist mode of production."[59] For Marx, importantly, the fundamental background of human thought and of the role of technology within it is not humankind's relationship with machines in the abstract or even humankind's relationship to nature. Rather, he prioritizes people's relationships with themselves through others.[60] As such, the person-person

---

56. See Callinicos, *The Revolutionary Ideas of Karl Marx*, 167–217.

57. Of course, this admits of many inflections in actual practice. While there is agreement on this principle, the implications of Marx's thought on these subjects are not agreed upon by all of his followers. See McLellan, *Marxism after Marx*.

58. Wendling, *Karl Marx on Technology and Alienation*, 170.

59. Ibid., 172.

60. Echoing this focus is Edgerton, *The Shock of the Old*, the recent account of technology in the last century. Edgerton's main thesis is that the real story of technology is how technology is actually used in human life rather than its impressiveness or use in the abstract. A good example here is the world-shaping impact of modern birth control

relationship is always the main thing, and the machine has the potential to become a legitimate servant by freeing humans from material concerns so that they may invest their labor-power and agency into meaningful tasks. Thus, as per above, the agency of the machine is alienated *human* labor, and never something in itself. Marx's disciples would go on to critique both of these theses—first that the machine can be redirected, and second that it reflects human (rather than its own abstracted) agency. Herbert Marcuse makes the first point, and Jacques Ellul (as we have already seen) the second. Let us here consider Marcuse.

Herbert Marcuse on One-Dimensional Humanity

What Marx did not appreciate, argues Marcuse, is the ability of the machine to create and to satisfy human needs in a way that effectively makes their humanity invisible even to themselves.[61] He writes:

> To the degree that freedom from want, the concrete sub-stance of all freedom, is becoming a real possibility, the liberties which pertain to a state of power productivity are losing their former content. Independence of thought, autonomy, and the right to political opposition are being deprived of their basic critical function in a society which seems increasingly capable of satisfying the needs of individuals through the way in which it is organized.[62]

(condoms, the pill). While fairly trivial and ordinary from a technical standpoint, their cultural significance is absolutely astounding.

61. Another fascinating post-Marxist figure is Georg Lukacs, who seems more ambivalent about the relationship between technology as the natural (as opposed to more consciously agentic) development of class-consciousness. He has sympathies with the early Marxist Rosa Luxemburg, who was able to appreciate the rather non-ideological syndicalist movements. See McLellan, *Marxism after Marx*, 171–80.

62. Marcuse, *One-Dimensional Man*, 2.

Technological society can make people happy, unmotivated to pursue change, even as it reduces true consciousness. Marcuse goes on:

> The means of mass transportation and communication, the commodities of lodging, food, and clothing, the irresistible output of the entertainment and information industry carry with them prescribed attitudes and habits, certain intellectual and emotional reactions which bind the consumers more or less pleasantly to the producers and, through the latter, to the whole. The products indoctrinate and manipulate; they promote a false consciousness with is immune against its falsehood. And as these beneficial products become available to more individuals in more social classes, the indoctrination they carry ceases to be publicity; it becomes a way of life. It is a good way of life—much better than before—and as a good way of life, it militates against qualitative change. Thus emerges a pattern of one-dimensional thought and behavior in which ideas, aspirations, and objectives that, by their content, transcend the established universe of discourse and action are either repelled or reduced to terms of this universe. They are redefined by the rationality of the given system and of its qualitative extension.[63]

It is important to see that, as for Marx, the ideology is carried along in practices rather than the other way around. Technology influences human thinking by reshaping the material conditions of humanity. These material conditions are comfortable, and they foster certain intellectual and emotional habits that make it very difficult for the sensibility that something is wrong to even develop. Indeed, even with respect to religion, Marcuse writes:

---

63. Ibid., 12.

The reign of such a one-dimensional reality does not mean that materialism rules, and that the spiritual, metaphysical, and bohemian occupations are petering out. On the contrary, there is a great deal of "Worship together this week," "Why not try God," Zen, existentialism, the beat ways of life, etc. But such modes of protest and transcendence are no longer contradictory to the status quo and no longer negative. They are rather the ceremonial part of practical behaviorism, its harmless negation, and are quickly digested by the status quo as part of a healthy diet.[64]

Technological culture, then, can incorporate its presumed negation into itself—but only by remaking the product after its own image and implicit values. As such,

Today, domination perpetuates and extends itself not only through technology but *as* technology, and the latter provides the great legitimation of the expanding political power, which absorbs all spheres of culture. In this universe, technology also provides the great rationalization of the unfreedom of man and demonstrates the "technical" impossibility of being autonomous, of determining one's own life.[65]

Marcuse, perhaps rightly, assumes that human moral, aesthetic, and philosophical thought tends to reflect human interests. And inasmuch as human activity and its products make us comfortable and feel free, there is little motivation to do or imagine anything in negation of this system. And so Marcuse engages the problem of raising class consciousness—persuading already contended humans that there are aspects of their nature that are left unfulfilled

64. Ibid., 14.
65. Ibid., 158, emphasis in original.

by technological society. In some ways, Marcuse appears cynical concerning the possibility that this can ever really occur.[66]

Summary of These Analytical Tools

We are now in a place to draw some of these themes together. While much could be said, I will focus upon three ways in which one might attempt to identify *how* it is that technology shapes beliefs—especially beliefs about the divine.

First, if human beings are fundamentally practical creatures, what are the implications? In the practical experience of those who live in the West, the ubiquity of technological artifice renders it barely even a background noise. It is rather tacitly imbibed as reality itself. We experience the world as what is revealed and presented to us in our technologies. We automatically engage it this way, even without thinking about it. Nature, for us, becomes an abstraction. For us, technology *is* what nature was to many generations of our ancestors.

And what does nature, then, reveal to us? It reveals to us a world full of convenience, a world in which unsavory items can be fixed by an enhanced technical apparatus, a world in which the heavier aspects of suffering and death are sanitized and rendered invisible (i.e., factory meats and old-folks' homes). And again, this is what the world seems like before we have started thinking about it. This grasp of things is more powerful than any thought—and it takes tremendous formation or discipline (or epiphany?) to see anything differently. Moreover, to the extent that personal and unscripted networks of trust (family, economy, local life, etc.) are replaced by technologically and system mediated person-person relations, the most primal agentic dimension of reality is muted. Against this backdrop, then, what is the initial plausibility of any God (or transcendental reality) who is not

---

66. This is why Marcuse goes on to locate emancipatory potential in the racial and cultural outcasts rather than in what would later be termed "majority culture." Ibid., 256.

suited to our convenience (perhaps even opposed to it)—and who is rather a dense and weighty reality outside of ourselves to whom the only appropriate posture is awe? Even further, what is the plausibility of any God at all—indeed—any fundamental person-like reality that can only be known by a sort of receptive hearing rather than an aggressively projected gaze?

Second, when we attempt to engage these questions, then, we must be attentive to the manner in which these plausibility structures (*pace* Taylor) have enframed (*pace* Heidegger) the ability of reality to answer back. One might get at the question this way. What does our practical engagement with the world shape us to expect the answer to our questions to look like? If Ellul is right, it shapes us to expect any answer to have the feature of techne itself—predictable rational efficient order. That is, no answer can actually look like a person. Of course, in asking reality to appear to us as impersonal rational ordering, it can certainly yield to us those dimensions of its being that appear to have these features— at least as we have defined them. And when it does, it is often assumed that we have been given everything it has to offer. But perhaps it is simply that our questions have destined or mediated a destiny that we have been set upon and that limits what can be revealed. Consequently, everything outside of techne is rendered invisible by its ceasing to be a matter of care, concern, and potential engagement to us. In our (mis)attunement, we cease to hear the call that exceeds those frequencies to which we are dialed in.

Filling this out, we must, third, say a word concerning the visible and the invisible. *Techne* is not always visible in the sense of physical presence, but it is visible in the sense that it is identifiable and predictable. It is always tied to concrete results or predictability—the link between which is control. This is not true of the mode of being we experience as personal, though attempts at social engineering have often tried to make it so.[67] But if our practical engagement with the world is one in which all things can be seen, and our philosophical questioning expects that any answer must take on the shape of a thing seen in the sense that *techne* is, we will likely render invisible dimensions of reality that are, as Heidegger puts it, more primal truths. Stated more critically, one gets the sense that reality is frequently thought to be explained when it has rather been explained *away* by reduction. It has produced answers determined by our questions. But as one might say of most modern people's relationship to humans themselves, perhaps we have lost the art of knowing what and how to ask. Or more accurately, perhaps our more basic defect is that we have forgotten how to take the posture of listeners to reality in a way that honors the phenomenon as such. One might hear this and think that the focus is on intense psychological experiences to be drummed up through immersion in nature. Rather, what I attempt to hint at is found in reflection itself, but a reflection that honors the full reality of the things we attempt to understand—rather than believing we have grasped the whole by grasping a part. In short, the path forward is in reality itself, if we are willing to let it tell us more than we have asked. But this already involves the agency of a servant rather than that of a master. In other words, it is the opposite of techne.

Thus far, we have drawn upon theorists of modern technology and labor in order to understand the manner in which each shape our perception of reality. In order to fully appreciate the lived worldhood of modern technoculture, however, and to fully appreciate its relevance to modern religious and/or a-religious consciousness, we would be aided in our inquiry by seeking to understand how and why spiritual realities were almost universally seen to be obvious in previous technological and labor

---

67. For an interpretation of reality that sees personhood all the way up, see David Bentley Hart, *The Experience of God: Being, Consciousness, Bliss* (New Haven: Yale University Press, 2013).

arrangements. If we can grasp this, it becomes clearer why the modern rearrangement of these things was quite naturally inflected in the direction that it has been. In the next section, therefore, I will unimagine the current order of things and then reimagine it against the backdrop of our human past.

GOD IN THE MIRROR OF THE WORLD:
THE MIGRATION OF DIVINE PRESENCE

The Cosmos Preborn: The Ancient World

According to Remi Brague, humans once had no world. Brague argues, drawing on Japanese, Egyptian, Akkadian, and many ancient Near Eastern sources and myths, that there is no word in these ancient languages that corresponds to the modern sense of world, or a total system of things that the human can ponder as an object.[68] It is this latter qualification that makes all the difference. The ancients certainly wrote about the origin of the lists of items that populated the realm of their experience, but (argues Brague) this does not include the distancing move required to contemplate the whole as an object before a subject. The ancient myths did not function as a sort of premodern theory of everything by which we are so fascinated. This explains why the details of ancient cosmogonies are the most diverse *precisely* where they fascinate us as at their most philosophical. The origin of all things is alternatively posed as (functionally) nothing, a chaotic unity, the sea, an egg, and so forth.[69] These were not part of our lived order—but precisely its contrast (a profound mystery). The cosmos did not suspend each of these things in itself as a ponderable unity. Rather,

---

68. See Remi Brague, *The Wisdom of the World: The Human Experience of the Universe in Western Thought*, trans. Teresa Lavender Fagan (Chicago: University of Chicago Press, 2003), 9–16. Here he differs from John H. Collins, "Cosmology: Time and History," in *Religions of the Ancient World: A Guide*, ed. Sarah Iles Johnston (Cambridge: Harvard Belknap, 2004), 59–70.

69. See the very helpful discussion of E. J. Michael Witzel, *The Origins of the World's Mythologies* (New York: Oxford University Press, 2012), 105–85.

the world was precisely where the chaotic unity, the sea, the void (etc.), was defeated, held back, or turned into something fundamentally different.

This sense of the whole, which is so natural for moderns, additionally requires a conception of humankind itself as central and significant in the cosmic community. An imagination formed without this conception would be less likely to feel that capturing the whole, in a proto-philosophical way, was a relevant exercise. Conversely, then, we would expect that the modern sense of cosmos might arise where the human mind was raised in significance. Certainly, it has been in the Western tradition, and its secular progeny have inherited (at least) this tacit sensibility. But one notes the relative insignificance of humankind in ancient mythologies. *The Epic of Gilgamesh*, among the oldest of our written tales, captures this in a haunting way. Gilgamesh, while a king and conqueror in relation to his people, is nevertheless subject to the decaying force of death, to the varying whims of the gods, and even to the fragilities of his own psyche. Fascinatingly, the epic ends with a hymn not to the king, Gilgamesh, but to the city he built:

> This is the wall of Uruk, which no city on earth can equal.
> See how its ramparts gleam like copper in the sun.
> Climb the stone staircase, more ancient than the mind
>   can imagine,
> approach the Eanna Temple, sacred to Ishtar,
> a temple that no king has equaled in size or beauty,
> walk on the wall or Uruk, follow its course
> around the city, inspects its mighty foundations,
> examine its brickwork, how masterfully it is built,
> observe the land it encloses: the palm trees, the gardens,
> the orchards, the glorious palaces and temples, the shops
> and marketplaces, the houses and public squares.[70]

---

70. Stephen Mitchell, trans., *The Epic of Gilgamesh* (New York: Free Press, 2004), 198–99.

Why the city and not the man? Arguably, answering this is a key to understanding the chief concern(s) of ancient cosmogonies. John Walton has written extensively on what he terms the "functional" versus "material" focus of ancient Near Eastern cosmogonies.[71] He states, "In the Ancient Near East, something did not necessarily exist just because it happened to occupy space."[72] Rather, existence for the ancients was predominantly conceived in terms of functions, that is, in their life-producing and life-sustaining activities. While it is possible that Walton overplays this contrast, his work minimally demonstrates that the question of functions was typically the most *emphasized* and *weighted* ancient ontological concern (though perhaps admitting of exceptions).[73] The items that populated the world in ancient myths represented progressive stages in an ordering process that culminated in life. And these stood in contrast to the chaotic unity or sea that was the opposite of life and within which it was destroyed.[74] The gods were often the first separated and separating agents. They formed the sky to hold back the chaotic waters above and the land to hold off the chaotic waters below. Yet within this claustrophobic bubble of space, it was still necessary to keep ordering. The default structure of the now-carved-out land was a barely life-sustaining wilderness. This must be cultivated into a weeded garden and ordered into agriculture. Humans were made to grow food, build houses, and climactically to build cities at the center of which would be a house for the gods (i.e., a temple)—in which cities humans themselves

---

71. Most extensively in John Walton, *Genesis 1 as Ancient Cosmology* (Winona Lake, IN: Eisenbrauns, 2011).

72. John Walton, *Ancient Near Eastern Thought and the Old Testament: Introducing the Conceptual World of the Hebrew Bible* (Grand Rapids: Baker Academic, 2006), 180.

73. John Currid's critique of Walton is among the most thorough: "Theistic Evolution Is Incompatible with the Teachings of the Old Testament," in *Theistic Evolution: A Scientific, Philosophical, and Theological Critique*, ed. J. P. Moreland et al. (Wheaton, IL: Crossway, 2017), 839–78.

74. See especially Jon D. Levenson, *Creation and the Persistence of Evil: The Jewish Drama of Divine Omnipresence* (Princeton: Princeton University Press, 1988).

were also fed and sheltered. In exchange for taking care of the gods through food and shelter, the gods would take care of human beings through the same (via good weather, protection from enemies, and the technical insights that aided humans in the further cultivation that was their reason for being).[75]

The center of this sense of reality was the city, which was not the farthest thing removed from nature (as we moderns commonly think of it) but rather its felt telos. Recalling the above question with respect to *The Epic of Gilgamesh*: *This*, then, is why the city and not the man. Differentiation and separation were for the sake of order and life, and the city was the clearest instance of life's fruition and protection from chaos—the primordial abyss. Distance from the city and the temple and movement, therefore, toward more sinister modes of divine presence were progressive movements toward chaos. Outside the city were certainly agricultural fields likely terminating in an unbounded wilderness (less cultivation, separation, and order) that eventually gave way to a vast sea, which itself smashed into the boundaries of anything life-sustaining at all. The chief concern was to maintain order and life, for the cooperative gods and humankind, in concert, to hold back the forces of chaos that threatened to swallow, from above and below, the differentiated space of life (as the wooden walls of a mine threaten to implode from the pressure of the mountain—and must therefore be vigorously and constantly maintained).

Indeed, this partnership with the gods underscores that it was not just the city but, indeed, the temple that was the true center of life-sustaining force. Note the centrality of the temple in the hymn cited above. *Enuma Elish*, similarly, culminates in the famous "fifty titles" of Marduk—likely part of a temple ceremony in ancient Babylon, where his temple was the most prominent feature in the

---

75. See Timothy Stephany, ed., *Enuma Elish: The Babylonian Creation Epic* (CreateSpace, 2014), which contains a wonderful ancient picture of this "economy" between the gods and humankind.

ancient city. While most humans have been aware that theirs was not the only city, it is worth noting that, for the ancients, order was always here where one's own life was sustained. Whatever was true of other cities, the bond with the gods experienced in the temple surrounded by *these* city walls (all together sustaining life) was felt to be the center of the universe. If that order of things expanded, then order expanded. It was, indeed, common (even among nomadic tribes in the Americas!) to conceive of temples, cities, or sacred objects as the pivot on which the axis of the earth turned. The center of the world was where balance was achieved, and it was achieved where humans felt themselves to be alive and flourishing.[76] That the center could be multiply realized again suggests a cosmic picture in which the primary question was one of order and life rather than of spatial orientation in a whole. One particularly fascinating image has been explored by Jon D. Levenson. He details the Israelite usage of the image of a navel to depict the placement of the Jewish temple in the cosmos. The foundation stone of the temple was sometimes conceived of as the foundation around which, or symbolically on top of which, the whole earth rested. And it was therefore this foundation that held back the chaotic waters under the earth. The foundation stone of the temple, on a cosmic mountain, was literally a cap on the forces of chaos—the removal or destruction of which would then risk a cosmic flood.[77]

It is a measure of our distance from this world that it seems so fanciful to us. And while an imperfect procedure, it is perhaps best for us to try to bring to consciousness (at least) two basic "way

76. This sense of being in the center can be seen in ancient Chinese cities and among the American Indians. See (respectively) Paul Wheatley, *The Pivot of the Four Quarters: A Preliminary Inquiry into the Origins and Character of the Ancient Chinese City* (Chicago: Aldine Publishing Company, 1971), and Ake Hultkrantz, *The Religions of the American Indians* (Berkeley: University of California Press, 1979), 28.

77. See Jon D. Levenson, *Sinai & Zion* (New York: Harper, 1985), 111–37.

things were" that seem particularly foreign—and that render this picture so implausible to moderns.

First, the ancient view of things really cannot be imagined without some sense of what we might call unboundedness outside of ordered phenomena. This prevents any sense of world as we think of it. There was no view from nowhere in which all things fit, but a fundamental phenomenal plurality beyond which was not a sense of the whole but rather boundless mystery. There was no world or cosmos that could be grasped in a moment of intellectual focus. Rather, there was simply the city, and outside of that the not-city, and outside of that, something even less ordered, a-culminating in a boundless sea of undifferentiated "we know not what."

Second, this sense of unboundedness was suffused with a horde of unpredictable agencies rather than predictable laws. Indeed, even the products of agents were themselves agents. Humanity, for instance, is both intensely agentic and a tool of the gods. Technology, likewise, was thought to be an insight from the gods concerning how things can be made to act when we ourselves perform a manipulating act of our own. Technology was the harnessing and ordering of an inner life-force (a "nature"). This perhaps felt indistinguishable from what we might think of as magic today. In any case, the major concern in this environment was the maintenance of order, of agents, gods, city, forest, nature, working together to maintain *and increase* an ecological and economic (in the broadest possible sense of the term) balance in which everyone's itches were scratched—but again, within the sphere of one's own concern. The gods whom humans served were local. Sinister non-local agencies could be held back by a well-sustained local order, its expansion then just an increase of that order. Fundamentally, *our* gods were for us while we were for them. Chaos was, then, held back through culture, liturgy, governorship, and so forth.

And it is here then that we are in a place to note why the divine presence and cosmic agency were most *prominently* associated with the city—in reverse of the modern trend. Certainly, there were gods who cared about the forest (sometimes fighting with gods who did not), but the gods were fundamentally ordering agents— and humans their form of technology. Human technology was borrowed insight or blessing (perhaps accounting for the ancient relationship between city building, technical problem solving, and rulership), and in it, humans participated in and perpetuated the divine ordering activity of separation and cultivation.[78] The basic existential reality, out of which this cosmic picture arose, was vulnerability. The ancient world was a world suffused with vulnerability. This was true not just of human beings but of the gods and of the cosmic order itself. Above and before all is the unbounded. Reality is an ultimate play or musical that can go from major to minor, comedy to tragedy, without any underlying sense of ultimate control, predictability, or eternally reliable cosmic order in the modern sense. The fickle gods could be alternatively vindictive, conquered, replaced, or killed. Cities could likewise be conquered, dynasties replaced, and temples destroyed. Flood waters could overwhelm, crops could fail, and rain could refuse its sustenance. In short, order and life could all cease. The very cycle of day and night, of seasons, and so forth, was not guaranteed by a law of nature but was a result of the constant activity of sustaining life in the midst of daily threats. The temple ceremonies, then, were perceived to be humanity's contribution (quite literally) to maintaining the order of the universe, the regularity of the solar system, the conquering of night by day every twenty-four hours—the holding back of death by fighting for life. In this sense, just as men were technology to the gods, so the gods were also a sort of technology

---

78. See James McClellan and Harold Dorn, *Science and Technology in World History: An Introduction* (Baltimore: Johns Hopkins University Press, 2015), 17–114.

to humanity—a latent power, harnessed through liturgy, for human ends. Humankind's participation in reality was suspended in an outside of me that one could not ultimately comprehend, control, manipulate, or even necessarily understand. Vulnerability was the most basic reality—reinforced by every aspect of human experience and never forgotten in the sweat and labor it took to maintain a flourishing life in its face.

It is difficult to imagine a story that captures this better than *The Epic of Gilgamesh*. Contained in it are themes of warring and fickle gods, vulnerable humanity, the prominence of death, and the care that even the king must take not only to mediate the gods to men but also to not violate his place in the order of life.[79] Yet the story is finally haunted with a deep sense of fragility, a disorienting resounding of death's echo in all of life. The only manner in which humans could answer back to this reality was to keep going and to keep working for the good of the city. In other words, humanity's calling was to cultivate whatever sustains and perpetuates flourishing life.

Minimally, then, what needed to change for the modern sense of divine absence to become possible was a loss of this sense of the primacy of the unbounded as well as the plausibility of its correlative agencies (the felt sense that the universe was composed of actors with whom one was in communication—whether they be trees or gods). The former shift occurred (mostly) in antiquity. The latter shift progressively occurred in early to late modernity. Let us consider these in turn.

The Cosmos Born: The World of Late Antiquity

We begin to see a fracture in the ancient conception in at least two sources—both of which are progenitors of modern Western

---

79. See, for this, Robert Bellah, *Religion in Human Evolution: From the Paleolithic to the Axial Age* (Cambridge: Harvard Belknap, 2011), 210–64.

culture.[80] The first, arguably more ancient, is the exceptional writing of the Hebrews.[81] The second, of course, is the tradition of thought that is typically seen to have originated in Greek philosophy. We briefly summarize both.

Though perhaps not exceptionless, the Hebrew tradition was nevertheless rare in the following respects.

First, the temple of YHWH was often conceived of as the whole earth, of which the earthly temple was just a copy. "Heaven is My throne and the earth is the footstool for My feet. Where then is a house you could build for Me? And where is a place that I may rest? For My hand made all these things, so all these things came into being" (Isa 66:1–2). It is highly likely that this is what is being described in Genesis 1, especially given the emphasis on YHWH's rest at the end of the construction project.[82] This would imply some structural order to all of creation.

Second, it is a matter of intense debate whether or not Genesis 1:1–2 would have us imagine YHWH bringing order out of the formless and void (seen as pre-existent) or whether the first verse, "In the beginning God created the heavens and the earth," should be seen as temporally prior to the formless and void stuff out of which

---

80. In speaking of Western culture, I mean not the nostalgic reification of so much contemporary discourse, but rather the sense in which it is used by Brague in *Eccentric Culture* to (in short) refer to Europe and its distinctive memories.

81. There is some debate, of course, about how old the Hebrew tradition really is. A helpful survey of the literature on this topic can be found in T. Desmond Alexander, *From Paradise to Promised Land: An Introduction to the Pentateuch* (Grand Rapids: Baker Academic, 2012), 1–112. One interesting implication of dating the Hebrew tradition early is that it would call into question Heidegger's reading of the history of philosophy. His aforementioned concept of the "destining of revealing" is filled out in his *Anaximander Fragment*, trans. David Farrell Krell in *Arion: A Journal of Humanities and the Classics New Series* 1.4 (1973/1974): 576–626. Here he speaks of the destining of the concept of being since the time of Socrates—a metaphysics of presence and subject/object that replaced their non-differentiation. However, if the Hebrew tradition is prior to the pre-Socratics, and if they distinguished undifferentiated being from divine Being, then one can leapfrog Heidegger's beloved pre-Socratics, putting firmly in place a significant piece of what would later make an ontology of presence possible. As I show below, however, this presence can be understood differently than in Heidegger's critique.

82. See Walton, *Genesis 1 as Ancient Cosmology*, 122–92.

God performs further ordering.[83] If the latter, this is extremely rare. If the former, there is still the rarity (though not absolute singularity) that YHWH does not himself arise from the chaotic state of non-differentiation.

Third, in the Hebrew tradition, then, the order of the universe is ultimately vulnerable to God—and therefore, humankind's vulnerability stands in relation primarily not to an impersonal structure but to an Absolute Agent. We are, of course, thinking here about monotheism and all that it ultimately implies. It is certainly debated whether one can find monotheism (versus the henotheistic primacy of one god) in the Pentateuch, but a modest judgment would be that the trajectory goes in this direction and that, at least by the time of the prophetic writings, monotheism is a given in Jewish thought.[84] In any case, the primary point, for our purposes, is that God is thought to be outside the unbounded and able to render it to nothing. In the ancient world, this would be as stunning as the concept of creation *ex nihilo* is to us today—and perhaps even imply it.[85] Levenson nevertheless argues that there is a tension here. While YHWH is victorious over chaos, chaos still threatens Israel and is therefore still existent after its defeat by God. But the image throughout the Hebrew Bible is always that it can only be unleashed if God so allows it (usually in judgment). The tension in the Hebrew Bible on this score also suggests the

---

83. On the question of whether Genesis 1:1 teaches creation *ex nihilo*, the most thorough treatment of which I am aware is Joshua Daniel Wilson, "A Case for the Traditional Translation and Interpretation of Genesis 1:1 Based Upon a Multi-Leveled Linguistic Analysis" (PhD diss., The Southern Baptist Theological Seminary, 2010). However, it is possible that the notion of creation *ex nihilo* did not take on great rhetorical significance (or conceptual clarification) until the earliest Christian centuries. See Gerhard May, *Creation Ex Nihilo: The Doctrine of Creation "Out of Nothing" in Early Christian Thought* (New York: T&T Clark, 2004).

84. On the development of Jewish religion, see Richard Hess, *Israelite Religions* (Grand Rapids: Baker Academic, 2007). On whether monotheism is ancient, this is highly controversial, but Winfried Corduan has recently resurrected the towering achievement of Wilhelm Schmidt on this subject in the former's *In the Beginning God: A Fresh Look at the Case for Original Monotheism* (Nashville: B&H, 2013).

85. See Walton, *Genesis 1 as Ancient Cosmology*, 139–52.

potential of a final victory over chaos, such as in Isaiah's vision of a "new heavens and a new earth" (Isa 65:17).

Fourth, this vision of YHWH as outside the chaos and as powerful over it also creates the possibility of history. It is fascinating that the Hebrew Bible opens with "in the beginning," as opposed to something like, "When there was nothing, God ordered chaos." The word choice is suggestive of an ending, as is the commission that is given to humankind in Genesis 1:26–28. While many cosmogonies in the ancient world have a quasi-historical character, their historical character usually leads up to a telos that is the very occasion of telling the tale itself. That is, many stories were composed to give a prehistory of a city or of a temple. But the final order of things was simply the preservation of the temple and the maintenance of cosmic order through its liturgies. At no point in the Hebrew Scriptures do we arrive at this finality. And while it does not leave the worldview of the cyclical, the cyclical nevertheless serves the linear in a sense that appears unique. It is in this vein, along with the Greek tradition of history writing, that the West developed a more explicitly linear historiography, the most iconic moment of which is Augustine's *City of God*.[86]

Fifth, implied in the previous point is that the Hebrew Bible makes the human-qua-human central in its cosmic geography and in the historical narrative that it develops. Unlike many cultures in the ancient Near East, it is not just the king but humankind itself that is said to be the image and likeness and son of God (Gen 1:26–28). Humanity is given a dominion and rulership over the earth that is nevertheless not a kind of dictatorship but the stewardship of a gardener—whose task of cultivation both serves humanity itself and is also constituted by guiding the forms of creation into their own fruition and ecological balance. A gardener both enjoys the fruits of a garden and also guides the garden to

---

86. On this point, see Baruch Halpern, *The Hebrew Bible and History* (New York: Harper & Row, 1988).

achieve its own perfection in itself. Humans are also portrayed as having a role to subdue the enemies of this order (personified in the Genesis account by the figure of the serpent).

Sixth, in this amalgam—and here we must be careful—one detects a proto-philosophical tradition in Hebrew thought that perhaps creates the foundations for (but not the actuality of) the fracture that Brague argues must be in place before we have a sense of cosmos in the modern sense. To wit, a person must be able to grasp the whole before himself as the subject. By the separation of God from chaos, and especially by separating his power from its power, one raises the possibility that God is *sui generis* in respect of being. And indeed, the covenant name of God, "I AM WHO I AM" (Ex 3:14), is difficult to read without thinking that "the question of being" (as such) had been raised by the ancient Hebrews.[87] That is, not a *view of*, but a *belief in* a whole in which all of reality was suspended—like words from speech. Even chaos itself does not act of itself but, rather, obeys what it is commanded to do in Genesis. Perhaps one way of stating the contrast is that the ancients tended to prioritize a sort of pure potency over any act. The Hebrew tradition tended to prioritize the pure actuality over the chaos of potentiality. Indeed, Robert Bellah lists Hebrew religion (by the time of the prophets) as an example of Karl Jaspers's famous axial age religions.[88] He, of course, also treats the rise of Western philosophy in this vein.[89] Let us, then, briefly consider the Greeks.

87. On the meaning of the divine name, see Andrea D. Saner, *"Too Much to Grasp": Exodus 3:13–15 and the Reality of God* (Winona Lake, IN: Eisenbrauns, 2015).

88. Bellah, *Religion in Human Evolution*, 265–323. However, for a critique of the concept of the Axial Age, see Iain Provan, *Convenient Myths: The Axial Age, Dark Green Religion, and the World that Never Was* (Waco: Baylor University Press, 2013).

89. See Bellah, *Religion in Human Evolution*, 324–98. When I first wrote this monograph, John Hilber's *Old Testament Cosmology and Divine Accommodation: A Relevance Theory Approach* (Eugene, OR: Cascade, 2020) had not yet been published. He would contend that there is some Hebrew notion of a whole that is implicit in Old Testament cosmology, but he does not argue that this was captured under a single term or concept. Brague considers this a highly interesting fact.

According to Brague, it is the Greeks (and particularly Plato) who are the first to speak of a world in the sense that the term is used today—a claim that there is a unity (captured in a single term) behind the whole that requires a distanced subject to imagine.[90] Arguably, Aristotle also gave the world a more proto-scientific account of agency (understood in terms of potency, act, and will)— which worked to rationalize sensibilities concerning cosmic agency that were far more fluid and, in modern perception, superstitious. Of course, these tendencies remained in the medieval world, but they grew alongside an Aristotelian discourse that had the potential to manage them to a modest degree—that is, rendering them ultimately ordered on a cosmic providential register (the world of Dante's *Divine Comedy* and Augustine's *City of God*).

Nevertheless, in neither the Hebrew nor the Greek tradition do we witness the loss of the felt agency of the cosmos. As such, the epistemic and existential relationship to the cosmos has the potential to remain very much what it was in the ancient era, even if the seeds have been sown for an alternative. Dante's *Divine Comedy* presents us with a universe far more mapped out even than our own, but one that situates and acts upon us rather than one subject to our manipulation. While the world was theoretically and theologically mapped out, the fundamental felt *relation* to that cosmos was nevertheless suffused with a more prominent sense of *immediate* mystery—a practical instinct that required items like modern housing and airplanes to change. Our universe is less mapped out in this very theoretical sense, but even its unknown particulars are pre-interpreted as belonging to the order of manipulable materiality rather than dreadful mystery. That is, it is less mapped out but more ordinary. It belongs to an order of things that is familiar to us and to which, in its wholeness, we imagine ourselves to be in a defined and controlled (rather than vulnerable) relation. Our *relationship* to the cosmos is as though we are outside of it looking

---

90. Brague, *The Wisdom of the World*, 17–25.

in on the system to which we relate as object. For the medievals, the mere act of looking up was far more wonder producing than it is for us—even though their picture was neater. That neat picture was suspended in an order of things to which humans were not practically oriented as object and in relation to which they felt tremendous vulnerability and lack of control. James K. A. Smith's summary of Charles Taylor is apt:

> 1. The natural world was constituted as a cosmos that functioned semiotically, as a sign that pointed beyond itself, to what was more than nature. 2. Society itself was understood as something grounded in a higher reality; earthly kingdoms were grounded in a heavenly kingdom. 3. In sum, people lived in an enchanted world, a world "charged" with presences, that was open and vulnerable, not closed and self-sufficient.[91]

While drawing upon the Hebrew tradition (which does not essentially localize God), then, the medieval Christian tradition nevertheless still predominantly associated God with the city, with architecture, with the realm of the ordered.[92] Medieval cities and communities were still suffused with the cooperation of God and humanity—with a transcendental purpose (even if the latter had more spiritual coding—for divine glory rather than for divine feeding). The world was still, in the words of some historians, enchanted. What looks to us like superstition was still nearly ubiquitous (angels, demons, fairies, nymphs, witches, etc.). And the world of things was still, albeit perhaps in a post-Aristotelian sense, perceived to be a world of agencies, some more free and some

---

91. Ibid., 27. More broadly, see especially C. S. Lewis, *The Discarded Image* (New York: Cambridge University Press, 1964) on the question of medieval cosmology.

92. See Taylor's discussion of the bulwarks of belief in *A Secular Age*, 25–89. Though note the tradition of desert fathers: Andrew Louth, *The Wilderness of God* (Nashville: Abingdon Press, 1991). Nevertheless, the desert is not perceived to be an adventure away from what will later become an impersonal city but is rather understood to be a site of renunciation.

less free—a chorus of communicators rather than an amalgam of machine parts.[93]

By way of transition, it is worth keeping the big picture in view. The ontological shift is important because while the human sense of absolute vulnerability remains, it is nevertheless suspended in an order that is fundamentally personal and rational (in the broadest sense of the term)—and in which humanity figures as an important feature.[94] The emergence of classical humanity from ancient humanity can be compared to the transition from childhood to the early stages of puberty. In the former (especially in the infant/toddler stage), the world is largely perceived as a boundless series of individuated experiences, scenes, trusts, and fears—with little sense of a whole. Late childhood (early pubescence) often involves a theoretical sense of the whole, but nevertheless as a mystery to be learned and journeyed. There is a sense of cosmic stability, trustworthiness, and a basic map of meaning. But there is no sense of control, familiarity, or fine-grained attunement to cosmic geography. What is required for *full* severance from the ancient sense of vulnerability, then, is a *gestalt* shift in the tacit understanding of what it means for a thing to be real at all—which is inevitably tied to one's practical orientation to reality. My reality is that with which I have to do, to engage. As I will argue below, I believe that this shift occurs progressively in the early modern to late modern periods. And I think we can best interpret it by understanding how the modern technocultural order (after the Industrial Revolution) changed humanity's sense of subjection

---

93. See Foucault, *The Order of Things*, 3–47.

94. It is possible that an Eastern parallel to this unique balance can be found in the great Chinese novel, Wu Ch'eng-en's *Monkey*. In my reading of it, one gets the sense of an extremely vulnerable universe, but one that is nevertheless fundamentally subject to an order outside the human capacity to fully grasp it (i.e., Rule of Heaven, which sometimes appears to be above the gods). This is the importance of the Scriptures—which instruct man in the ways of Heaven. Also of note is the predominantly urban (or at least) garden character of the realm of the gods, contrasted with the large amount of wilderness that monkey and his crew must cross in the ordinary terrestrial plane. Wu Ch'eng-en, *Monkey*, trans. Arthur Waley (New York: Grove Press, 1970).

to felt agencies outside of themselves. Simplifying to the extreme, the world became a world of things at hand rather than a world of actors to which the human was subject.

The Cosmos Come of Age: The Modern World

The shift above was described as something like the transition from early to late childhood. The shift I hope to describe here could be called analogous to the transition from late childhood to early adulthood—to juvenility. Bound up with this is a felt change in the degree to which humans are independent and free from agencies, authorities, and threats outside of themselves. Juveniles are wont to imagine themselves invulnerable. This is, of course, a change in perception rather than in reality.

This transition, away from a world of enchanted agencies to a world of manipulable machine parts (or, more recently, processes), has often been identified by historians as the disenchantment of the cosmos. Whence this epistemic and ultimately existential shift? As I claimed in the first chapter, there are as many analyses of this phenomenon as there are accounts of it—in its relationship(s) to the Reformation, early modern science, late medieval natural philosophy, scholasticism, nominalism, Neo-Platonism, the Baconian scientific method, and sundry other moments in the massive period of change that is early modernity. And so I must focus only on points that, it seems to me, are at least highly relevant to understanding this break. After laying out this broad outline, I will (in the next section) seek to fill out this picture with a more fine-grained phenomenological analysis of the lived world of modernity.

First, one precondition for this eventual break is a reconception of the city's relationship to God. Several shifts in early modern Europe made this conception possible. Of chief importance was the fracturing of the Holy Roman Empire into a mix of city-states that each confessed a different faith. What united them thereafter was not necessarily their submission to the papacy or even to a

particular creed but often rather their common temporal interests.[95] This new context creates the possibility, but not the necessity, of reconceptualizing the role of the temporal order as having
its more immediate telos in human flourishing rather than in the
spiritual kingdom of Christ. This reconception was instantiated
predominantly in Britain, Holland, and America—public religion
reimagining itself largely in relation to Luther's earthly kingdom
and only in a significantly qualified way to his spiritual kingdom.[96]

   Second, simultaneous with this international situation and its
latent possibilities was the development and reception of Bacon's
scientific method—often identified as the foundation of modern
science. But of central significance in Bacon's method was the
reconceptualization of humanity's posture toward nature. Nature
was rendered an instrument for humanity—at least in a provisional
sense. The fruition of the scientific method was technological in
nature—as the powers of nature were harnessed for human flourishing. Of some relevance is that Bacon was explicitly critical of
Aristotle's approach to nature and to human knowing, emphasizing
practical use rather than philosophical reflection on nature's *inner*
potency (i.e., individual "natures"). Of course, this posture bore
tremendous fruits. It was not uncommon in the eighteenth and
nineteenth centuries for Europeans to feel that they were living
in an era of extreme advances in human knowledge and mastery
over their own destiny.[97] The advances in medicine, for instance,
were seen as effectively creating a different world. And it was a
world that had been formed out of the options made available
by the early modern political environment. The order of *techne*
(which involves increased *control* over mere predictability) was

---

95. This is a significant theme for Taylor in *A Secular Age*.

96. It is difficult to identify a work that traces this theme sufficiently, but one that I
think captures precisely the right shift in political principles is Littlejohn's *The Peril and
Promise of Christian Liberty*.

97. Note the general optimism of the *philosophes* in Peter Gay, *The Enlightenment: The
Science of Human Freedom* (New York: Norton, 1996).

then perfectly fitted to the order of the penultimate—*as* which the urban was being reconceived and experienced.[98]

Third, this reconception makes it possible to view the city not only as for man but also of humanity. Rather than an echo of divine activity, it becomes an icon of *human* activity. Though one might see modern urban architecture as scratching a sort of transcendental itch, the transcendental itch is nevertheless located and represented as the imminent order. The skyline of New York City would have seemed like a portal to the gods to an ancient person, but in our instinctual modern reading, it fundamentally represents humanity and its achievements. Increasingly, the city belongs to the order of the immanent rather than to the order of the transcendent.

Fourth, nature (conversely) is sentimentalized throughout this period.[99] Especially among elites and persons no longer fighting the most immediate battles of survival, gardens take on the connotation less of a proto-city (as they were in the ancient world) than of a proto-wilderness. Increased sentiment towards animals develops. As man is increasingly shielded from the life-threatening aspects of nature via his technologies, so the wilderness is reconceived as a sort of place of primal and originary order rather than of primal chaos. It is no longer a site of renunciation, but a site of serenity and spiritual resonance. Indeed, in the nineteenth century (especially in Romantic literature), it is in uncultivated nature that God is to be found, rather than in the city, which echoes the voice of man rather than the voice of God. One can see something of this transition in Thomas Hardy's *Jude the Obscure* (1895), where the city (while exciting) is the place of freethought, temptation,

98. Taylor's *A Secular Age* is largely concerned with showing how early-modern Protestantism tended to emphasize the telos of much of human activity in the benefit of one's neighbor. While this was not at all divorced from a theological foundation or end, the focus on man-qua-man as an end was significant. For Taylor, this makes possible (but not inevitable) the severance of these ends.

99. See the masterful treatment of Thomas, *Man and the Natural World*.

and the loss of faith. The countryside is where God may be found, though by the time of Hardy, barely so.

Fifth, the city, progressively reduced to the temporal order, ultimately threatens to swallow even the personalism of the countryside. At roughly the same time as people begin to speak of the urban jungle,[100] they also begin to speak of nature as "red in tooth and claw" (Tennyson). As in ancient perception, then, the city still tends to set the standard for humans' understanding of reality in general—and therefore their understanding of the wilderness and of the wider world. Only now the latter increasingly represents a progressive diminishment of the city's felt impersonality rather than its felt agentic character. Nature, then, is a more diminished blind process rather than a more diminished mode of personal agency (as it was for our ancestors).[101] This is a particularly important point, and I will unpack it below in my claim that our modern self-projection onto the cosmos is a matter of projected impersonality rather than a projected agency.

Sixth, we are now in a place to suggest one of two primary features of the epistemic-cum-existential shift that constitutes modernity. The previous points render our modern condition possible, but not inevitable. I would argue that this point (especially in its relationship to labor—which I discuss below) makes our modern condition all but inevitable. It is often suggested that our former enchantment changed when human beings were able to predict the alleged agencies of the cosmos, presumably rendering them less agentic. I do not think this is quite a sufficient move. Regular prediction might shift one's perception of just how rigid particular modes of agency were, but the perception was still that natures communicated by acting. Furthermore, medieval natural

---

100. On which, see Joseph McLaughlin, *Writing the Urban Jungle: Reading Empire in London from Doyle to Eliot* (Charlottesville: University Press of Virginia, 2000).

101. It is fascinating the note the dialectic between machine and life in this period—a dialectic that we are still seeking to work out. See David Channell, *The Vital Machine: A Study of Technology and Organic Life* (New York: Oxford University Press, 1991).

philosophers were constantly trying to predict the course of nature and even to influence the activities of angels and demons—rendering *them* predictable.[102] And so, alternatively, I would argue that the real key to the progressive change and sense of things that have shifted in the West in the last five hundred years is a change in the human ability to *control* these alleged agencies rather than just to predict them. If a person is not only able to understand a thing but to use it for his own ends, that same thing might increasingly be perceived less like an agent to which one is reciprocally subject (as agent to agent) than like a tool that is rather *entirely* subject to that person's agency and ends. In emphasizing this, I (of course) echo many claims made by Ellul and Heidegger. Here we see a significant shift in the human's immediate practical sense of things. As the modern era progressed, droughts, which were formerly signs of divine judgment, were now possible to control because of one's tools. Indeed, in our day, it is now normal to even *seek out* the desert for aesthetic purposes. Death was felt to be less and less a threat (through medicine, infrastructure, etc.), and comfort and distance from nature a more ubiquitous and extensive given. The philosophical waters were made even murkier when ecclesiastical invocations of divine judgment for increasing philosophical blasphemies or for the exploitation of nature went unrealized. This rendered even the (presumably) most agentic aspects of the cosmos effectively silent and invisible. The real story here, then, is the story of modern technoculture and its implicit postures toward the real.

Inasmuch, then, as nature continued (and continues) to yield to human control, the instrumental posture toward nature appears to be reality-revealing. The world has subjected itself to humanity and given its fruits. And this suggests that we have carved reality at

---

102. See David Lindberg, *The Beginnings of Western Science: The European Scientific Tradition in Philosophical, Religious, and Institutional Context: Prehistory to A.D. 1450* (Chicago: University of Chicago Press, 2008).

the seams by relating to nature in this manner. This relationship, of course, has never been absolute. But the continued holding of this posture and the increased proliferation of its technological fruits cannot but have had a massive effect on the Western sense of what it means for a thing to be real at all. Our posture toward nature, *which is itself reinforced by the technologies that mediate that relation,* ultimately shape our imagination concerning the real. Science and technology are not fundamentally distinct, an insight that is suggestive as it pertains to the role that scientific discourse has taken in our era.[103]

And so, what does it mean for a thing to be real in the modern order? In my judgment, the modern technological order tacitly communicates to us, day in and day out, that reality (the sort that actually concerns us), belongs to the order of the manipulable—subject, in principle, to human agency. We saw in Heidegger that modern technology is the destining of revealing such that nature answers back to me in the shape of my questions (i.e., uses) for it. That it appears resonant with the realm of material manipulation has everything to do with how we have approached reality in the first place. For Ellul, technique is a pattern of thought that changes everything it touches—a reduction of reality to the terms of the rational and ordered and the efficient. What does not fit this mold is ultimately invisible.

It is not that there is no longer a philosophical argument for invisible realities. On the contrary (in my judgment), many classical arguments are compelling, but they belong to a discourse that is unnatural to us and was quite natural (teleology, etc.) in its original context.[104] As such, their persuasive power depends upon accounting for this disjunct and attempting to reharmonize our reality instincts with the conclusions of our free minds. This is

---

103. See Lelas, "Science as Technology."

104. I give a philosophical argument but make this point about discourse at length in *Enduring Divine Absence,* 26–62.

because we have been shaped to relate to the cosmos and to perceive the cosmos only (or almost only) in its manipulable dimensions, which is to say that dimension in which human agency can, in principle, interfere. As such, any aspect of it that does not conform to this dimension is perceived to be nonexistent. Or, stated differently, the least personal aspects of reality become the only realms of concern and care for us.[105] Inasmuch as these are that as which we perceive the real, it is natural for us to feel as though anything else is superfluous. We fancy our explanatory itch scratched when it has rather been numbed.

In any case, it is my claim that this is a large part of why atheism, for instance, and an urbanized modernity are highly correlated. It is here that one can move around in a world that has been controlled for the human and that consequently forecloses the experience of agency that has classically reinforced the notion of God by making personhood seem like a fundamental property of all being. This is especially the case by the 1960s, by which time the majority of those living in the West experienced lifestyle comforts that were historically unimaginable to their ancestors just a few generations before. In any case, this point is made clearest to us as we consider our own immediate context. I, for instance, live in an air-conditioned house. When a storm comes that would have been a crisis to my ancestors, I do not even flinch. I can hardly imagine what it is like to get food or water anywhere else but a grocery store or a tap, the products of each appearing, for all practical purposes, as by magic (albeit I assume of the demystified, technical sort in the hands of an anonymous, different sort of clergy). When I experience nature, it is manicured nature, whether it be

---

105. This is especially exacerbated to the extent that we achieve immediate satisfaction and relief in these things. Though the writer of the ancient proverb was not referring to atheism as such, there is insight in the statement, "Two things I ask of you, Lord; do not refuse me before I die: Keep falsehood and lies far from me; give me neither poverty nor riches, but give me only my daily bread. Otherwise, I may have too much and disown you and say, 'Who is the Lord?' Or I may become poor and steal, and so dishonor the name of my God" (Prov 30:7–9).

the neatly placed trees in my neighborhood, the mowed lawn, the pruned bushes, or the nonthreatening sky. When I walk outside to the bus, the notion that my path is lit, that I walk on smooth concrete, that I am in a vehicle that transports me at high but efficient speeds, does not even enter my consciousness. This is reality to me. I *know* that it is technologically mediated, but that is only when I am thinking about it. When I am simply moving around in it, it is simply the world. One could go on to speak of technologically mediated encounters with health, death, and other persons. Even the most agentic aspects of reality (human relationships) are increasingly subjected to media, surrogates, and options that are historically unprecedented and mechanistic.[106] That on which I rely is less family and neighbor than institution, expert, and system. To put it bluntly, the world is a world for me. I do not find myself in a big, mysterious world suffused with agencies to which I am subject and around which I must learn to co-navigate with my immediate community. I find myself in a world almost entirely tool-i-fied, a world of my own (agentless!) subjectivity before an increasingly silent cosmos.

Seventh, then, my argument is that it is this shifting background noise that constitutes the existential space within which modern persons develop their sense of the divine in relationship to nature and to the city. And this noise is fundamentally impersonal. This is the era of Freud's *Civilization and its Discontents* and Albert Camus' *The Stranger*. The former puts the irrational at the very heart of civilization. The latter captures the indifference of the cosmos—a fundamental truth that filters down into the most basic of human realities.[107]

---

106. See Nicholas Carr, *The Shallows: What the Internet is Doing to Our Brains* (New York: Norton, 2011).

107. The theme of divine absence in the face of an indifferent cosmos is also beautifully explored in the films *The Grey*, directed by Carnahan (2012), and *Melancholia*, directed by Lars von Trier (Magnolia Pictures, 2011).

Still, I have only described that background noise in a general way. Implicitly, I have highlighted the centrality of humankind's practical or lived orientation to the world in the formation of his plausibility structures. But to understand this more thoroughly, we need to reflect upon humankind in its active relationship to its tools. As such, we need to fill out the key sixth point above (concerning control) with a discussion of the modern individual as an active laborer. It is worth reiterating that the early modern move to the city was largely related to policies of enclosure and to the ensuing relationship of laborers to the jobs that so define our era. And so the modern experience of urbanity and industrialism was always mutually implicated by, and in the individual's relationship to, his own labor. In the following section, then, I aim to describe the active dimension of our engagement with the modern order phenomenologically—because it is to people in their actual (though not always felt) agency that the world most primally manifests itself.

THE WORLD IN THE MIRROR OF MODERN LABOR AND TECHNOLOGY

Phenomenological Analysis

I develop two claims in this section: (1) In the default practical involvements cultivated by it, the modern technocultural order shapes human beings to see *themselves* in others and in the world rather than to see *others* in others and *the world* in the world. (2) This projection of the self is a matter not of our projected personhood, agency, or activity but of our projected impersonality, subjection, and passivity. The religious consequences are obvious. A world read as irreducibly impersonal is one with which any instinctual sense of the divine is in tension.

Stating my claims so curtly affords me the advantage of anticipating a probable counterclaim (even reaction) and to show why, while it is misguided as a critique, it is a uniquely fitting starting point for my analysis. The counterclaim might be developed as follows: Is this not the age of communication? Are we not surrounded more than ever by personhood in at least two very prominent senses? First, the items that populate our world are very clearly made by persons. Further removed than our ancestors from the harsh world of nature, the basic furniture of our little cosmos is no longer sun, moon, stars, and trees—but lights, groceries, beds, houses, buildings, cellphones, computers, tables, coffee mugs, shoelaces, and so on. Second, many of these technologies mediate increased contact with humans (and an increasing number of them) in ways that our ancestors would have thought either magical or at least overwhelming. We can speak to persons in another country. We have hundreds or thousands of "friends" on social media. We keep in touch with our intimates throughout the day via texting, emails, and phone calls. We have the ability to more easily stay in touch with persons whom we might otherwise forget. This is not to mention that we live in extremely populated cities or suburbs and that the population of the world in general has increased many-fold. Several prima facie observations could be made in relation to this objection, but instead of taking this route, it is preferable to consider these phenomena more fully—to ascertain if they do not rather make the point than confute it.

Taking up the first point, then, what of the proliferation of man-made objects? Do we not, in them, see *others*, and what is more, other *persons*? The answer to this depends entirely upon what we mean by see. We, of course, are abstractly *aware* or, if you will, *know* that these items are made by other persons. But arguably, we do not *relate* to them in this manner. Our tacit sense of their sheer *givenness* predominates. Numbed to any instinctual sense of the contrast (and relation) between the makings of people and the makings of the world, the makings of people feel very much to us what nature might have felt like to our ancestors. The erosion of this sense of difference can be accounted for by the vast proliferation of modern technologies to the point that there are very few things in our experience that are not heavily inflected through some (usually more than one) technical apparatus, but—and this is key—a technical apparatus involving enormous amounts of human agency that is out of sight and out of mind for us.

Still, why should such erosion necessarily mediate impersonality? Our ancestors, after all, detected agency in rocks and air and celestial bodies. Quite right, but since (for them) human *labor* was irreducibly meaningful, the comparatively non-agentic aspects of the cosmos—experienced in the mirror of such labor—were simply felt to be less free locations of active being. Immediately *for* humanity itself, such labor is naturally coded as human participation in the ordering project of the god(s). What has changed in our context is not merely technology in the abstract but our relationship to our own making (and therefore the sense of "what the world is like" carried along in those practices).

Let us explicate this point with more clarity. We are almost entirely removed from the actual persons who make the products that mediate our experience. For the most part, the products are just "there," and the human-making aspect of them is erased from our awareness except in the most abstract ways. But perhaps more importantly, the products that populate and mediate our experience do not have the marks of craft. In claiming this, I do not mean anything sentimental—as perhaps one might imagine in the arts and crafts usage of the term. I rather mean that most products are (1) mass products for mass humanity rather than *this* product for *me* and (2) actually made by persons who often lack *investment* and *engagement* in their making (except accidentally). This is, of course, to invoke Marx's comments about alienation from labor, but it is also to go a step further. This systemic alienation does not just mean that the hands that made my computer, or (as the case may be) managed the machines which made my computer, are unshaken and imaginary to me (not to mention appropriated by ends other than those of the hands' possessor).[108] What is also

---

108. Even the technical designers are often driven more by projected consumer convenience and sales potential than by craft as such. And, of course, good craftsmanship

ordinarily missing in this is what Richard Sennett has identified as a state of *engagement* in labor.[109] A lack of *investment* can be largely correlated with the fact that the maker (at whatever level) is ultimately subject to pressures larger than his own making—but a lack of *engagement* highlights the fact that such pressures do not tend to allow for craft *for the sake of* craft. The marks of human making are as much imperfection as perfection, dissonance as much as harmony, uselessness as much as usefulness, the sense of producing as such rather than producing *for*. Richard Sennett calls this "doing a good job for its own sake." We might add that good must here be defined by the ends of the maker rather than the pressures of the market or the projected demands of the consumer. Indeed, these might be in tension.

But this sort of engagement in craft for its own sake, in making for its own sake and according to one's own values, is the paradigm of *personal* involvement. It is the paradigm of agency. To the extent that our labors are removed from this, to this extent they are impersonal. This is a key point. There was a connection between these things for our ancestors as well—who presumably posited some gap between the makings of the divine and the divine itself (Barfieldian "original participation" notwithstanding).[110] But precisely because their relation to the world and to others was connected and engaged, this gap did not affect their tacit sense of the reality of divine agency as the foundation for their own. They felt themselves to be finitely participating in prior activities and meanings that were *in the public world itself* (the world being or approximating the infinite plentitude that grounds all particular meaning). Lacking this resonance, such meanings appear to us as mere projections. And so, ironically, what we *actually* project

---

might be particularly marketable. While most items that populate our experience traffic in a place of planned obsolescence, there is certainly a market niche for fancier cabinets and shrubberies that are not as texture-less and decay-laden as most modern products. On the modern dynamics of work in late capitalism, see Sennett, *The Corrosion of Character*.

109. See Sennett, *The Craftsman*.

110. See Barfield, *Saving the Appearances*.

back onto others and onto the world, by contrast, is impersonal in character.

It is important to note that we do not experience this order only passively. This given and prescribed world is something in which we are caught up and to which we actively contribute with our own labor. Therefore, the failure to achieve engagement is a matter of both the specific *content* of much of our activity and the order to which it belongs. To be sure, it is not that engagement is impossible. Nor is it that previous engagement could not be monotonous (which is *not* the opposite of engagement in the above sense). It is rather that such engagement is neither necessary nor easily available (even in its primal forms such as growing one's own food for survival). And lacking necessity and urgency (apart from a sublimated anxiety concerning our lack of meaning), the activity of most humans tends to amount—when taken as a whole—to *passively* being carried along (even when being *active*) in forces that they neither understand nor feel the ability to shape. Even monotonous labor, when it is in the full possession of the laborer, is irreducibly shaped by the laborer who *means* it. By contrast, this sense of being carried along in our activities is a significant piece of what I am trying to account for.[111]

Moreover, recalling Ellul's discussion of the impact of techne on the human, the outsourcing of our networks of trust to institutions and experts necessarily reduces the human engagement that we even mediately (rather than immediately) have to the nature of techne itself. The world after the image of a parent or sibling

---

111. Astute readers will note the contrast to the control that I have otherwise argued constitutes the modern condition. What unites these is that what is controlled for us are those immediate items of concern and care, but with the compensatory effect that we are carried in our narrative, labor-structure, and sense of the whole. We might control particulars but are passive agents of the whole in relation to which we experience ourselves as having little capacity to alter our world. Moreover, even the tools of control are default givens in our lived world—and objects of will only relatively. In short, our world-making experience of superficial control forecloses our awareness of a deeply sublimated and scripted dependence.

is different from the world after the image of a boss or coworker. What was formerly a matter of trust in relation to persons who could not be reduced to their social function is now a matter of unchosen dependence on persons whose pedigree is guaranteed by systems, experts, and institutions—and whose relation to me is largely reduced to their utility within a shared network.[112] And so, just as I confront the world as a sort of passive material to be shaped by my will via the technologies that mediate its relation to me, so also (inasmuch as my contact with other persons is shaped by these structural features of my involvement) even persons proper tend to be reduced to passive material for manipulation. I can block on social media. I can turn off the television. I can hang up the phone. I can decide not to text back.[113] And this gets at the second point of the objection with which we started this section and further highlights the reciprocally reinforcing relationship between *other* and *world* in relation to which I develop my sense of reality in general.

In sum, the world of our experience is neither one that confronts us as agentic nor one in relation to which we usually feel like difference-making agents in the fuller sense. And this is important because as Sennett writes, "We become particularly interested in the things we can change."[114] Lacking this sense, the world seems less and less like it calls for the sort of engagement that is the fullest mark of personhood.

We have almost sketched out a preliminary framework, but not quite. What remains to be made explicit (though just implied

---

112. This is largely the argument of Giddens, *The Consequences of Modernity*.

113. It is remarkable to observe that social media demonstrably tends to reduce humans to an abstracted collection of identities that are projected on the public forum. And this public forum becomes a site of judgment (likes and dislikes) abstracted from the whole thing that constitutes what it means to be human. As a consequence, not a few persons have observed that our social circles are becoming ever more an echo chamber. This can be contrasted to the pub culture in the United Kingdom, where some social tension is absorbed in the temple that is the pub. Since most homes are in walking distance to a pub, a larger amount of social tension is mediated by persons "smashing into one another," being confronted by the reality that persons are not reducible to their identity-projections and such.

114. Sennett, *The Craftsman*, 120.

above) is the claim that a human's self-conscious sense of agency and self-possession is fundamentally developed in *response* to the felt active personhood of others. This qualifies my claim that the world is largely understood via my own makings. While true, our making is always a response to something prior—most fundamentally to other persons in relation to whom we experience and engage the potential of the world. And so there is a reciprocal relationship between our I/thou relations and or I/it projections. Our first experiences are of being spoken to and cared for by a community. We learn to become our own agents by navigating around others who can confront us and frustrate our own ends. Siblings learn life and love in the primitive motions of unavoidable negotiation and bonding. To the extent that the world is structured in such a way as to avoid what was formerly unavoidable, we are not impelled to possess our own agency. We cultivate a passive relation to our very own activity. While we can technically shape the (felt) impersonal order according to the promptings of our will, we increasingly *find ourselves* not in the default setting of agentic self-possession but rather as carried along even in our own *actual* agency! And if others appear to us to be the same (since our primary relation to their agency is mediated and prescripted by unseen agencies outside of either of us), then what will be reflected back to us in the mirror of the other is precisely our own being as manipulable and non-agentic—the ultimate agent a faceless system or process or set of laws.

We are, of course, speaking about an experienced relation to the world and to others rather than giving a causal account of who or what *actually* makes this world. Implicit in what I have just claimed, that our own agency is shaped by the felt agency of the other, is that the world itself (as experienced) is the chief causal element—though, as we shall see, in the mode of *tendency* rather than irreversible or absolute determination. My claim, then, is that we are engaged in such a way as to erase the kind of active engagement (non-alienated labor) that makes the world seem personal.

Conversely, in this parody of a primal encounter with the world, we are shaped to imagine that our relation to the world is one of a manipulator of passive material, but in such a way as to anxiously experience this possession of agency as a power without direction—an impersonal force in which we are caught up and with which we have little sense of what we are to do: What shall I do today? Should I go to this school or that? Should I marry this woman or that? What should my career be? Under erasure is the felt facticity of that which orients us in the world—the engagement of others as others and the world as the world, with their respective callings upon us that shape our individual performance of life.

At this point, we have (I think) at least preliminarily painted our picture. Because its agency is hidden, our world is one to which we relate predominantly via our will. But cultivated as passive participants in our own willing (because unengaged by the world), we tacitly perceive our own lack of true activity in the mirror of the world itself. In short, the world and the other are impersonal because we are. And, to bring the argument full circle, this accounts (then) for why reality does not tacitly seem like a manifestation of divine personhood.

Narrative Manifestation

In making these claims, I attempt to give discursive utterance to anxieties that have more frequently been given voice in narrative. In Thomas Hardy's *Jude the Obscure*, the titular character converses with his urban lover, Sue, who declares her love for a newfound rural environment: "I rather like this ... outside all laws except gravitation and germination." Jude replies, "You only think you like it; you don't: you are quite a product of civilization." She retorts, "Indeed I am not, Jude. I like reading and all that, but I crave to get back to the life of my infancy and its freedom."[115] What renders this scene compelling is not merely its manifestation of an urban/rural

---

115. Hardy, *Jude the Obscure*, 139.

158

CHAPTER THREE

contrast but its hint that we can never really go back prior to the effects of modern civilization once we have tasted it. To imagine otherwise is to engage in nostalgia. And yet, this longing remains. Karel Capek captures this beautifully in his early-twentieth-century play *R.U.R.*, famous for introducing the word "robot" into English (via translation). Contrary to utopian fantasies about the benefits of machines and robots performing all of human labor, the central human of the narrative, Alquist, refuses to stop laboring. When asked why he builds a brick structure, he replies, "There's something more decent about laying just one brick than drawing up plans that are too big."[116] This singular move saves Alquist's life. As the robots become self-conscious and eradicate their human overlords, Alquist alone is preserved because the robots perceive that he works—like one of them. Perhaps alienation from labor receives no better exposure as insanity than in Kafka's *The Metamorphosis*, wherein Gregor Samsa (its protagonist), recently transformed into a giant beetle, is chiefly concerned that he will not make it to work on time. While this is a picture of high-pressure wage slavery, Dave Eggers's *The Circle* portrays the comic insanity of relatively engaged labor that nevertheless requires that humans transform themselves into extensions of digital devices and their logic. In none of these is technology an abstraction, but in all, it is seen in its capacity to mediate the world to humankind in people's active use of their tools. And for each, humanity increasingly becomes an impersonalized parody of itself.

In my judgment, two particularly poignant pieces of literature capture the reality-shaping impact of modern technology and labor, and particularly what Heidegger meant by the "destining of revealing" (or "unhiding"). One is Kurt Vonnegut's *Player Piano*, and the other is John Updike's *In the Beauty of the Lilies*. Vonnegut imagines a world in which the United States dominates the world after World War II and wherein most jobs have been eradicated

---

116. Karel Capek, *R.U.R.* (Rockville, MD: Wildside Press, 2010), 37.

by machines. What is relatively unique in his story is that it is a book about inequality, but not inequality of economics. To be sure, there are the rich and the poor. But the poor are all given a basic subsistence on the back of machines and work menial jobs as they are assigned. The managers of machines (increasingly downsized) have the more intellectually fulfilling labor and higher incomes. Nevertheless, the complaint of the quasi-Proletariat is not that they are not paid enough but that their labor does not contain a "sense of participation, the sense of importance."[117] One character prophesies the highly volatile situation of men in such a condition: "Sooner or later someone's going to catch the imagination of these people with some new magic. At the bottom of it will be a promise of regaining the feeling of participation, the feeling of being needed on earth—hell, *dignity*."[118] This inequality of meaning, however, is only apparent. The chief protagonist, a prestigious machine plant manager named Paul Proteus, grows increasingly disillusioned with his reality. A technologically mediated world shapes humans according to its image. Paul's wife Anita is described as having the "mechanics of marriage down pat."[119] Paul has a passive relation to his socially manipulating wife and takes up reading novels about men accomplishing things in the wild. Paul has lost "the sense of spiritual importance in what they were doing; the ability to be moved emotionally, almost like a lover, by the great omnipresent and omniscient spook, the corporate personality."[120] "People are finding," states one character, "because of the way the machines are changing the world, more and more of their old values don't apply any more. People have no choice but to become second-rate machines themselves, or wards of the machines."[121] Men become machines.

117. Kurt Vonnegut, *Player Piano* (New York: The Dial Press, 1991), 91.
118. Ibid., 92, emphasis in original.
119. Ibid., 17.
120. Ibid., 63.
121. Ibid., 290.

In Updike's highly underrated narrative (with which I began this book), the "destining of unhiding" (or revealing) is unveiled by its focus on what I believe is an insufficiently explored driver of this destiny—modern film. Updike tells the story of four generations of an American family alongside their complex relationship to the history of American cinema. In a matchless description of lost faith, Updike narrates the story of Clarence Wilmot—an early-twentieth-century Presbyterian minister whose faith left him despite his desperation to hold onto it. Experiencing the personal and familial consequences of his newfound atheism, Clarence finds solace in the new attraction of the cinema house. "Gutted by God's withdrawal," Clarence "felt himself fading away, but for the hour when the incandescent power of these manufactured visions filled him."[122] A generation later, however, Clarence's son Teddy has little affection for the cinema.

> Life was endlessly cruel, and there was nobody above to grieve—Father had proved that. And life's central event, propelling men and women through their days and nights, was an unthinkable collision of slimy, hairy parts that should be kept forever hidden. The cinema wished to leave nothing hidden, to throw nakedness up on the screen, and grief, and fistfights and explosions and violence, and even corpses and monsters, played by Lon Chaney. Terror would attack Teddy even in the middle of hilarious and romantic sequences, as he realized that these bright projections were trying to distract him from the leaden reality beneath his seat, underneath the theatre floor. Death and oblivion were down there, waiting for the movie to be over. Not so, these movies tried to say. Life was not serious; it was an illusion, a story, distracting and disturbing but at bottom painless and merciful.[123]

---

122. Updike, *In the Beauty of the Lilies*, 107.
123. Ibid., 148.

More like her grandfather, Teddy's light-hearted daughter grows up to be a movie star and to neglect her child for the sake of her career. Raised late after the advent of cinema and (deeply) shaped by it, her child (Clark—the fourth-generation Wilmot) constantly imagines his life to be like a movie. Moving from trivial pleasure to pleasure, scene to scene, Clark is surprised to find himself attracted to a cult that repudiates the majority of modern technology. Clark changes his name, joins the cult, and completes the cycle of disenchantment-cum-enchantment initiated by his great grandfather. What makes Updike unique is his development of a technology's impact over several generations and the manner in which it deeply shapes the human psyche—helping to shape the very experience of the world itself. Or, as Heidegger might say, film destines that world by enframing it in such a way that only certain of its features are revealed and/or distorted. In a relevant sense, men become movies.

Excursus on Film

By way of transition, it is worth reflecting upon the medium of film as an especially poignant technology in relation to which our basic picture of reality is revealed to us. This is particularly the case because I want to conclude this chapter with a more extended reflection upon the theme of presence and absence in relation to which we, as I have argued, often navigate the question of God. And in my judgment, film is particularly important for coming to grips with that discourse.[124] This is because we might say that

---

124. On film's underrated impact on our perception of reality as well as our ordinary behavior, see B. J. Bushman and L. R. Huesmann, "Short-Term and Long-Term Effect of Violent Media on Aggression in Children and Adults," *Archives of Pediatrics and Adolescent Medicine Journal* 160, no. 4 (2006), 348–52; Torben Grodal, *Embodied Visions: Evolution, Emotion, Culture, and Film* (New York: Oxford University Press, 2009); Veronica Hefner, "From Love at First Sight to Soul Mate: Romantic Ideals in Popular Films and Their Association with Young People's Beliefs About Relationships" (PhD diss., University of Illinois at Urbana-Champaign, 2011); Colin McGinn, *The Power of Movies: How Screen and Mind Interact* (New York: Pantheon Books, 2005).

the question that frames this essay ("What does it mean that a thing is real?") might also be converted into the question, "What does it mean that a thing is present or absent?" To the extent that the ubiquitously consumed medium of modern film shapes our instincts on this question, it is worth briefly reflecting upon as we move toward taking final stock of modern presence and absence discourse.

Jacques Ellul reflects upon film in a general argument concerning the relationship between image and reality. Specifically with respect to vision and action, Ellul writes, "Sight moves to action."[125] He says further:

> Sight previously showed me reality as a thing present to my consciousness; now it urges me to be a presence myself, in relation to this reality. I will use all the information that sight has conveyed to me, as I change this universe of images by creating new ones. I am a subject, not separated from what I look at. Rather, what I see becomes part of me, as my action involves me in what I see.[126]

Sight is "only a presence. It bears witness to something 'already there.'"[127] It makes the universe a universe-for-me.[128] This will shape Ellul's evaluation of film. One could argue that film contains speech as well as sight, but Ellul argues that "speech is basically presence. It is something alive and is never an object. It cannot be thrown before me and remain there. Once spoken, the word ceases to exist ... The word is never an object."[129] Words in film do not involve one in a dialogue, and they can be listened to over and over. It is objectified speech. In it, we are spectators of a reality

---

125. Jacques Ellul, *The Humiliation of the Word* (Grand Rapids: Eerdmans, 1985), 6.
126. Ibid., 6–7.
127. Ibid., 9.
128. Ibid., 10.
129. Ibid., 15.

that is not reciprocally aware of us. Inasmuch as movies contain words, then, they are more object-like than interpersonal speech.

What, then, is the reality, *as* which film presents itself, like? Ellul argues:

> The film viewer is placed in a state of emotional accessibility that opens him wide to influences, forms, and myths. Because of the images that draw him into the story, he is liberated from the restraint usually placed on some of his instincts. He projects his personal desire onto the world, because these desires wear the mask of everyday emotions. Since this situation occurs repeatedly, its effects are long-lasting ... Obviously every frequent film-goer is not thus poisoned, but his personality is modified by the world of images whose company he keeps, as they superimpose themselves on the real world.[130]

The world of film tends to make of the world, film. Ellul later asks:

> How can we avoid being impressed by the direct authenticity of the scene before us? We are not indifferent and disciplined enough to resist being carried away by this presence. I especially distrust those who say they do not get carried away by this influence. Such people are just embarrassed by their fragility.[131]

On the one hand, Ellul argues that the potential long-term effect of film is to render our world more objective ("concrete" and "for me"). Film participates in the image-centricity of Western culture and perhaps also the egocentricity of it. Film makes us feel as though its visions are real. We are good at bracketing out this sensibility in terms of visual effects but not in its more subtle portrayals of justice, love, and self-fulfillment—all of which influence

---

130. Ibid., 119.
131. Ibid., 138.

us in significant ways. On the other hand, however, Ellul seems to argue that film so reduces the world only by its ability to wrap its concretion in the mythological.

I have argued that we have already been shaped to think of reality as belonging to the realm of the material and the manipulable. To the extent that Ellul rightly exegetes our world, more than being merely pushed into this realm, film (and its parallels) addicts us and attunes us to it—particularly in its capacity to function as a surrogate for the absorption of those aspects of human existence that are otherwise neglected in our modern order. And in its capacity to scratch these itches, film attunes us to a particular model of what it means that a thing is present to us. And so, in our final section, we will supplement our question concerning the real with its inflection in the discourse of presence and absence—which discourse (as I have been arguing throughout) strongly relates to our conception of God and his plausibility.[132]

PRESENCE, ABSENCE, AND THE METAPHYSICS
OF SIGHT AND SOUND

The modern presence/absence dialectic is complicated because it has more than a single pedigree. As we saw in the previous chapter, it names the contrast between a personal and an impersonal cosmos in much nineteenth-century discourse. However, in the work of Martin Heidegger and in his philosophical successors, it takes on the larger and more primal connotation of the human's attempted grasp of reality as a whole. The former sense of presence and absence is the modern parody of a late antique relation to the world's felt agency. The latter sense parallels and inverts the late antique sense the mind of humanity is adequated to a cosmos in its

---

132. Ironically, the image is starting to lose its authority in modern culture. The technologies of the image have become such that fantasy can be made to look like reality, and this has thrown us into a frenzy of concerns about fake news and the reliability of sources of information—instincts concerning which are quite complicated and highly related to the influences of those who have formative power over us.

wholeness and structural integrity. For Heidegger, the absentiality of the whole in the experienced part is a constitutive part of being human.[133] Let us attempt to put these pieces together.

Heidegger's notion of presence (later inflected by Derrida in his emphasis on the presence and logo-centricity of modern metaphysics) is developed early in his magnum opus, *Being and Time*, wherein he critiques classical metaphysics:

> According to the tradition, *existentia* ontologically means *being present* [*Vorhandensein*], a kind of being which is essentially inappropriate to characterize the being which has the character of Dasein. We can avoid confusion by always using the interpretive expression *objective presence* [*Vorhandenheit*] for the term *existentia*, and by attributing existence [*Existenz*] as a determination of being only to Dasein.[134]

Of first importance, Heidegger associates the tradition (i.e., Western philosophy since Plato)[135] with an ontology of presence. To exist is to be present. He goes on to call objective presence an interpretive expression, suggesting that the object-like nature of the existent thing is the point of emphasis. An object is present before and can be manipulated by a subject. Focused as he is on the relationship between being and temporality, Heidegger notes that the Western tradition privileges the present, the time that is directly at hand and in which objects are present to us.[136]

---

133. I am indebted to Peter Escalante for helping me to distinguish these levels of presence and absence discourse.

134. Martin Heidegger, *Being and Time*, trans. Joan Stambaugh (New York: State University of New York Press, 2010), 41, italics in original. All pagination references are to the English edition rather than to their German equivalents within the margins of the English edition. In what follows, my reading of Heidegger is significantly indebted to Charles Bambach. See his *Heidegger's Roots: Nietzsche, National Socialism, and the Greeks* (Ithaca, NY: Cornell University Press, 2005).

135. See the use of the term in Heidegger, *Being and Time*, 19–25.

136. See ibid., 24–25.

In contrast to this notion, Heidegger wishes to posit the phenomenology of Dasein. He writes, "*The 'essence' ['Wesen'] of Dasein lies in its existence [Existenz].* The characteristics to be found in this being are thus not present 'attributes' of an objectively present being which has such and such an 'outward appearance,' but rather possible ways for it to be, and only this."[137] Dasein is not an object that appears (presumably before a subject) and that has attributes attached to it (the latter being ontologically derivative). Not "present," Dasein, or the human being, is rather entirely and only its own possibility—namely, to "to be." Dasein is not present because it is not an actual thing. As Heidegger goes on, "Dasein *is* always its possibility. It does not 'have' that possibility only as a mere attribute of something objectively present."[138] Heidegger will even provocatively state, reversing Aristotle, that "higher than actuality stands *possibility*."[139] For this reason, Dasein bears a relation to the future that pulls all the potentiality of the present into itself. And as a consequence, human "being" is not an object and cannot be reduced to the scientific discourses that attempt to so reduce it.[140] The futural orientation of Dasein locates its plenitude of being in potency—in the possibility of being's manifold revelation.

Heidegger's phenomenology of Dasein is largely concerned with an interpretive and existential holism that attends the manifestation of being to Dasein. Rather than attributes of objects, Dasein is rather "being-in-the-world"—a phenomenal analysis that attempts to sever the boundary between subject and object, and even between object and attribute. The latter are rather interpretive movements suspended atop a more primal ontological attunement.[141] As we have already seen, in his later "The Question

---

137. Ibid., 41, italics in original.

138. Ibid., 42.

139. Ibid., 36, italics in original.

140. Ibid., 44–49.

141. Heidegger summarizes this theme in ibid., 53–62.

Concerning Technology," Heidegger will speak about modern technology (itself rooted in the Western tradition's ontology of presence) as the "destining of revealing."[142] Whatever our *primal* attunement to it, our *derivative* explicit relationship to being might nevertheless be an objectification of it (and, by implication, of human "be-ing"). Technology is a mode of bringing forth, itself a sort of presencing,[143] which only allows being to speak within the enframing that has been explicitly and actively set upon it.[144] And while being does manifest within our enframing, it is also largely rendered invisible. Yet it is precisely humanity's destining of revealing that manifests the facticity of the beings so reduced—and therefore highlights the possibility, if human beings will let being be, of a more original and originary revelation in art and poetry.[145]

Martin Heidegger's critique of the Western ontology of presence is perhaps the most important moment in twentieth-century philosophy. It is therefore significant to note a number of philosophical voices that articulate a notion of presence that echoes some of Heidegger's own positive insights without discarding the notion altogether. One wonders, indeed, if Heidegger's phenomenology of presence as object is his own "destining of revealing." It is possible that one could locate the problem in Heidegger's tendency to use (even in his positive philosophy) models and metaphors of manifestation, light, and seeing.[146] Ironically, this has been a privileged metaphor in the Western tradition,[147] and it would seem that Heidegger does not fully emancipate himself from it, though, as David Michael Levin argues, there are resources

---

142. Heidegger, "The Question Concerning Technology," 335.

143. Ibid., 317.

144. Ibid., 325.

145. Ibid., 337–41.

146. See, for instance, *Being and Time*, 67, and "The Question Concerning Technology," 338.

147. See Hans Blumenberg, "Light as a Metaphor for Truth," in Levin, ed., *Modernity and the Hegemony of Vision*, 30–62.

within Heidegger's own philosophy for such an emancipation.[148] Whatever the case, we will here consider a few attempts to articulate a phenomenology of "presence" that perhaps deflate some of Heidegger's critique of the Western tradition—even if it can still be argued that he has some positive offerings for it.[149]

As a preliminary consideration, it is worth highlighting the patron saint of those who privilege the ear instead of the eye—Martin Luther. In his early *Lectures on Hebrews*, Luther attempts to understand why, in Hebrews 10:5, the Greek Septuagint changes the Hebrew "You have opened my ears" to "You have prepared a body for me." His etymologies and exegesis are complex, but his conclusion is worth quoting at length:

> God no longer requires the feet or the hands or any other member; he requires only the ears. To such an extent has everything been reduced to an easy way of life. For if you ask a Christian what the work is by which he becomes worth of the name "Christian," he will be able to give absolutely no other answer that that it is the hearing of the Word of God, that is, faith. Therefore the ears alone are the organs of a Christian man, for he is justified and declared to be a Christian, not because of the works of any member but because of faith.[150]

Luther speaks here with reference to distinctively Christian identity, but he opens the way for others to consider the relationship between sound and human identity in general. This is particularly

---

148. See David Michael Levin, "Decline and Fall: Ocularcentrism in Heidegger's Reading of the History of Metaphysics," in *Modernity and the Hegemony of Vision*, 186–217. Heidegger's tendency in this regard is particularly paradoxical, in my judgment, given his contribution to the philosophy of language.

149. It is interesting to note the influence of Heidegger on self-professed naïve realists like Charles Taylor and Hubert Dreyfus as well as Thomists like Robert Sokolowski and W. Norris Clarke.

150. Martin Luther, *Luther's Works Volume 29*, ed. Jaroslav Pelikan (St. Louis: Concordia, 1968), 224.

so since it is through the ear that we hear speech—without which we would not be human at all. The twentieth-century philosopher Eugene Rosenstock-Huessy subversively inflected Descartes' *Cogito* with "I respond, although I will be changed."[151] More recently, Michael Horton has developed a theological phenomenology of the human being as one who is spoken to and answers back.[152] Let us, then, develop how an orientation in the ear and to sound might modify the manner in which we consider the notion of presence.

Jacques Ellul's reflections (discussed above) are clearly relevant here. Sight brings the human being into contact with objective presence before her. Sight is fundamentally continuous, present, active, and bound to laws of necessity.[153] Hearing, by contrast, is dialectical. Vision does not contradict vision, nor does image stand in tension with image. But sounds conflict in our ears. Statements conflict in relation to one another. And yet, here is a realm that is experienced as freedom and, most importantly, in which the human being is originally passive. In vision, I experience the world as that upon which I actively gaze. In sound, I experience the world as acting upon me. But it is ironically the word presence that Ellul uses to communicate this:

> Thus speech is basically presence. It is something alive and is never an object. It cannot be thrown before me and remain there. Once spoken, the word ceases to exist, unless I have recovered it. Before it is spoken, the word places me in an expectant situation, in a future I await eagerly. The word does not exist on its own. It continues to exist only in its effect on the one who spoke it and on the one who

---

151. My access point to this is via Peter Leithart, *The Baptized Body* (Moscow, ID: The Canon Press, 2007), 124.

152. Michael Horton, *Lord and Servant: A Covenant Christology* (Louisville: Westminster John Knox, 2005), 89–156.

153. See ibid., 5–47.

recovered it. The word is never an object you can turn this way and that, grasp, and preserve for tomorrow or some distant day when you may have time to deal with it.[154]

One can hear echoes of Heidegger here. The word places me "in a future." While vision is spatial, the word is oriented toward time and is a more primal mode of attunement to the world. And yet, for Ellul, the word is nevertheless a presence, though not (as he insists) an object. Here we see a departure (at least semantically) from Heidegger.

The relationship between "presence" and "the word" is perhaps never more powerfully developed than in Walter Ong's *The Presence of the Word*. There are many parallels between Ong and Ellul, but Ong emphasizes the "person-hood" of the word more than the simple passivity of our primal attunement to sound. "Since sound," Ong writes, "is indicative of a here-and-now activity, the word as sound establishes here-and-now personal presence. Abraham knew God's presence when he heard his 'voice.' "[155] Again:

It is true, of course, that the primary quality of extension, which is registered so directly by touch and sight, is more permanent or abiding than other sense qualities, and in this sense more real. Yet if we define reality in these terms, we become largely incapacitated for dealing with persons. Persons are potentialities, sources of power, and, although they may be extended in space, this is not what gives us our sense of them as persons, for extension in space is essentially passive. Persons, moreover, precisely as persons, are

---

154. Ibid., 15.

155. Walter Ong, *The Presence of the Word* (Albany: State University of New York Press, 2000), 113. It is fascinating to consider that there is perhaps little distinction, in the human infant's original experience of the world, between sound and the voice. Even the former, however, are predominantly sounds of a person. I doubt that it is overly speculative to suspect that the world, for infants, is almost entirely agentic-for-me and only progressively develops into an object-for-me.

eminently real. The most elementary psychological data make clear that our relations with other persons are powerful determinants of our actions if they are not indeed the most powerful of all determinants. Since voices manifests the person at a kind of maximum, hearing puts us in contact with the personal grounds of actuality of reality in a specially intense way.[156]

Important to note is Ong's use of the concepts of potency and act here. For Heidegger, Dasein (indeed, being) is primarily potentiality (which is above actuality). Ong adds in the dimension of the potentiality of the other in relation to the potentiality of the human being. The potentiality of the other-qua-agent sources my own potentiality-cum-actuality, that is, the "personal grounds of actuality." He uses this language again later:

Picturability is not the measure of actuality. For the universe, or at least our part of it, is filled with presences, which form the real stuff of our awareness but which of themselves cannot be pictured. Being-in-space is not of itself presence in the full sense of presence, that is, the sense of simultaneous at-oneness and otherness which another human being can bring to me.[157]

Taking these points together, it seems that the actuality of the other is a potentiality for me—as an agent that acts upon me. As actual (i.e., real), the other can potentially act upon me in such a way as to reduce my own potentiality to actuality. Is this not the same as to shape my identity? Moreover, does this not make the experience of reality irreducibly and primally personal?

It is worth taking stock at this point to ask whether these alternative formulations really represent a substantive rather than a merely semantic contrast to Heidegger's notion of presence.

156. Ibid., 173–74.
157. Ibid., 308–9.

Heidegger's seeming conflation of presence with object is suspended in his phenomenology of Dasein—which is not a subject related to an object (even to another person) but is, rather, a hermeneutical and factical whole. The question then becomes whether Luther, Rosenstock-Huessy, Horton, Ellul, Ong, and such only find a way to articulate their respective notion(s) of presence by maintaining the very subject/object dichotomy that Heidegger has attempted to deconstruct. In my judgment, the answer to this is "no." Rather, what becomes manifest in these works is that Heidegger's model of subject/object is spatial and objective rather than aural and personal. And it is here that we must be attentive to the fluidity of presence/absence discourse, two versions of which were highlighted above. In my judgment, it would be better to speak of these authors as articulating a "I/not-I" dichotomy rather than a "subject/object" dichotomy. The human being is immediately aware of being acted on by what is "other-than-myself." The other is immediately grasped as other by Dasein—even if often reduced (illicitly) to a mere determined and grasped object. The most immediate and important point, however, is that the latter is a derivative move from the former.

In any case, it does seem to me that there is something in Heidegger's phenomenology that is missing (at least as far as I am aware) in these authors' own positive formulation(s). While it is true that they make the presence of the personal "other" primary and the order of "objective presence" secondary, it is unclear how these two orders of being are related or in what common "being" they are suspended. This is precisely the sort of question that Heidegger asks and answers in his phenomenology of Dasein and particularly in his primary focus on the potentiality of being's manifesting as the ground of all factical being. Still, perhaps it is precisely the objectification of "presence" that then moves Heidegger to render the ground of being as presence-less and therefore apersonal. That is, because his problem is determined by objective presence, his conclusions are haunted by its ghost (even if only by negation).

One wonders, however, what philosophical fruit might be grown in the following twofold query. (1) Does a personal (rather than an objective) phenomenology of presence-otherness have implications for those aspects of being that are not typically considered personal? (2) If so, how can we articulate the meaning of the being in which both are suspended?

The first question is addressed in the post-Heideggerian Thomism of W. J. Norris Clarke, whose *The One and the Many* is perhaps unimaginable apart from Heidegger's holism. For Clarke, the agency that the above thinkers have articulated in their phenomenology of the word is an agency echoed in all beings. Clarke's central insight is that *what* a thing is is *how* it communicates itself in the community of beings. Note the verbal metaphor. The only way in which any being is (which is the same thing as to be manifest) is in its communication of itself among the community of beings. A non-communicating being is no being at all. Hence, what is most distinctive about human being (i.e., speech) is a distinctive mode of a fundamental property of all being (i.e., communication). This moves one step toward the holism characteristic of Heidegger—only this is a holism of presence (albeit grasped in particular manifestations of the whole rather than in the whole qua itself). All beings are present without being objects because all beings are agents acting upon Dasein. All can agree, then, that the objectification of presence is a derivative mode of being's manifesting, but presence as such is not.

Nevertheless, we are still speaking of "beings" in an *ontic* way rather than "being" *ontologically* considered (as Heidegger makes the distinction). Heidegger's holism is not merely a holism of Dasein but a holism of the Being of which Dasein is an irreducible aspect.[158] We have already noted that Heidegger's stated problematic and privileged metaphors move him toward a deflationary account of the personal other and of presence, and this is

---

158. I am taking on an older tradition of capitalizing Being to refer to this concept (only for the sake of clarity in English).

profoundly manifest here. For Heidegger, Being (which manifests itself to Dasein as Being's site of revelation) is pure potency—the opposite of which (for Heidegger) would imply an object. One might conceive of this, by analogy, as something like a quantum field that manifests itself in particular instances. But, as in the analogy, the difficulty is that a quantum field is still an actual state of potency—perhaps even an objective state. Indeed, it would seem inconceivable and incoherent to assert otherwise about any state of potency. Potentiality is actual potentiality. But this does not mean actuality is an object that admits of manipulation. On the contrary, our primal mode of attunement to actuality (*pace* Ong) is that we are subject to it as asserting itself upon us. Our answering back is derivative both ontically and ontologically.

Approaching the second question more explicitly, then, it would seem that rather than being suspended in pure potentiality, the being-of-communication is suspended in pure actuality, indeed, pure presence—but not in pure *object*. Pure actuality is the Being in which potentiality itself is suspended, of which communicating beings are free *poieses*. Objectivity is, then, a second-order derivative mode of our encounter with them—a reductive destining of revealing within an already projected whole.[159]

This circumvents Heidegger's deconstruction of Western theology. God is not an ontic being who creates more ontic beings, nor is his description as the "ground of being" rooted in a notion of objective presence. Rather, one might say that God is a pure act of absolute communication. It is for this reason that the Gospel of John inflects the Genesis account by referring to God as communicating, being next to, and even being the "Logos" (John 1:1). This both appropriates and subverts the Western concept of the term

---

159. For a significant Thomist engagement with Heidegger, especially in the latter's notion of Being as "abyssal," see the recently translated work of Ferdinand Ulrich, *Homo Abyssus: The Drama of the Question of Being* (Washington, DC: Humanum Academic Press, 2018).

before it.[160] God is the supreme infinite and eternal act of communication in which all communicating beings are suspended as purely and utterly contingent—whether quantum fields, Dasein's potentiality, or our primal attunement to voice and touch that constitutes our original relation to the world.

It is precisely this suspension in infinite plenitude that situates another of Heidegger's main concerns, human interpretation. As George Steiner writes, "Our encounter with the freedom of presence in another human being, our attempts to communicate with that freedom will always entail approximation. So will our perceptions, our decipherments of articulated imagining."[161] Steiner's essay *Real Presences* is a wager (as he often puts it) on *Logos* as the transcendental precondition for the reality of communication—in which we all participate. He writes, "The archetypal paradigm of all affirmations of sense and significant plentitude—the fullness of meaning in the word—is a Logos-model."[162] Indeed, in the Christian tradition, it is precisely the infinite communication of God-to-God in the *Logos* that *freely* echoes forth into the absolutely contingent communication of God-to-creation. What John depicts with respect to the *Logos*, Genesis 1 depicts with respect to finitude. God speaks and potentiality obeys. "And God said" ends in "and it was so." The contingent order answers back.

There is one exception to this. In the Genesis account, one creature is made whose answering back is a matter of concern for it. While darkness, sea, earth, and animals obey their calling—only humankind is constituted by discourse, by the ability to destine revealing or, even worse, to lie. The relation of this to the human faculty of will is an important theme of the next chapter. For our present purposes, this faculty is constitutionally related

160. See also Paul Ricoeur's reflections on the ancient Near Eastern "phenomenology of manifestation" versus the Hebrew "hermeneutics of proclamation," in his *Figuring the Sacred: Religion, Narrative, and Imagination* (Minneapolis: Fortress Press, 1995), 48–67.

161. Steiner, *Real Presences*, 175.

162. Ibid., 119.

to individuals' ability to have their own being as a project for themselves. The image of God in the Genesis account is largely a calling. Authenticity to our very own nature, then, is found in in the union of our freedom and our extraspective response to that calling which brought the human being forth from nothing[163] and which is therefore a resonant frequency in the very constitution of Dasein's being-in-the-world. And so while the human can lie, this is only because the human is also the only being that can say "yes" to being's manifold communication and communion.

In any case, divine absence discourse is arguably related to a notion of presence that prioritizes visible, material, and manipulable modes of presence rather than personal and aural ones. Divine absence, on this account, would involve God's failure to speak rather than to appear. It is worth considering, then, that the monotheistic tradition has largely emphasized God's revelation of Himself in words—not as *opposed* to visible manifestation, but as the *model* and *paradigm* of a presence that is an irreducible property of being (i.e., communication).[164]

THE ARGUMENT AS DEFLATIONARY FOR ATHEISM

Having made the above extended and perhaps ponderous argument, it is worth briefly summarizing the claims I have made over the last two chapters. I have claimed that there is a significant correlation between the rise of the plausibility of atheism in the second half of the nineteenth century in the West, and the movement of Europeans and Americans at the time to post-industrial urban areas. Moreover, this emerging atheism tended to find its home among the lower classes (albeit the intellectually skilled

---

163. There is possibly a parallel in the biblical "nothing" (formless and void) to Heidegger's pure potentiality.

164. A fuller account would need to account for what this might mean for the beatific vision, which has been often described in ways consistent with these emphases (since such vision is not a gaze, but a gift). See Hans Boersma, *Seeing God: The Beatific Vision in Christian Tradition* (Grand Rapids: Eerdmans, 2018).

among them)—and is therefore correlated with the alienation of their labor following (in many cases) the impact of enclosure laws. We see another rise in the prevalence of atheism around the 1960s, only this time the primary site of its spread seems to be among the middle class. I have accounted for this double movement (first) by arguing that humanity's active relationship to the world (as meaningful) was foreclosed in the context of alienated labor, increasingly making the world seem as though it were impersonal and belonging entirely to the realm of the manipulable—and (second) by arguing that as this alienation was compensated for via greater, but more comfortable, dependence on the order of techne, so those features of the world that reinforced God via the world's own imposition were increasingly muted (leading both to an increased sense of divine absence and to a general existential crisis in Western culture). Alienated in their activity, humanity consequently experienced even their very own selves as lacking fundamental agency and personality. Moreover, the progressive displacement of historic networks of trust with modern ones helped to remove a fundamentally personal dimension of existence while also removing that site wherein humanity has historically tended to achieve and enact their own sense of agency (in response to others who are not reducible to their role for me).

To illuminate all of this, I have considered several theorists of labor and technology whose categories helped us to interpret our situation. I went on to contrast our situation with that of our ancestors and to account for our progressive emergence from a very different arrangement. Next, I sought to get inside what it is like to be a modern person and to experience the modern world in modern labor, finally concluding with an analysis of recent presence and absence discourse, suggesting that (even here) such discourse has been shaped by our particular attunement to reality as material and manipulable. Is it possible that Heidegger's critique of an ontology of presence would have fallen on deaf ears prior to the world of industrialism?

While I have focused on atheism, it is important to note that this era also spawned parallel developments in religion (Taylor calls this the "nova effect"), though largely relegating it to the realm of the subjective. As the world was deemed less and less a communicative act, and therefore as God was erased, the realm of the divine and the spiritual were progressively confined to smaller and smaller spaces within the house of humankind.[165]

The import of the argument is deflationary for atheism in the following sense. If my argument is correct, it suggests that much of what makes atheist claims plausible and much of what makes religious claims implausible is related to our tacit (and arguably distorted) attunement to reality. This, of course, depends upon the independent veracity of the arguments for religion. However, even if they are persuasive in themselves, my argument would suggest that these will ordinarily fail to persuade unless we bring the topic under consideration into self-conscious reflection. And even if one is persuaded by my argument, it is not as though such persuasion would remove the kinds of belief pressures that I have been discussing. In fact, it is unlikely that these will vanish apart from a significant (and likely long in the future) shift in basic features of the modern technocultural arrangement or human habit relative to it. In the meantime, what is there to mediate between our alienated consciousness, our reality-distorting cultural comportment, and the conclusions of our mind?

I will suggest in the next chapter that rather than pining nostalgically for the past, persons motivated to maintain orthodox religious faith in our current context must recognize the unique role that their will must take in the maintenance of their religion. This is not because the arguments themselves are unpersuasive but because they nevertheless only appeal to a portion of the human. Required is the integration of the person in mind, body,

---

165. See, for instance, Ross Douthat, *Bad Religion: How We Became a Nation of Heretics* (New York: Free Press, 2013).

and soul—and this takes strategy (in a word, will). One midcentury atheist-cum-Christian recognized the importance of this in his recounting of his relationship to philosophical arguments for God before his conversion:

> In philosophy class I learned the traditional metaphysical proofs for the existence of God. When I took my comprehensive examination, the professor questioned me, probably because he knew I was a Communist, about those proofs, and I got the highest mark. But my knowledge of these proofs did not existentially concern me any more than the a priori categories of Kant or the monads of Leibnitz; these were questions one studied to pass an examination and not to take a personal stand on. Many years later, when I had become a Catholic and was studying theology, imagine my surprise to find my teachers explaining these same proofs and affirming that they truly and irrefutably proved the existence of God. It had been my experience that they prove nothing to one who does not have faith.[166]

In emphasizing the human will, however, I have no intention of (still) implicitly granting the superiority of the state of humanity prior to modern technoculture. Not only would this reflect some ingratitude, but it would also fail to properly evaluate modern atheism or (crucially) ancient religion and culture. Rather than seeing the present situation as a bad thing to be overcome by an approximation of the past, I will argue that it is worth seeing the present as an opportunity to shape a future that could not have been attained without going through this stage of human development in relation to our own religious faith. In short, to evaluate our current situation and to strategize in relation to it involves a larger reading of the end of human religion. In conversation with Martin Luther and Dietrich Bonhoeffer, then, I will (in the final evaluative

---

166. Ignace Lepp, *Atheism in Our Time* (New York: MacMillan, 1963), 16.

chapter) argue that those who want to maintain orthodox religious faith in the current technocultural order ought, counterintuitively, to be at least somewhat thankful for rather than threatened by the modern condition. In order to make this argument, I will contend that modern Christians cannot orient themselves relative to the modern plausibility of atheism without orienting themselves relative to its causes and correlative symptoms. The tendency of modern religious persons is to treat atheism as merely an idea to be refuted rather than a way of seeing the world that derives from *common* plausibility structures—the latter of which cannot be engaged or changed without far more than ideological contestation. As I will argue, especially important in this engagement is confronting an underappreciated aspect of modern alienation—to wit, not only alienation from our own labor but alienation from participation in the historical development to which our labor belongs. It is, then, to this evaluative task that I now turn.

FOUR

Orthodox Protestantism in a World Come of Age

THE REMAINING STUBBORNNESS OF ATHEISM'S PLAUSIBILITY

In the previous chapter, I offered a deflationary account of the plausibility of modern atheism or materialism. I argued that its plausibility is dependent upon the manner in which late modern technoculture has shaped us to perceive what reality is like. However, this under-determines a full evaluation of modernity, not to mention our practical and ideological orientation within it. To unveil our cultural architecture is not to change that architecture. Explaining these pressures is not the same thing as making them go away.

And so we are left with the need to evaluate the phenomena (and our task in light of them) that we have sought to understand. Such evaluation, of course, cannot be divorced from one's goals and vision of the world. And such goals are inevitably informed by one's particular intellectual and spiritual provenance. In my case, the particular location from which I perform the task of evaluation is that of my own classical Protestant tradition. Consequently, while my evaluative remarks might have implications for a much broader audience, they are calibrated to matters of concern that belong to this particular community (i.e., those desiring to maintain intellectually and spiritually honest orthodox Protestant religious convictions in a late modern context).[1]

Presumably, persons trying to orient themselves relative to modern "bulwarks of unbelief" from this vantage point will want to know what it might look like to resist what they take to be an intellectual or spiritual temptation, and they will also want to know what it might mean to cultivate the human project in a direction that could eventually manifest in renewed and more (in their view) truthful plausibility structures. My argument in this chapter is that engaging atheist ideas is only a modest portion of this task. The bulk of the task is addressing those dimensions of the world (per chapters 2–3) that render atheism plausible in the first place. Suggestive along these lines, I will proceed herein in three steps. First, I will briefly highlight some fairly prominent attempts to cope with the features of the late modern world that I have identified. Second, I will (also) briefly offer a preliminary critique as well as a clarified statement concerning the problems themselves. Third, then, I will more thoroughly fill out my own suggested alternative developed via a particular inflection of Martin Luther's paradigm of two kingdoms, and I will supplement this with special attention to a neglected dimension of modern alienation—that is, alienation from the history to which we belong. As I will argue, it is in the latter that orthodox practitioners might attain their most initial and immediate sense of religious and practical orientation.

Attempted Copings

There are several strategies that have been developed in order to cope with the existential complexities of late modernity (often found in the same persons or movements). First and foremost are those that attempt to undo the modern order and to approximate

---

1. Among others, Thomas Oden, *The Rebirth of Orthodoxy: Signs of New Life in Christianity* (New York: HarperCollins, 2003), noted the broader trend toward the recovery of "orthodox" versions of the major faiths in the modern West.

that stage of human history when we did not face these temptations. The alter ego of this attempt is that which sees modern existential crises as overcoming a mostly negative past, such that modern anxieties are a matter not so much of loss but rather of as-yet unrealized gains. The former reaction is fundamentally conservative. The latter is fundamentally progressive in its self-evaluation. I will argue below that each fails to achieve cultural maturity in the following way: Conservative thought easily concocts an idealized phantasm of a past, risks ingratitude for many present goods, and, most importantly, bears an immature relation to the unbounded—the adventure and journey of learning to navigate the unexpected and the surprising. Progressive thought, on the other hand, easily dismisses and misunderstands the past via its own ideological projections and scapegoating, fails to be honest about some goods that risk being lost in late modernity, and, most importantly, bears an immature relation to the limits that structure our relation to the unbounded. The former tends to be all Gesetz, and the latter tends to be all Geist.[2] Wisdom, however, is the attunement between these two poles of human action and vocation.

Often, the above tendencies are given narrative voice in relation to the theme of enchantment. As I pointed out in the first chapter of this book, one of the most common narratives of modernity on offer emphasizes the interruption of an enchanted Middle Ages by late medieval nominalism, the mediating impact of the Reformation, the culminating evisceration of the Enlightenment, and finally the fruit of this in our modern mechanized world. On the one hand, I have critiqued this methodologically—emphasizing that human behavior is not merely the epiphenomenon of some chief idea—but this narrative is also defunct for more trivial reasons. For example, the Reformation critique of massive superstition did not (and does not) preclude a tacit awareness of the agentic dimensions of

---

2. Here one might think of the poles represented by (at least certain fans of) Wendell Berry on the one hand, and Ray Kurzweil on the other.

reality. Many of the critics of the Reformation on this score (and even the fairly sympathetic Charles Taylor) appear to have affection not merely for re-enchantment but for a modern version of superstitious folk religion.[3] And we are historically irresponsible if we fail to note the tremendous intellectual and spiritual (not to mention the political) bondage that attended these sensibilities.[4] More importantly, however, it is presumably worthy of note that this projected past was not actually religiously ideal in the way that some might hope an enchanted world to be. Said differently, if enchantment is supposed to solve our problems, and the past was enchanted, then the results are rather underwhelming. Presumably, the Christian account of Old Testament Israel, the New Testament Church, and medieval Europe would have it that all three lived in comparatively enchanted contexts, but in none of these do we find human beings more in tune with God than we do in our own time. Indeed, we find precisely the same tendencies to religious hypocrisy, nominalism, and idolatry.[5] The negative photocopy of this narrative of enchantment is one that seeks re-enchantment via social engineering and technological progress. Because I will comment more on this below, I will not unpack this further here.

Moreover, as Marcuse was wont to emphasize (highlighted in the previous chapter), the late modern order easily absorbs its own critique, packaging various lifestyles into its machinations and for its ends. One cannot help but get a sense that a lot of recent attempts at calibrating late modern religious orientation are irreducibly bourgeois and boutique in their practical emphases.[6]

---

3. On this theme in Taylor, see Horton, "The Enduring Power of the Christian Story."

4. In general, see Michael Bailey, Fearful Spirits, Reasoned Follies: The Boundaries of Superstition in Late Medieval Europe (Ithaca, NY: Cornell University Press, 2013).

5. I make this point more thoroughly in Enduring Divine Absence, 63–94.

6. Most prominently in recent discourse, Rod Dreher, The Benedict Option: A Strategy for Christians in a Post-Christian Nation (New York: Sentinel, 2017), or the practical suggestions of James K. A. Smith in any of his works on postmodernism or liturgy. There is insight to be found in each, but it is difficult to find their appeal beyond a particular class of persons. Interestingly, this increasingly and ironically includes even the appeal to the

That is to say, they are easily objects of intellectual and practical consumption rather than insights that aid in the bestowing of internalized principle and moral self-possession—the transgressive potential of which far exceeds the capacity of predigested intellectual peer pressure to encourage *truly* radical action.

Before getting into my larger critique, however, there is one further observation to be made. That is, in concert with what has just been said, it is important to note the relationship between even the comparatively intellectual versions of these movements and intellectual authority. On the conservative side are attempts to recover a great Western tradition, all sorts of resourcing projects, or (in more evangelical circles) an emphasis on the primacy of one's worldview as that fundamental and prerational (in the typical sense of the term) commitment to an authoritative source of knowledge by which we know all things.[7] The progressivist alternative to this is to be located in Giddens's treatment of modern dependence on experts (particularly, in our context, technocrats).[8] That is, each option involves what William Bartley has termed a "retreat to commitment."[9] Foreclosed in each of these mental motions is epistemic self-possession—a refusal to claim competence without processing the world for one's own self. And my fundamental critique of this, once again, is that each of these reactions represents a refusal to be mature. The first option under-imagines the future, and the second option over-imagines it. And this failure of imagination (to the right and to the left) highlights a problem that will inform a large portion of my response—that we are

minorities on whom Marcuse wagered revolutionary potential. See Darel Paul, "Diversity: A Managerial Ideology," *Quillette*, February 19, 2018, http://quillette.com/2018/02/19/diversity-managerial-ideology/.

7. Popular, for instance, among a certain conservative subculture is David Nobel and Jeff Myers, *Understanding the Times: A Survey of Competing Worldviews* (Colorado Springs: Summit, 2013), a text that has sold more than 500,000 copies (in various editions) for circa twenty years.

8. See especially Giddens, *The Consequences of Modernity*, in which this is a key theme.

9. William Bartley, *The Retreat to Commitment* (New York: Knopf, 1962).

alienated from the history to which we belong and therefore fail to self-narrate our own relation to it. In all of the below, then, it is this particular problem that I hope to confront.

The Ordeal(s) Clarified

Given what has been said above, what is needed in our circumstance is an act of will to clarify our minds concerning both the problems that we face and the precise nature of our calling in light of them—in order that the latter might be embraced and reinforced through chosen practical orientation. In a word, what is needed is wisdom, the bond between the *Gesetz* that is the primal structure of our world involvement and the *Geist* that unfolds within and into it. And here I still posture my analysis generally because our problems and challenges are common, even if our solution(s) or coping(s) are not. With a view to this, let us clarify the challenges of late modernity and then describe what a contemporary Protestant response might look like. I want to highlight three interrelated aspects of our challenge in late modernity.

First, the default setting and situation of modern Western existence is that of an at least partially stolen dominion. While the alienation I have highlighted is rarely *total*, it is worth highlighting the fact that it is not ordinarily possible for a person to relate to the world and to its resources apart from mediation via others who already own or control access to most of it. Another way of saying this is that anything we might call "the commons" has all but disappeared. Moreover, to the extent (especially) that this ownership and these resources are aggregated into fewer and fewer hands, the dispensing of these resources (access to which is accomplished via participation in modern labor systems) is fundamentally a matter of dependence, but of a sort that is abstracted and distanced from immediate social relations (i.e., unlike the dependence of family members on one another). The inevitable result of this is that more and more humans are alienated from their own making, from the world, and from others whose primary experience of the world (like ours) necessitates highly scripted involvement in modern social structures—with the compensatory erasure of ever increasing lifestyle options. This is, of course, to mimic the traditional Marxist (though also conservative!) critique of wage slavery, but I also want to fill it out a bit more.[10] Preliminarily, it is worth noting that this critique under-determines any practical statement concerning what can be done about it. As well, none of this need imply that modern technological and labor systems are not far more comfortable (and in most cases, even preferable) to the average life of any human in the past. But granting this does not, on the other hand, imply that we risk losing no historic goods, or that retrieving and cultivating them requires going back.

Second, while the above problem has largely been exacerbated by the use of technologies that aid in the subjection of some men to other men, some of our technological problems have "taken on a life of their own" (not in spite of but *via* human agency) and, contra Marx, are not entirely reducible, at this point, to being a mere means. Just as in American slavery, the institution was so bound up with the entirety of Southern culture that it was nearly impossible (even if morally necessary) to let go without disintegrating the entire civilization. Like a scaffolding holding up an impressive edifice, the latter cannot survive the collapse of the former. As Jedediah Purdy and others have argued, our mode of world-involvement has created dependencies upon our technology *while at the same time reshaping much of the world itself.*[11] And

---

10. On the conservative critique of wage slavery, see Christopher Lasch, *The True and Only Heaven: Progress and Its Critics* (New York: Norton, 1991); John Hughes, *The End of Work: Theological Critiques of Capitalism* (Malden, MA: Wiley-Blackwell, 2006); Peter Kolozi, *Conservatives against Capitalism: From the Industrial Revolution to Globalization* (New York: Columbia University Press, 2017); and Tim Rogan, *The Moral Economists: R. H. Tawney, Karl Polanyi, E. P. Thompson, and the Critique of Capitalism* (Princeton: Princeton University Press, 2017).

11. See Jedediah Purdy, *After Nature: A Politics for the Anthropocene* (Cambridge: Harvard University Press, 2018). See also the eco-histories of William Cronon, such as *Changes in the Land: Indians, Colonists, and the Ecology of New England* (New York: Hill and Wang, 2003). A particularly alarming trend is the drastic decline in male sperm count in

what this means is that we cannot simply let go of our technologies without significant catastrophe. Urban density, for instance, depends on the success of extremely modern farming methods—the privation of which would cause an enormous feeding crisis. And so we bear the burden of having created conditions of technological dependence that we cannot easily let go of. Moreover, this problem is compounded by the fact that we lack obvious sites of collective action. Much of what constitutes these forces transcends the regulation of states, and (in any case), states are increasingly fragmented from within by groups who are technologically enabled to live, think, and get their information from independent sources—increasingly dissolving any hope of collective persuasion and consequent action.[12] We are alienated, then, both from the world (necessarily mediated to us via our technologies) and from other persons (removed as we are from unchosen and stubborn collective sites of action and self-directed common projects). Marx, of course, predicted much of this, believing that a global communist society would arise from the ashes of capitalism's internal instability.[13] I argue, however, that Marx failed to sufficiently capture a third dimension of our alienation—alienation from the history to which we belong. And given this failure, his positive prescription is suspect.

Third, then, analysts of modernity often miss that alienation from one's labor, one's world, and other persons simultaneously foreclose one's sense of belonging to and participating in history. Labor is historical in that it (in a primal sense) involves humans in a project that predates them and that they cultivate into the not-yet. This is also true of embodied (rather than increasingly virtual and

the last two generations in the developed world, a trend that (if it continues at its current race) would drastically threaten the survival of our species. See Daniel Noah Halpern, "Sperm Count Zero," *GQ*, September 2018.

12. See Jonathan Haidt, *The Righteous Mind: Why Good People are Divided by Politics and Religion* (New York: Vintage, 2013).

13. The most accessible treatment of Marx's thought (which captures this element well) of which I am aware is Callinicos, *The Revolutionary Ideas of Karl Marx*.

outsourced) connections to other persons and to particular places. Concrete persons, especially one's family connections, put one in continuity with the past for the sake of the future. One's sense of the past is immediately heightened in particular locations that have all the markings of human endeavor, to which one contributes one's own markings. Involvement in this project is tantamount to what it means for a person to be home. A felt lack of involvement in it is to be existentially homeless, such that Peter Berger could refer to modern consciousness as the "homeless mind."[14] In our alienation from the concrete particulars of local communities and families, we lose any sense of propulsion from coherent structures that are prior to us. In our alienation from our own labor and makings, we lose any sense of orientation toward a future that summons and draws us. To address this requires addressing both dimensions of this dilemma. So-called conservatives almost always only address the former, and so-called liberals almost always only address the latter. As said above, the alleged right is all *Gesetz*, while the alleged left is all *Geist*. The task of the free and modern individual person is to achieve a mature and attuned relation to both poles and so to achieve a sense of belonging to the human history that more primally possesses us.

A CALIBRATED RESPONSE: PRIMAL AGENCY

Preliminary Orientation

My argument is that we will not adequately address any of the above problems without addressing all three. I have implicitly commented on their interrelation already. And while addressing one point can be an access point for addressing the other two, I will argue below that our historical alienation is a neglected access point for getting into the larger problems we face. In what follows,

---

14. Berger, Berger, and Kellner, *The Homeless Mind.*

then, I explicate what a modern orthodox Protestant response to all of the above might look like.

I take my point of departure from Martin Luther's famous theory of the two kingdoms. The historical significance of Luther's doctrine of the two kingdoms (spiritual and earthly) is often missed as merely a seminal notion of the separation between church and state. This vertical and institutional reading has been much critiqued in the last few decades.[15] Rather, for Luther, the distinction is largely horizontal. It names two simultaneous and inter-related modes of human existence. Luther's spiritual kingdom is that dimension of human existence in relation to which humanity (in his view) is spiritually free and bound only to God. Luther's earthly kingdom is that dimension in which humanity possesses an earthly life—involving duties to neighbors, authorities, and so forth. The crucial thing is that, for Luther, humanity dwells in both of these realms simultaneously.[16] This would later develop into the language of the external and internal forums (or fora).[17] Post-Reformation political theory and jurisprudence was largely a matter of adjusting existing political structures to this fundamental insight in all of its implications (reinforced, of course, by practical necessity).[18] Arguably, this project is still unfolding.[19] In any case, necessary for Luther is that the concrete and historical existence

15. Most importantly, see William Wright, *Martin Luther's Understanding of God's Two Kingdoms: A Response to the Challenge of Skepticism* (Grand Rapids: Baker Academic, 2010).

16. Putting Luther in larger historical context (especially that of Augustine), see Robert Crouse, *Two Kingdoms & Two Cities: Mapping Theological Traditions of Church, Culture, and Civil Order* (Minneapolis: Fortress Press, 2017).

17. This connection is made in particular by Torrance Kirby, *Persuasion and Conversion: Essays on Religion, Politics, and the Public Sphere in Early Modern England* (Leiden: Brill, 2013), 36–50.

18. Toulmin's *Cosmopolis* emphasizes some of the contextual factors, such as the religious wars. A helpful genealogy of Protestant political thought on this score can be found in Harold Berman, *Law and Revolution II: The Impact of the Protestant Reformations on the Western Legal Tradition* (Cambridge: Harvard Belknap, 2006).

19. The corpus of Remi Brague is especially useful for thinking through the stage we are currently at in the unfolding of the Western project. See his *The Legitimacy of the Human* (South Bend, IN: Saint Augustine Press, 2017).

of the whole Christian person mediates between these realms.[20] Implied therein, then, is a theory of the relationship between soul and body the role of religious practices in reorienting the mind while the mind (in turn) motivates religious practices, and, most importantly, how the reality of the spiritual forum limits any claim of person over person in the earthly kingdom. We can do no better in our attempt to orient ourselves than to slowly exegete Luther's famous statement at the beginning of his 1520 treatise *The Freedom of the Christian*: "A Christian is a perfectly free lord of all, subject to none. A Christian is a perfectly dutiful servant of all, subject to all."[21] Unfolding the meaning of this famous statement, I will first look at how late modern persons seeking to maintain orthodox faith might find orientation in relation to the internal forum. I will, second, look at how they might find orientation in relation to the external forum. Finally, I will comment upon modern historical alienation—which history is the horizon against which the concrete historical humanity mediates between the internal and external fora. In all of these points, I aim to highlight the broader significance (in our context) of exercising our faculty of will and agency in reconciling the disjunction between reality signals received by the mind and contrariwise cultivated instincts. This is obviously not only important for Protestants, though I will inflect this concern through the discourse of that particular community.

The Internal Forum: Acts of Remembrance

Arguably, of chief importance for the person who is interested in maintaining religious orthodoxy in a late modern technocultural context is the act of remembering. That is, because what we can

---

20. Perhaps the most sophisticated outworking of Luther's seminal insight is to be found in the magisterial Richard Hooker. See Littlejohn, *The Peril and Promise of Christian Liberty*. A helpful treatment of Luther's concept of mediation between the visible and invisible can be found in Jonathan Trigg's development of the theme of "trysting places" in his *Baptism in the Theology of Martin Luther* (Leiden: Brill, 2001), 13–60.

21. Martin Luther, *Three Treatises* (Minneapolis: Fortress Press, 1990), 277.

know with the mind is not always reinforced by the structures of our experienced cultural and historical reality, and because the latter reality-signals are—if my argument is correct—demonstrably distorted in some respects, then the will takes on a unique role in helping the mind to interpret and reinterpret the world such that its signals are re-narrated and integrated rather than left in a degree of significant tension. For the persuaded Christian, of course, this involves the calibration of one's instincts to the story and structure of the world as articulated in classical Christian discourse.[22] Here I suggest, therefore, the content of four important acts of remembrance that, in concert, re-narrate the world to the Christian mind in such a way as to call into question the otherwise tacit response to the world in the context of modern alienation. First, such a person must recollect the arguments for and the nature of God's being. Second, one must recollect the primal created freedom of humanity and its relationship to history. Third, the Christian must have an honest assessment of humanity's misuse of its freedom. And fourth, per Christian acceptance of divine revelation and promise, such a person must recall that the deepest human quandary is ultimately not resolved by human attunement to the divine but via divine attunement to the human. Because these can seem like an imposition upon (rather than an honest reading of) reality, it may be important to recollect this material and arguments for it with some frequency. The resultant re-enchantment of the mind (internal forum) motivates the embodied practices (external forum) that reinforce and, in their increasing reciprocal influence, carry along a renewed world-narration in them.[23]

---

22. As an explication of principles, see Joseph Minich, ed., *Philosophy and the Christian: The Search for Wisdom in the Light of Christ* (Landrum, SC: The Davenant Trust, 2018).

23. This perhaps has something to do with the enormous preponderance of texts of apologetics in our time, though the market for these runs the risk of cultivating superficial analysis.

A. God as *Actus Purus*

The most important act of remembrance concerns the fundamental nature of being, because it is within this discourse that the classical doctrine of God has been articulated.[24] As discussed in the first chapter, within the early to late modern period, the very definitions of causality and of God subtly shifted. The notion of God, in contemporary treatments, belongs to a discourse concerning causality in which the latter is conceived along the lines of a great series of dominoes (God being the first domino relative to creation). Or, said differently, God belongs to conversations about whether there are marks of divine design in the created order.[25] Classically, however, the doctrine of God belonged to a discourse concerning being as such. The arguments of Anselm and Thomas Aquinas cannot be understood in light of modern design arguments, nor can their understanding of what a cause is. God, in classical Christian discourse, is not thought to be a being alongside other beings—simply conceived of as the greatest member of the class of beings. Rather, God is conceived of as Being as such, the necessary non-existence of nothing (or alternatively, as the ground of being(s)). The evidence for God, then, was to be discovered not primarily in the probabilistic gap between what can be taken as random and what can be taken as designed but rather in the absolute and necessary gap between the potential non-being of all finite things (things that do not exist by definition and in themselves) as juxtaposed with the fact that they nevertheless *actually* exist. The import of this (for

---

24. To speak of a classical notion of God brings up the debate over Hebraism and Hellenism, which I cannot treat here. I have elsewhere edited a volume on this theme. Joseph Minich and Onsi A. Kamel, eds., *The Lord Is One: Reclaiming Divine Simplicity* (Landrum, SC: The Davenant Trust, 2019).

25. For an analysis and critique of this discourse, see Cunningham, *Darwin's Pious Idea*. For treatments of the question of God's existence that get the question just right and competently deal with objections, see Edward Feser's two volumes, *The Last Superstition: A Refutation of the New Atheism* (South Bend, IN: Saint Augustine Press, 2008), and *Five Proofs of the Existence of God* (San Francisco: Ignatius Press, 2017).

medieval thinkers) was that Being is personal, the gap between non-necessary existence and actual existence only accounted for in terms of the personal willing of *necessary* Being itself (or God) in respect of finite things.[26]

Why this act of remembrance? There are two reasons. First, when one understands the classical doctrine of God, the evidence of the divine is no longer conceived of along the lines of manifestation versus hiddenness (as in the conundrum of divine design). Rather, the fact of the divine is a matter of a clear understanding of being as such. And divine presence need no longer be conceived of along the lines of (more or less spatially and visually conceived) manifestation versus the lack thereof—that is, evidence. Rather, divine presence now belongs to the question of communion with (rather than the being of) God, and the mode of that communion is perhaps most primally and intuitively to be conceived of as speech and language. It is not arbitrary, therefore, that the Gospel of John conceives of God's own self-relation and personal relation to historical actors in the metaphor of the Logos (John 1:1–18)—a metaphor that is prior to and the foundation of the same author's use of the "light" metaphor just a few sentences later (obviously paralleling the similar priority in the account of Gen 1:1–3). The solution to divine absence/silence, then, is not necessarily a vision but, even more fundamentally, a word.[27]

The second reason is counterintuitive but is related to the first. Our own mode of being is historical, and this is especially true of that dimension of our being that participates in speech—by means of which we relate to the past and the future in the present. What is counterintuitive, however, is that the classical (and here, specifically Christian) doctrine of God gives an ontological account of the necessarily historical nature of finite being. I say this is

---

26. I have developed this point at length in *Enduring Divine Absence*, 26–62.

27. See Michael Rea's recent *The Hiddenness of God* (New York: Oxford University Press, 2018).

counterintuitive because it is often thought that modern process philosophy and theology, which essentially historicize God, provide the dynamic categories that appropriately account for the divine echo (or self-unfolding) in finite reality.[28] As I will argue below in the section on historical alienation, however, it is precisely the non-historical character of the divine that gives being to history as its other ground and end. I mention the specifically Christian (rather than generally monotheistic) provenance of this claim because Christian theology gave a particularly robust account of finitude and its capacity for developing (including historical development) in its long-hammered-out Trinitarian discourse. In articulating the divine persons of the Godhead as God's own purely actual, eternal, and changeless self-unfolding and self-relation, classical theism highlighted a sort of motion in God that, while not historical in the sense of implying development or change, nevertheless highlights that pure actuality is not, as it is often conceived, pure *non*-activity. That is, God is not to be thought of as a static, boring, or sternly focused sky-curmudgeon. Rather, we are closer to understanding pure actuality if we conceive of God as doing everything rather than doing nothing. The reason that Christians posit no change in God is not because God is thought to be limited but precisely because he is thought to be infinite—admitting of no possible increase. The self-relation and self-delight of infinite-God in infinite-God, then, is a sort of purely actual infinite and eternal motion that finds its echo in finitude—in creation *ex nihilo*. In classical theology, the infinite and necessary self-relation of God (which is how to think of the Trinity) is the divine ontological foundation for the finite and non-necessary other-relation of God

---

28. On relational trends within the doctrine of God, see Roger Olson and Stanley Grenz, *Twentieth Century Theology: God and the World in a Transitional Age* (Downers Grove, IL: IVP Academic, 1992). On panentheism in general, see John Cooper, *Panentheism—The Other God of the Philosophers: From Plato to the Present* (Grand Rapids: Baker Academic, 2006). A sympathetic Thomist response to process philosophy can be found in W. Norris Clarke, *The Philosophical Approach to God: A New Thomistic Perspective* (New York: Fordham University Press, 2007).

with respect to creation.[29] But as finite and admitting of increase and change, the finite echo of God's infinite life necessarily takes on a historical character. History is finitude, particularly human finitude, approximating (via experience and the donation of what is not the self) the perfection and fullness of God's own consciousness. And so God's self-revelation in creation takes the form of a story, a process, a motion from potential being/perfection to actual being/perfection as the finite endlessly approximates and unfolds into the Infinite that it will never comprehend.[30]

B. The Original and Primal Freedom of the Human Person

If the first act of remembrance concerned the Christian's attunement to reality as inflected through modern alienation, this one concerns common human alienation as such. To wit, whether one takes the original Genesis account as proto-historical or as merely mythological, it is nevertheless meant to give us a normative picture of the relationship between persons and their

---

29. As Bavinck so ably puts it, "Without generation, creation would not be possible, If, in an absolute sense, God could not communicate himself to the Son, he would be even less able, in a relative sense, to communicate himself to his creature. If God were not triune, creation would not be possible." *Reformed Dogmatics Volume 2*, 420. On the Trinity and the question of being, see David Bentley Hart, *The Beauty of the Infinite: The Aesthetics of Christian Truth* (Grand Rapids: Eerdmans, 2003).

30. This insight helps to bridge the gap between Lessing's famous ditch between the accidental truths of history and the necessary truths of reason (a gap which, in any case, is an instance of Hume's distinction between fact and value). To wit, Being simply is personal and meaningful. Moreover, in a Christian notion of the historical process, while there are significant stages in historical development, there is never a ceasing of being part of a process as such. As there is a difference between the rate of change and substantive difference between childhood to adulthood to old age, at no point (not even in the eschatological state) do humans cease in their capacity to grow. Contextualizing Hume, see the fascinating comment on the moment in which Hume becomes possible in Foucault, *The Order of Things*, 60. On Lessing, see Gordon Michalson, *Lessing's Ugly Ditch: A Study of Theology and History* (University Park: Pennsylvania State University Press, 1985), and Toshimasa Yasukata, *Lessing's Philosophy of Religion and the German Enlightenment* (New York: Oxford University Press, 2002).

own makings.[31] The infinite freedom of God in his creative act is therein portrayed as echoed in the finite freedom of humankind in its own makings on top of what God has made.[32] Humans were made for meaningful and free labor in order to cultivate order out of non-order—to participate and to be engaged in the unfolding of the historical process via their access to and ability to change the world of which they are the stewards.

Implied here is a claim that has been given utterance (though sometimes in a confused way) in early-to-late modern discourse. That is, on Protestant principles, the primal freedom of humanity is both spiritual *and political*. Moreover, these are organically related. Spiritual freedom vis-a-vis one's relationship to God in the conscience limits the rights of any earthly despot to coerce human conscience, but inasmuch as the conscience is inevitably given artful expression in human life, the former freedom implies a limitation of earthly authority vis-a-vis the concrete historical individual as such. While the latter exists in given organic relations to family, law, and the state, these are emergent features of one person's free relation to another.[33] Moreover, this is simply a

---

31. The most intelligent treatment of how to read Genesis is C. John Collins's excellent *Reading Genesis Well: Navigating History, Poetry, Science, and Truth in Genesis 1–11* (Grand Rapids: Zondervan, 2018).

32. On the theme of the image of God in humanity as including humanity's labor, see Peter Gentry and Stephen Wellum, *Kingdom Through Covenant: A Biblical-Theological Understanding of the Covenants* (Wheaton, IL: Crossway, 2018), 668–70.

33. It is worth asking how infants, for instance, fit into this picture. Our most primal experiences are of dependence on others in overlapping networks of trust (over the more hermetically sealed, independent, and chosen sites of community so common today), but even these are the result of human choices and have, as their implicit end, the cultivation of individuals who will to maintain and perpetuate their communal relation. It is significant, on this account, that the narrative of Genesis 2 portrays the cultural commission as prior to Adam's relation to Eve. This establishes some independent relation to the human commission that is served by the union of marriage rather than the reverse. Moreover, the primal independence of the individual human is evidenced by the fact that such relations can be severed. Here, of course, I am speaking of an independence in respect of human activity and self-possession rather than any absolute cultural independence (a realm in which we rather tend to be appropriated). In any case, ideally, thick cultural bonds (in a healthy society) do not need to work in tension with this kind of individualsm. Part of why

fact of human experience. In fact, neither the conscience nor the bodily activity of humanity can be *ultimately* coerced. One person can revolt against another. A person can leave her family. A human being is primally, for good or ill, a perfectly free lord of himself, subject to none.[34]

As we will see in the next point, this does not at all imply that people cannot misuse their freedom (they do). Nor does it undermine the legitimacy of the family, the law, or the state. Rather, it points to the simple reality that the capacity of each of these is limited and suspended atop the implicit and continued submission of free actors. Even in the case of despotic rule, men freely respond to bodily threats for the sake of self-interest. This example highlights, however, that the fact of humanity's essential and ineradicable freedom does not imply a free *relation* to objects of their concern. The art of statecraft, then, has really always been discourse concerning the legitimate use of collective agency in relation to individual agency for the sake of both the individual and the group.[35] That is to say, to the extent that a free individual

dependence within families and local communities, for instance, is different from other sorts of dependence is that (a) the individual is not reduced to (and therefore discardable relative to) his social role and (b) there is a thick sense in traditional communities of holding a child or an individual's access to the world and its resources in reserve for her. This is most obvious in something like "inheritance," but the basic idea is that access to the world, to the means of relating to it, and to participation in the body politic is a birthright rather than a commodity controlled by some people who decide other people's access to it. We can take for granted, of course, that the negotiation between communal and individual identity varies highly by custom and context. I credit Alastair Roberts for introducing me to the distinction of "overlapping" versus "isolated" networks of trust.

34. This underdetermines the ethics of our actual employment of freedom, however. Modern philosophy has been particularly interested in existential freedom—even as it relates to suicide. One might get the impression in Camus, for instance, that the profoundest liberation is to be found in the knowledge of one's ultimate control over one's own life (that choosing to continue living is ultimately up to the self). But this is a shallow and egoistic individualism that terminates in the self rather than outside the self. The profoundest experience of our primal freedom is rather to be found in the alignment of that freedom with goods that are greater than and outside the self—but pursued by and united with it. On this theme, see D. C. Schindler, *The Perfection of Freedom: Schiller, Schelling, and Hegel Between the Ancients and Moderns* (Eugene, OR: Cascade Books, 2012).

35. This was famously demonstrated by Otto Gierke concerning medieval political theory in his *Political Theories of the Middle Ages* (New York: Cambridge University Press,

can legitimately aid or illegitimately infringe upon another free individual, the collection of free individuals (in the interest of each and of the whole) collectively pool their agency for the flourishing of all. And it is precisely this that helps to illuminate the especially illicit dimension of modern labor. It is only because it is so ordinary to us that we feel no scandal at the fact that human capacity, calling, and innate potential for cultivation are obscured and replaced by the prescripted roles of some men for other men or at the fact that many late modern men possess little primal access to the world (but rather have an access mediated by others). While this cannot ultimately eradicate humanity's essential freedom or calling, as I will argue below, it nevertheless so removes people's consciousness of their primal relationship to their own freedom that their basic sense of participation in the human project (not to mention unjust prevention of involvement in it) is numbed out of their consciousness.[36] Conversely, a body politic that is numb to this infringement will inevitably be numb to the attempted seizure of conscience as such—which is ineradicably related to its expression in primal world-involvement.[37]

1987). And even in ancient polity, the king could fail to embody his people well, with terrible consequences. See the excellent discussion of Bellah, *Religion in Human Evolution*, 210–64.

36. This point need not be considered ideological. To say that we experience a sort of stolen dominion is simply to point out that most persons depend, for their survival, on the expenditure of an enormous amount of their life's energy in the service of another, accomplishing projects that are not an extension of their own aspirations or spirit or immediately linked to their survival. Our labor is unlike the man who builds a fence and enjoys the fruit of his energy, cultivating a space to be enjoyed by self, neighbor, and posterity. Rather, we typically participate in large processes (the whole of which we rarely understand) by doing thing after thing in order to maintain a flow. And while there is an enormous amount of psychological energy invested in maintaining this flow, most of our participation in it is entirely replaceable by others. In short, in our labor, we do not feel ourselves to be difference-making agents—leaving behind accomplishments that (in both their perfections and imperfections) bear our fingerprints.

37. As I will argue below, this is a problem in modern progressivism—which is ineradicably tied to achieving a parody of eschatological individualism (a society of maximally free agents) by negating it in the present, politically. This is inevitably justified in terms of suppressing those who would damage others through political imposition or social engineering. The problem is that any good parody of eschatological individualism must result from protological individualism, not through disregarding free individuals but by

In highlighting the primal freedom of human beings in relation to their own labor, this act of remembrance also highlights the essentially historical nature of humankind considered both individually and collectively. This is because labor is essentially involvement in history. It is the cultivation of what is prior to one's self, changing it into what remains after one's self. In the Genesis account, history is built into primitive labor in that the divine command is to fill the earth, subdue it, and rule over it. This is accomplished especially in the acts of being fruitful and multiplying, highlighting the cultural and collective end of human families in service of a large human project (Gen 1:26–28). And this project is not just a norm or a myth but a fact of human experience. Indeed, in some cases, its facticity falsifies myths that emphasize the essential stability of a social order for which history serves as a mere backdrop. Humanity has always transcended any attempt to declare an end to history in any tribe, nation, or empire.[38] In Christian theology, this is because the human always pursues the infinite. Clearly, this dimension of being human can have catastrophic consequences, and so this leads naturally into our third act of remembrance.[39]

---

persuading them toward a common project. Moreover, one suspects that progressivist individualism is dependent upon its own gatekeepers and technocrats who, even at the end, must mediate the world to mass humanity.

38. One of the implications of this is that when discussing natural law in relation to human nature, we must recall that human nature has development built into it—which complicates what is good vis-à-vis human nature. This is most obvious when we speak of something like the ordinary growth cycle. Some things are good and natural for infants that are not good for adults, and vice versa. But this individual growth is paralleled in the growth of humanity as such. To be sure, there is the essential form of humanity as an embodied political and discursive animal, but in Christian theology, humanity will eventually find itself in a stage of its own collective political and discursive life that will involve a co-reign with God over creation sans the need, for instance, for marriage (which is related to the protological stage of the human project in such a way as to have an in-built end).

39. On the contrary, Robert Pogue Harrison, Gardens: An Essay on the Human Condition (Chicago: University of Chicago Press, 2009), ix–xi, argues that gardens are a suspension of history—a haven from its crushing weight. This is right and wrong. Life and happiness are had where aspiration for more and development cease in a moment. But in precisely this sense, they represent the ultimate good toward which history marches— manifest partially and modally as a present object of consciousness in a particular thing.

C. Humankind's Abuse of Its Primal Freedom

However we interpret the dimension of human existence that is highlighted in the Judeo-Christian story of the fall, most human beings recognize a juxtaposition between our moral possibilities/dignity and our moral performance and inclinations. That is, human beings misuse freedom and labor in such a way as to harm themselves, their world, and others.[40] And so in any attempt to be attuned to injustice and alienation versus the necessary structures that prevent human destruction, we must factor in this aspect of our reality.[41] I will comment more below upon how even human prevention of evil has its limits, but for the moment, it is important to note that modern discussions of alienation can confuse the precise meaning of alienation as a sort of catch-all of human problems and therefore dangerously treat the solution to our problems as one of overcoming conditions that are definitive of the pre-alienated path forged via humanity's concrete historical existence, and against which humanity possesses very little

---

In this sense, all history moves toward what is already intuitively grasped and enjoyed (in part) in human rest and enjoyment (including engaged labor). Said differently, the end of history is manifest in the particulars all along the way. The telos to which history tends is imminent in each being-qua-being in a different mode—in the mode of the particular to which the whole moves. The particular precedes and succeeds the whole. But these moments and rests go away and are reduced to mere longing. By contrast, eternity preserves the capacity for development and increase (and in that sense, history), but not in the form of longing. Rather, it is in the form of full satisfaction. In Christian theology, each cup is full in the eschatological state, but one's cup can grow. This 'is not the ceasing of history but a different stage of it. But it is a stage already stamped in our protological consciousness as aspiration, just as earthly history will be stamped in heavenly consciousness as memory.

40. As I will argue below, many modern sociological and anthropological reconstructions preserve some implicit fall in human history. Whether one takes this as myth or not, Paul Ricoeur was most certainly correct to say that "Evil becomes scandalous at the same time as it becomes historical," quoted in Henri Blocher, *Original Sin: Illuminating the Riddle* (Downers Grove, IL: InterVarsity Press, 1997), 56. That is, if evil were simply given together with being as such, rather than a form of intrusion into it, then evil would simply be co-extensive with the nature against which evil must presumably be measured for a coherent definition (contra reducing it to a matter of mere sentiment or will).

41. In our morally cynical age, it is difficult to feel scandal at the moral and personal habits we take for granted. But this is a failure to adequately contemplate and explore the self in relation to what is known and valued to be the good, as one discovers in (for instance) Augustine's *Confessions*.

power. To make this point clear, it is important to clarify the difference between what we might call humankind's ancient exile and modern alienation.[42]

We can more clearly grasp what is distinctive and interesting in Marx's doctrine of estrangement by comparing it with myths and philosophies that predate him—or at least that are not responding to him. One could go about this in several ways. There is the obvious case of Buddhist philosophies that posit that reality itself or even the self simply *is* alienation. The relief is through a path (an important metaphor). Nirvana is *not* usually understood merely in negative terms but in positive ones as well. Connotations of return and home can be associated with this release from suffering and the cycles of rebirth. And it is this cluster of metaphors (home/path/return, etc.) that I think will help us get to the larger question at hand. Alienation centered around these terms can perhaps best be captured in the metaphor of exile.

The tradition with which Western persons are most familiar in this vein is, of course, that of the Hebrew Bible—with its stories of Israel in Egypt, the Jewish people in Babylon, and (most importantly) Adam and Eve being removed from the garden. Let us consider this last story for a moment.[43] In the second chapter of Genesis, God creates Adam from the dust of the ground *outside the garden*, and *then* makes the garden, and *then* places Adam inside the garden (Gen 2). The significance of this is that God has taken Adam from an uncultivated ground, started a work of cultivation, and then placed humankind inside that project to continue and expand it. Adam is to serve and keep the garden. In the larger task as described in the first chapter of Genesis, Adam is to fill the earth (apparently expanding God's original cultivating

---

42. I am thankful to Peter Escalante in helping me with this formulation.

43. There is an extensive literature on Genesis and human labor. My own reading has been significantly influenced by the unpublished writings and lectures of, and personal correspondence with, Alastair Roberts.

project across the uncultivated spaces of the world, which were presumably the first things he saw).

And yet, Adam's fall (the nature of which is much debated) gets him expelled from the garden into the land "from whence he was taken" (uncultivated space) in Genesis 3. What is more, rather than responding to his labors, the earth will fight him (weeds/thorns for Adam and enhanced labor in childbirth for Eve). Nevertheless, the basic project of cultivation remains, even as the earth frustrates humankind. This is evidenced by the fact that the same Genesis 1 is repeated to the second Adam, Noah, in Genesis 9.

From then on, at least two themes dominate the Hebrew Bible (or *Tanak*). On the one hand, there is the theme of exile. On the other hand is the theme of humankind's attempt to recover the Edenic home by virtue of their labor overcoming the uncultivated and frustrated earth. And there is an ambivalence about the latter. There is often a positive attitude about technology, the development of cities, and so forth. But there is a critique of the pretension that these can get us back home. The story of Tower of Babel is perhaps the iconic instance of this. In short, there is a continued task as well as its limitations in relationship to recovering home. What emerges from this tension, however, is some parody of the oft-cited statement, "You can never go home again." Once left, the nursery of Paradise is not to be recovered. It is interesting, on this score, that the attempt to achieve Paradise is normally sought not in a garden but in a city (as in Babel). Even in the Christian New Testament, the new heavens and earth are pictured as a city—the climax of the cultivation project that began in the garden (Rev 21–22).

Before comparing and contrasting this to Marx's notion of alienation, it is worth giving a few more examples of this theme outside explicitly religious discourse (suggesting, perhaps, that it is a structural and universal piece of human self-narration). Paul Shephard locates the human fall in the move from a hunter-gatherer state to a sedentary agricultural state. In other words, it was the move *to the garden* that was the original exile from our natural condition! He writes, "Agriculture removes the means by which men could contemplate themselves in any other than terms of themselves (or machines). It projected back upon nature an image of human conflict and competition and then read analogies from that to the people."[44] Murray Bookchin, on the other hand, argues that the original fracture was social. It was the ancient move from equality to hierarchy that constitutes the primal wound. And like Shephard, Bookchin claims that this original wound eventually issues forth in a human-world projection: "A world so completely tainted by hierarchy, command, and obedience articulates its sense of authority in the way we have been taught to see ourselves: as objects to be manipulated, as things to be used. From this self-imagery, we have extended our way of visualizing reality into our image of 'external' nature."[45]

In each of these stories (all perhaps parodies of Ferdinand Tönnies's and later Émile Durkheim's more famous *Gemeinschaft/Gesellschaft* distinction), there is an implicit imagining of a sort of originary harmony that was interrupted by either a human practice or social organization. Of importance, however, is that none of these persons imagine that the solution to such a thing (indeed—if there be one at all) involves the re-primitivization of humanity—except in parody. Rather, the typical move is to imagine a sort of going backward *by* going forward—a move from Paradise to the New Jerusalem (a new state of home).[46]

How might we compare this to Marx's notion of alienation? It seems to me that they link in the following manner. The traditional

---

44. Paul Shepard, *Nature and Madness* (Athens: University of Georgia Press, 1998), 114.

45. Murray Bookchin, The Ecology of Freedom: The Emergence and Dissolution of Hierarchy (Palo Alto, CA: AK Press, 2005), 450.

46. One could also mention Freud's *Civilization and its Discontents* here. On theoretical reflection upon primitive humanity relative to "modern" humanity, see the unfinished project of Arthur Lovejoy and George Boas, *Primitivism and Related Ideas in Antiquity* (Baltimore: Johns Hopkins University Press, 1935), and George Boas, *Primitivism and Related Ideas in the Middle Ages* (Baltimore: Johns Hopkins University Press, 1948).

theme of exile (which is nearly ubiquitous in world literature) involves the curse of frustrated labor. People are not alienated from their task of world-cultivation as such but are to perform it in a state of frustration and tension—not to mention self- and other-inflicted vice. Many traditions reflect upon monotony, decay, humanity's narcissism, and so forth. Nevertheless, humanity's task is not (as such) lost. They have their primal dominion—only over an earth that rebels against humanity in the way that humanity rebelled against God (at least in the Hebrew telling).

What Marx's theme of estrangement highlights is the actual loss of involvement in that project by means of mediated contact with the world. On the one hand, we are exiled from home. On the other, we are also forced to be involved in a project that does not move toward (or even parody!) its recovery. Our tasks, for Marx, cease to belong to the human story that progresses from the Garden to the New Jerusalem (though he would certainly not put it in these terms). What we see after Marx is a blend of these themes in much twentieth-century literature. On the one hand, there is a continuation of the more general human sense of frustration, monotony, and so on. But there is an added sense of meaninglessness and removal from the relationship between this monotony and some historical or cultural end. Said differently, there is the loss of a common project and therefore, as I will argue below, of history.

Grasping this distinction is essential to calibrate those aspects of our common quandary that are so innate that we cannot eradicate them, and those that are accidental modes of our exile that can be overcome historically via human action. Only by a realistic evaluation of this can we distinguish between a necessary prevention of evil and a hubristic seizure of the dominion of some people by other people. We will seek to more fully grasp the former in the next section. For Christians, the latter puts in stark relief the importance of our fourth act of remembrance, that (per the

Christian story) human alienation and the end of the historical process are a matter not of humanity achieving the finite but of the infinite giving of its own plenitude to humanity. That is, the emphasized motion is one not of ascent into the divine but of divine descent into communion with humankind. This is already the structure of creation *ex nihilo* as such, but it is echoed in divine self-involvement with humanity as created and as fallen.

D. God as *Pro Me*

In this final act of remembrance, the Christian sense of desperation results in both the refusal to overcome exile by illegitimate means (that only perpetuate the deepest of human problems) but also in the hope that this can nevertheless be overcome by a divine act. This is not merely a punt of human responsibility in lieu of anticipated divine action but a refusal to hubristically take upon oneself a task for which one is unfitted by a realistic assessment of one's own capacities and inclinations.[47] Divine activity in creation, the sustaining work of providence, and the merciful preservation of humankind in lieu of the latter's ill-will are all seen to provide the grounds for the hope that divine activity can both resolve the problem of our exile and bring the human project to its completion. This last point of remembrance echoes the other acts of remembrance in highlighting the necessity of God's free divine activity, but also his *inclination*, to create of nothing, to preserve as something, and to complete that creation despite human failure. In the conscience and in the mind, therefore, such persons believe themselves to be most attuned to reality to the extent that they recognize a fundamental goodness of Being and a loving disposition of God to ensure that human history reaches its climax—the enjoyment of

---

47. I will say more about transhumanism below, but it is worth highlighting that its aspirations depend (in large part) upon treating human vices as a matter of biological limitation and lack of perspective rather than a matter of irrational spiritual will—a pure will to power that cannot be engineered away—an ill-meant *desire* deeper than the epiphenomenon of a biological urge.

God. If the first act of remembrance takes Protestants to Aquinas and to God as *actus purus*, this last act takes them to Luther and to God as *pro me*.[48]

With these acts of internal conscious reflection (for attunement to reality) in place, we can move on to consider acts of attunement in the external forum—the acts of the body fitted to acts of the mind. As we will see, these acts are reciprocally influential on one another. Together they constitute a strategy for internal and external calibration and world re-narration (carried along in Christian practices, motivated by the mind).

External Forum Qua Individual

If the above point exegeted Luther's comment that the Christian is the "perfectly free lord of all, subject to none," we will shortly explicate his corresponding claim that the Christian is the "perfectly dutiful servant of all, subject to all." The site of mediation between these realms is, however, the concrete historical existence of the whole person (body and soul), including the ineradicable and primal freedom mentioned in the second act of remembrance highlighted above. As such, strategizing concerning the external forum requires treating both its relation to the individual free person and the corporate dimension where that freedom is used or sacrificed for service—or limited to prevent evil. Concerning individual people in their freedom, then, we note several important elements of *embodied practice* in which a re-narration of the world is approximately carried on. These, again, highlight the importance of the will in mediating between our distorted tacit sensibilities and our persuaded convictions concerning the nature of reality.

---

48. This combination is the genius of the Protestant tradition. See Michael Allen, "Divine Fullness: A Dogmatic Sketch," *Reformed Faith and Practice* 1, no. 1 (2016), 5–18; Manfred Svensson and David VanDrunen, eds., *Aquinas among the Protestants* (Oxford: John Wiley and Sons, 2017); and Jordan Cooper and Dan Lioy, "The Use of Classical Greek Philosophy in Early Lutheranism," *Conspectus* 26 (September 2018), 1–27.

First, if the contention of the previous chapter is correct (that modern labor tends to result in the projection of our own impersonality), then the irreducibly agentic and personal character of being (not to mention basic justice) will be cultivated and reinforced to the extent that our embodied participation in it arises from a primal access to the world and an ability to engage it directly via craft (that is, to change something that we want to change). While workers' rights movements in the last century have certainly helped to ameliorate some of the ill effects of alienated labor, this has been accomplished largely by outsourcing those problems to other countries; but even if the latter could be overcome, we have still only numbed rather than dealt with our most essential ailment—that the world feels less and less like a garden (with all the cosmic picture that this implies) and more and more like a system driven by blind (and therefore ironically impersonal) will. To the extent that we can respond to the world as it elicits (via nature and culture) our own capacities for its perfection, to that extent it will self-narrate in such a way that our tacit instincts will begin to reconcile with the conclusions of our minds.[49] However, I will argue below that Christians (and in another sense, humans generally) have a primal calling from which we cannot be alienated even in principle, and which provides orientation in the context of alienated labor that shows no sign of abating in the near future.

Second, of particular importance to the modern person interested in the maintenance of orthodoxy is faithfulness in the classical Christian disciplines such as prayer, meditation upon Scripture, charity toward one's neighbor, the confessions of one's sins, and faithful attendance of worship. As James K. A. Smith has argued in an important trilogy of works, the embodied and liturgy-like repetitive practices of humans help to shape and cultivate the

---

49. In this way, ownership and engaged labor tend to go together. There is a different level of care (and therefore even a different level of awareness) that obtains between the rented and the owned home. On modern labor generally, see Richard Sennett's below-mentioned works on craftsmanship, as well as *The Corrosion of Character*.

imagination.[50] This point requires caution because what I highlight here is not the religious aspect of bourgeois lifestyle criticized by Marcuse (completely absorbable into late capitalist machinations) but rather a comprehensive way of life that renders one's relation to modern systems uncomfortable while at the same time standing out as a dignified and embodied prophetic critique of the same.[51]

Third, of particular importance here is the commitment (sometimes very difficult) of living outside of oneself in one's neighbor. Luther says (again in *Freedom of the Christian*) that "a Christian lives not in himself, but in Christ and in his neighbor ... He lives in Christ through faith, in his neighbor through love."[52] This is done first of all in any act of cultivation and craft that terminates in the common world (whether family or civil society) rather than merely in one's own enjoyment. But further than this, and particularly difficult in our own context, is the commitment to a generous hospitality—a difficult-to-achieve lifestyle that leaves space for others to interfere and that contains the boldness to interfere in the lives of others. These sorts of encounters are artificially replaced in our era by work relationships, social media, and so on. But these cannot truly achieve the dimensions in intra-human relation that are achieved in the free response to persons in unchosen proximity to oneself. Perhaps this dimension of human relationships is preserved to some extent in modern churches. But most lives are dominated by the clock and by disembodied or tailored relationships that suffocate our mental and psychological bandwidth for anything deeper. To have space for the latter, however, requires commitment and strategy. And to the extent that we smash into and are smashed into other humans, one's sense of "what reality is

---

50. See Smith, Desiring the Kingdom, Imagining the Kingdom, and Awaiting the King: Reforming Public Theology (Grand Rapids: Baker Academic, 2017)—which project is summarized in his You Are What You Love: The Spiritual Power of Habit (Grand Rapids: Brazos Press, 2016).

51. On this theme, see Peter Escalante and Joseph Minich, "Philosophy as a Way of Life: Reforming the Quest for Wisdom," in *Philosophy and the Christian*, 461–513.

52. Luther, *Three Treatises*, 309.

like" will inevitably and progressively change. Overlapping thick networks of trust belong to a cosmos quite different from scripted and chosen (rather than given) non-overlapping sites of limited common interest.

These above acts of individual will and commitment help (individually and in aggregate), then, to re-narrate the world to ourselves. However, humans are social animals, and the particular dimensions of our quandary that we highlighted at the beginning of this chapter cannot be dealt with by individuals alone. While it is difficult to imagine, necessary for ultimately addressing our problems is corporate activity in a world where very few sites of corporate activity remain. And it is about this difficult matter that we attempt to strategize next.

External Forum Qua Community

It is here especially that we must grasp the meaning of Luther's comment that the Christian is the "perfectly dutiful servant of all, subject to all." Free individuals are claimed by, acted upon, limited by, and called forth through others and through the world. According to W. J. Torrance Kirby and W. Bradford Littlejohn, Luther's doctrine of the two kingdoms, as developed in the jurisprudence and political circumstances of the early modern period, resulted in the slow emergence of a public sphere—the goal of which was the governance of the body politic via persuasion.[53] While this was initially quite limited, the public sphere progressively broadened in most Western countries to include protection for freedoms of the press, religion, speech, and so forth.[54] It is worth taking our point of departure in this section from these

---

53. I have mentioned the works of Kirby and Littlejohn above. See also the work of Andrew Pettegree, *The Reformation and the Culture of Persuasion* (New York: Cambridge University Press, 2005).

54. Much of the dot-connection in this history is yet to be written well. One could helpfully consult the sources in the previous note, as well as John Witte, *The Reformation of Rights: Law, Religion, and Human Rights in Early Modern Calvinism* (New York: Cambridge University Press, 2008), and Nelson, *The Hebrew Republic*.

sites because implicit in them (normatively rather than historically) is the sensibility that the health of any human collective depends upon the continued free persuasion of free people. This opens human society to the danger that its way of life can be argued against, that its first principles can be critiqued. And so there has always been a tension between the existence and the regulation of the public sphere. But at their most confident, human societies can permit the critique of their orienting ideals to the extent to which they are confident that such ideals are persuasive enough to motivate common and collective action, to solicit the consent of free people. Indeed, the long-term stability of public authority finally depends on the honesty and public responsibility that such a political and social program demand and reward.

This point underscores, however, one of the difficulties of our late modern period. That is, the public sphere has become so diversified and hermetically sealed (in an era of fake news and echo chambers) that it is extremely difficult to achieve any common frame of reference within which we can adjudicate public disputes. Urgent for the flourishing of the late modern human race, then, is the continued cultivation of a culture of persuasion alongside mutual non-partisan investment in sites that adjudicate conflicts. This, of course, depends upon an ethic that honors humanity's primal freedom and does not seek to herd other people like sheep through psychological manipulation. In other words, contrary to the aspirations of social engineers, this view would suggest that an urgent need of our human race is a sense of our limits with respect to one another.[55] Maturity involves not only the capacity to perform a particular action (the control of some people by other people, disproportionate access to social manipulation, etc.) but also the refusal to do so. This refusal and self-limitation is a

---

55. This, of course, implies not the non-existence of elites or of power differential but rather the self- and other-imposed limits of these as they infringe upon the sovereignty of others. What this looks like, of course, highly varies by culture and circumstance.

matter of both individual and public responsibility.[56] This is maturity born of a chosen persuasion with respect to the good.[57] And once again, this means simply that we adjust our political principles to fundamental realities, that we cannot (after all) seize, but only illicitly manipulate, the consciences of free persons. Human happiness depends upon the recognition of this truth, and the happiest societies implicitly or explicitly assume it.

This corporate responsibility is particularly urgent in light of the second problem highlighted at the beginning of this chapter. It is not entirely obvious how we might address the problems in the world that we have created for ourselves. Much of the relation to the world and to others that we have created cannot be undone since our survival (down to the manner in which we currently grow food) depends upon systems that we neither understand very well and which are not in any single person's hands. Attempting calibration to our problems within this context is enormously difficult.

Nevertheless, here I suggest ten integrating hypotheses that are necessarily inadequate and tentative—lacking (as I do) perhaps not the earliest experiences of adulthood but the adornment of gray hair that refines one's discursive fumblings about:

First, there does seem to be significant evidence that there is something about modernity that extends or intensifies or renders more ubiquitous the premodern exile or monotony themes I have discussed. It is not that the latter disappear or that the former is always as prominent. The play these themes are given in the modern novel, in modern film, and in modern poetry suggest—minimally—a *felt sense* of some crisis of meaning that was not as

---

56. See the below discussion of *Ecotopia* for an example of this.

57. See also the theme of hope as elucidated in the writings of Christopher Lasch and Jacques Ellul. Concerning the former, consult Eric Miller, *Hope in a Scattered Time: A Life of Christopher Lasch* (Grand Rapids: Eerdmans, 2010). Concerning the latter, consult Van Vleet, *Dialectical Theology and Jacques Ellul*. Resonant with these, see Frederick Turner, *Culture of Hope: A New Birth of the Classical Spirit* (New York: Free Press, 1995).

obvious in the past. To be sure, there might have been more obvious misery or a crisis concerning the justice of God, but this is quite different from a crisis of meaning as such.[58]

Second, it is plausible that crises of meaning have something to do with shifts in human labor—that is, in Marx's larger sense of *labor*. This has been variously expressed. Richard Sennett's phenomenology of labor, Christopher Alexander's reflections on the healing power of making and architecture (see below), Robert Pogue Harrison's essays on gardens, or Karel Capek's reflections on labor in his famous *R.U.R.* all, in my judgment, variously get at a fundamental structure portrayed in the early chapters of Genesis. This structure is captured in the controversial term "dominion." The fear, of course, is that this implies some exploitive or damaging relationship to the earth or to other persons.[59] It rather implies a self-possession of one's own involvement in the human project, begun (in Genesis) by God and continued by human activity with an end-view in the final city. Again, this basic involvement in the human project is preserved in the exile from Eden—and it cannot be absolutely eradicated (see below). But to the degree that humans lack a felt *direct* involvement in the human project, there will inevitably be a crisis of meaning.

Third, the conflation of the problems of alienation and of exile run the risk of either (1) despairing of a human solution to the former or (2) being optimistic about a human solution to the latter. The former option breeds quietism and the latter breeds totalitarianism. I expand on these options in the next two points.

Fourth, even if the latter cannot be reduced to the former, the person-person and even person-self relation is always prior to the person-techne relationship in order of being. To speak of

---

58. Taylor's *A Secular Age* gets at this larger development adequately. The "crisis of meaning" in modernity was also a major theme of Max Weber. See Michael Symonds, *Max Weber's Theory of Modernity: The Endless Pursuit of Meaning* (Burlington, VT: Ashgate, 2015)

59. See, for instance, Lynn White's classic "The Historical Roots of Our Ecologic Crisis," *Science* 155 (1967), 1203–7.

technology that has gotten out of control is to speak, in large part, of the extension of some *person's* (or people's) agency over other persons as having gotten out of control. While these might not easily be distinguishable in an individual's existential relationship to technology, this distinction is nevertheless true as such. If this is the case, it would seem that ethical concerns about technology ought to be (at least initially) calibrated in terms of ethical concerns about persons. In this, I am more sympathetic to Martin Heidegger's treatment of the solution to our quandary than I am to that of Jacques Ellul. As I pointed out in the previous chapter, Ellul does not believe that our modern crises can be solved via any human action, and especially not any action involving technique. Heidegger ends his famous essay on technology, however, with a quote from his beloved Hölderlin. To wit: "But where danger is, grows the saving power also."[60] If technology gotten out of hand is a result of human activity, then resolving it must also be accomplished via human activity, which is not (however) simply to say that we can or must stop doing" what we have done—since this might be impossible. The burden of maturity is to press forward with a keen sense of limits and the approximation of the good in this specific context and situation. That is, the burden of maturity often reduces to the boring advice, "be wise," which is often misunderstood as an endlessly elastic aphorism. On the contrary, while not positive law or its deductions, the wise thing is often specific and fine-grained but obvious only to those who have cultivated and achieved the vantage point to see it. This might suggest something about the necessity and urgency of a society caring about and cultivating the wisdom of its members. Such cultivation, of course, is itself the object of wisdom (requiring knowledge of how wisdom relates to the family, custom, when self-imposed rather than other-imposed tutelage is called for and vice versa, etc.).

---

60. Heidegger, "The Question Concerning Technology," 333.

Fifth (corresponding to the mention of totalitarianism and the end of exile above), the implication of the previous point is that modern technology does not *inherently* alienate individuals from their labor—and might even be a part of the solution to modern alienation. However, this can only be the case to the extent that a person's access to it is limited by another person's access. This is part and parcel of a larger ethic that suggests the goodness of limits and boundaries. The privation of these limits tends to be associated with a sub-class of individuals who seek to overcome the more basic problem of exile by human means. Here, C. S. Lewis's cynicism (*not* of technology as such but of certain person-person relations) is warranted.[61]

Sixth, if the alienation of labor is a matter of the relationship between one person and another, then it would seem that its privation is *also* a matter of the relationship between one person and another. In this sense, echoing the above, any solution to this problem (which, again, is distinct from the problem of exile) is necessarily a matter of an individual's action in relation to another—whether directly or by instrument. That is, the solution is *essentially* ethical and only *accidentally* or instrumentally technical.

Seventh, even if collective action is difficult in modernity, it is not impossible. To the extent that we fail to take it, this says something more fundamentally about the character of human beings than it does about their tools. Such solutions are most obvious at a local level—and might even involve the use of technology to cultivate collective agency and human involvement. It is also possible by means of the *subversive* use of technology. Social media is not good for certain things that it can nevertheless be used for. Sidney Lumet's *Network* (1976) provides an interesting example of film criticizing the cultural impact of film.

61. In both *The Abolition of Man* (New York: HarperOne, 1974) and *That Hideous Strength*, Lewis famously claimed that "What we call man's power over nature turns out to be a power exercised by some men over other men with nature as its instrument."

Eighth, to speak of human responsibility is only to downgrade technology from a *determining feature* of human behavior, not from its status as a *significant factor* relative to the crafting of human behavior. On the one hand, one might say that an alcoholic is responsible to avoid alcohol. On the other, we might say that this would be more difficult if the whole world were a liquor store. Similarly, it is easy to speak of responsibility with respect to the person-person relationship in the use of modern technologies. It is quite another to declare that many technologies could "just as well" be used for this as for another thing. In fact, some are obviously more suited for some people alienating other people than for improving common access to the world. Putting the matter this way might help elucidate the dilemma more fully: While it is true that our use of technologies says something about our character, it is also possible that we have a very strong tendency to *defective* character (and here we get back to the theme of limits). Walter Miller's *A Canticle for Leibowitz* classically asks this question of humans. On the eve of the earth's second nuclear annihilation (far in the future), a ship leaves the earth with all of the secrets of humanity's knowledge. A character considers:

> The closer men come to perfecting for themselves a paradise, the more impatient they seemed to become with it, and with themselves as well. They made a garden of pleasure, and became progressively more miserable with it as it grew in richness and power and beauty: for then, perhaps, it was easier for them to see something was missing in the garden, some tree or shrub that would not grow. When the world was in darkness and wretchedness, it could believe in perfection and yearn for it. But when the world became bright with reason and riches, it began to sense the narrowness of the needle's eye, and that rankled for a world no longer willing to believer or yearn. Well, they were going to destroy it again, were they—this garden Earth, civilized

and knowing, to be torn apart again that Man might hope again in wretched darkness. And yet the Memorabilia was to go with the ship! Was it a curse? ... It was no curse, this knowledge, unless perverted by Man, as fire had been, this night.[62]

This passage is fascinating for captivating the tension between humanity's knowledge and their capability to be responsible with it. Indeed, in some interpretations of Genesis 3, Adam was meant to eventually partake of the tree of the knowledge of good and evil (representing kingly judgment). His sin was not the eating as such but rather the seizing of such before he was ready and mature.[63]

In any case, the above suggests a prima facie plausible relationship, in my judgment, concerning the relationships among technology, religion, and alienation. Modern technology did not create modern alienation, but it rendered cultivating it far more tempting—perhaps too tempting for human beings to resist. One could make similar observations about the juxtaposition between humanity's tendency to think about long-term consequences and our technical ability to do so. Relative to religion, there is some reason to posit a relationship between the development of modern technology and the religion of the West.[64] But the relationship is not that of religion-cum-technology-cum-alienation. Between the latter two terms lie human agency and tendency-cum-temptation.

Ninth, part of human responsibility is, then, to reflect upon what humans can responsibly handle. This means reflecting not merely upon normative limits but rather upon what we might call existential limits. The question we must ask is not what we might be *able* to do but what we will *tend* to do. And within this consideration, we can fittingly reflect ethically upon various technologies.

---

62. Walter Miller, *A Canticle for Leibowitz* (New York: HarperCollins, 1959), 303.

63. See William Wilder, "Illumination and Investiture: The Royal Significance of the Tree of Wisdom in Genesis 3," *Westminster Theological Journal* 68, no. 1 (2006), 51–69.

64. See Peter Harrison, *The Fall of Man and the Foundation of Science*.

Here, reflecting upon modern philosophers of labor and architecture is especially helpful—thinking through the manner in which our makings enhance versus hinder human communion (see below). Even if human agency remains primary, we must still ask what kinds of humans we are attempting to cultivate, what kinds of actions we want them to accomplish, what behaviors we want to reward, and so forth. And then we must cultivate structures that solicit those behaviors naturally and make their contrary more difficult (i.e., custom). And yet we must be cautious here. While character can manifest itself in techne, techne can only cultivate an already existent *seed* of character. That is, the techne-character relation is not automatic. Nevertheless, the cultivation of a well-oriented soul has the reciprocal effect of rewarding and nourishing those dimensions of human character (still metaphysically prior to it) that will, in turn, manifest in meditation upon the importance of human limits. Persons so oriented are more likely to consider the relationship between these limits and the flourishing of their neighbors. Under-determined in this point, however, is the role of any specific collective agency (the state, etc.) in facilitating this task. This under-determining is not primarily, however, a function of my favored political philosophy but is rather rooted in the conviction that whatever this might practically look like will highly vary by context, culture, and custom.

Tenth, whether or not we think that humans can overcome the problem of modern alienation, there is no other option but to try. The consequences of already made human decisions are such that we find ourselves in a situation requiring a sort of cultural and technological adulthood that we might very well not be able to handle (a la *A Canticle for Leibowitz*). Whether we are up for it does not matter, however. Again, Heidegger's "But where the danger is, grows the saving power also" captures our condition. Our tools have in many ways improved the world. And they will go on improving the life of many persons. It is nevertheless the case that, through them, we can tend to ill-cultivate our souls and our fellow men. But the path through this dilemma is a sort of bearing up, a fine-grained attunement to the boundary between our limits and the needs of others—to be the perfectly dutiful servants of all. The Christian, moreover, rests contented within human limits in the expectation that the final hope of history is not dependent upon humanity's hubristic seizure of it (which, in any case, inevitably destroys rather than redeems).

Examples of this sort of balance can be found in recent authors who seek to strategize concerning the continued development of the public sphere, the craft of cooperation, ecology, and so on.[65] Most fascinating, in my judgment, are those whose reflection upon cities and upon architecture have, as their telos, the cultivation of cooperating humans. Joseph Rykwert argues that "historical and/or economic 'forces' have always been the aggregate products of the choices that were made by individuals."[66] As such, he is insistent throughout his work that whatever gripes we might have with modern cities, labor structures, or technology, the only way to change these is through human decisions. Jonathan Rose likewise takes this perspective and suggests five dimensions of what he considers a well-tempered city.[67] In light of the world's increasing urban shift, Rose considers such a rubric very urgent. Most interesting, in my judgment, is the work of Richard Sennett, who has continued to think through the features of a good city and of meaningful labor. These come together when we think of cities

---

65. I have mentioned several above. Jedediah Purdy, *For the Common Things: Irony, Trust, and Commitment in America Today* (New York: Vintage, 2000), and Joel Salatin, *The Marvelous Pigness of Pigs: Respecting and Caring for All of God's Creation* (New York: FaithWords, 2017).

66. Rykwert, *The Seduction of Place*, 9.

67. See Jonathan Rose, The Well-Tempered City: What Modern Science, Ancient Civilizations, and Human Nature Teach Us about the Future of Urban Life (New York: HarperWave, 2016).

as a craft.[68] Crucially, Sennett can imagine non-alienated labor in a good city, but not the end of human exile. He writes:

> Lurking in the civic problems of a multi-cultural city is the moral difficulty of arousing sympathy for those who are Other. And this can only occur, I believe, by understanding why bodily pain requires a place in which it can be acknowledged, and in which its transcendent origins become visible. Such pain has a trajectory in human experience. It disorients and makes incomplete the self, defeats the desire for coherence; the body accepting pain is ready to become a civic body, sensible to the pain of another person, pains present together on the street, at last endurable—even though, in a diverse world, each person cannot explain what he or she is feeling, who he or she is, to the other. But the body can follow this civic trajectory only if it acknowledges that there is no remedy for its sufferings in the contrivings of society, that its unhappiness has come from elsewhere, that its pain derives from God's command to live together as exiles.[69]

Here we see at once some vision of a community which is nevertheless not finally at home. This modest achievement, nevertheless—for some persons—still requires a relationship to labor that is not owned by another for survival. One irony is that city-planners are often accused of cultivating alienation by philosophers of architecture. The necessity of a connected relation to architecture is an especially prominent theme in Christopher Alexander's work. In his judgment, *places* must be actively made and cultivated by

---

68. Sennett's trilogy on craftsmanship, especially in relation to human cooperation and city building, is a profound project along these lines. See *The Craftsman*; *Together: The Rituals, Pleasures and Politics of Cooperation* (New Haven: Yale University Press, 2013); and *Building and Dwelling: Ethics for the City* (New York: MacMillan, 2018).

69. Richard Sennett, *Flesh and Stone: The Body and the City in Western Civilization* (New York: Norton, 1996), 376.

the persons that inhabit them. He attributes an almost magical power to this relation:

> When a group of people make their environment for themselves, this has massive consequences. Because they are bringing forth the real content of their own existence, becoming aware of what their bodies know, this activity allows their instincts to reveal previously undreamt-of knowledge about themselves. This has a liberating and transforming effect on their consciousness, and ours. How this social process works is not yet well understood.[70]

Similar reflections about the relationship between architecture, intimacy, and space can be found in Alberto Perez-Gomez.[71] Nevertheless, what is captured in the aggregate of these city-planners and architects is, most basically, a sense of a common human project. Each of them hints toward the idea that this requires a kind of intimacy between individuals and their labor that would seem ruled out *not* by modern technology as such but by economic systems that do not automatically permit people to have their own participation in the common human project as an *immediate* (i.e., unmediated) object for themselves. Nevertheless, most of these authors do not appear to imagine that this re-cultivated world will overcome the problem of exile.

A fascinating literary example of this perspective might be found in Ernest Callenbach's *Ecotopia*.[72] Callenbach imagines the Pacific Northwest seceding from the United States and writes a fictional account of a journalistic report of their society a few decades after the fact. Worthy of note is that, on the one hand, Ecotopia

---

70. Christopher Alexander, *The Battle for the Life and Beauty of the Earth: A Struggle between Two World-Systems* (New York: Oxford University Press, 2012), 481–82. Alexander was fond of saying that "making is healing."

71. See Alberto Perez-Gomez, *Attunement: Architectural Meaning after the Crisis of Modern Science* (Cambridge: MIT Press, 2016).

72. Ernest Callenbach, *Ecotopia* (New York: Bantam, 1990).

contains many technologies (some quite advanced), but there are limits to the use of technologies—particularly any that would make some men the subjects of other men. There is relatively common access to and ownership of the human project—but the latter is mostly conceived of in *concrete* orientation to people and place, rather than in terms of abstract *policies*. For instance, pertaining to racial dynamics, Callenbach imagines west-coast minorities wishing to have their own towns and communities.[73] This is not portrayed as *forced* from either side, but *chosen*. There are similar portrayals of what many modern theorists might consider non-utopian dimensions of gender and violence. In essence, Callenbach depicts a society with non-alienated labor but also with a sense of *limits* as it pertains to humankind's more primal exile. The goal is a social order, a cosmic economy, in which humankind cultivates and cares for the flourishing of that over which it is lord and which in turn serves humankind (i.e., trees make houses and animals provide food for a steward that in turn preserves and cultivates the flourishing of each species). This latter point underscores, as well, the importance of a relationship to the world's ecology that allows the latter to shape our perceptions of what reality is like. This, of course, requires both access to such spaces and the crafting of societies in which such realities impose themselves upon us.[74]

In any case, and this brings us full circle to our discussion above concerning the public sphere, the only *imminent* hope for this collective action is that humans cultivate a positive vision of finitude and of the limits of men with respect to other men. And as suggested in point seven above, certain technologies might very well be an aid in this, but only if situated within the trump-card of

---

73. This is perhaps a reflection of the fact that West Coast civil rights movements in the twentieth century tended to emphasize Black independence and nationalism. Here I benefit from the insight of Jeffrey Schulze.

74. Scott Martin makes this point in a lovely way in his little article, "The Spiritual Dangers of Disconnecting From Creation," The Gospel Coalition, February 4, 2019, https://www.thegospelcoalition.org/article/the-spiritual-dangers-of-disconnection-from-creation/.

good collective humane values rather than the consumptive will of illicitly empowered individuals. Perhaps herein are to be located principles for a hospitable face of nationalism (or concentric circles of local government as opposed to any imperialist trajectory) that protects the agency of humans against the manipulations of interfering would-be sovereigns, but in such a way that recognizes that we inhabit a shared world, a cosmic economy that humans serve through cultivation, and which (in turn) sustains them for such service.[75] The question that the human race has yet to answer is whether it is possible for the late modern technological order to sustain the feeling that one is a part of a local, national, and global (not to mention cosmic) economy—extended out from the primal site of home as concentric circles of home. In this vision, the global would not replace the nation, nor the nation the local community, nor the local community the family, but each would grow into the other as the free relation of one with another (for the sake of a common project greater than all). Progress is not the eradication of one of these spheres in the service of another but the preservation of each smaller piece in service of the whole. The service of the distant neighbor is achieved through the service of the immediate neighbor, and so forth. Furthermore, a mature corporate relation to technology cultivates a felt economy in which my labors are engaged precisely because they are felt to matter. What might this imply? Minimally, it means that it is clear to individuals where they

---

75. An important recent work in this vein is that of Yoram Hazony, *The Virtue of Nationalism* (New York: Basic Books, 2018). Hazony distinguishes particular nationalisms (which might very well be illicit) from a theory about the goodness of *nations* as such. Moreover, nationalism is to be distinguished from the nation-destroying juggernaut of *imperialism*, with which it is often conflated. Important along these lines is a robust sense of human custom. Customs represent a sort of dance that a given people have as their way of life and flourishing. They are built up over very long periods of social reward and rebuke, and they tend to be allied to cultural temperament and values. Part of the quandary of globalism is that it disintegrates local custom and forces many persons and peoples who have learned a particular dance to coordinate with others whose dance" is profoundly different. Some good things can emerge from this, of course, but the point is nevertheless that the diversity of human dances can be seen as a good in itself. They are different ways of performing the one human project locally considered.

link up into a system, into a nation, into the world, and so forth. This is to imply not mental comprehension but rather lived coherence. A world so approximated will, in my judgment, be a world in which modern atheism is less and less plausible—because our attunement to reality (and the character of reality itself) will be perceived to have an irreducibly agentic and meaningful character. And it is in Christ's command to love one's neighbor as oneself, I will argue below, that we find our first orientation to this—both as a normative calling as a power unleashed in history.

However, a vison of the good arises not spontaneously from the human soul but from a sense of calling that gives both immediate and broader direction. Named in the term "calling" is not a chosen path but a sense of the world as summoning and wooing the human soul in relation to what is larger than it, and in relation to which humans can become self-forgetfully engaged in extraspective love. But it is precisely the ability of the world as such to *summon* us that is increasingly foreclosed in modernity—removed as our participation is from its inherent meanings. This is in respect of not only its innate and immediate meanings but its ends. Here again we confront our alienation from the history to which we belong. This must be addressed because our sense of historical belonging clarifies both our end and our immediate tasks via the calling implicit within it. That is, humans cannot get along well without a sense of their own story and their place within it. Indeed, for human beings, a lack of history is unbearable (not to mention dangerous). For persons interested in the cultivation of *new* "bulwarks of belief," then, the problem of historical alienation must be dealt with head on. As such, it is finally to our alienation from history that we now turn.

The Existence of God in a World Come of Age

A. The Problem of Historical Alienation

In classical Protestant thought, as mentioned above, the site of mediation between the aforementioned internal realm of conscience and the external world of social and ecological action is the concrete and historical human person propelled out of himself as called by an "other" in order to participate in what is more than the self. Without this, the human tendency to the adoration of ego or will is difficult to avert, inevitably resulting in the endless individuation that so defines modern Western culture (a tentatively safer bet, admittedly, than the collectivist will-worship of previous imperialisms).[76] However, if humans were made for the infinite, they can never truly settle for this. And for this reason, it is necessary to give an account of the inevitable individual and collective journey that the self and that the human race ineradicably aspire to. That is, it is necessary to account for the human relation to the history in which we are always already caught up—especially in light of our confused relation to it. The goal in doing this is to discover what immediate practical orientation (relative to Protestant goals) might look like. And so, via the detour of explicating the problem of historical alienation more thoroughly, we will (by the end of this chapter) suggest more concretely what such immediate orientation might look like. Presently, we begin our journey with John Lennon.

"Imagine there's no heaven. It's easy if you try." John Lennon's 1971 hymn of progressivist secular globalism is famous for its attempt to imagine an end of earthly history without reference to heavenly or infernal postulates. And yet, commentators usually

---

76. This individualism is, of course, a corporatism in individualist skin—a universal liberal self performed in public "expression." This individuation has been noted by Judith Halberstam, *In a Queer Time and Place: Transgender Bodies, Subcultural Lives* (New York: New York University Press, 2005), 16–18.

miss the significance of the line "It's easy if you try." Arguably, hundreds of years from now, if this song is preserved in the annals of the Western musical canon, future historians will dissertate far more on the line "It's easy if you try" than on "Imagine there's no heaven." "It's easy if you try" captures a feature of the late modern West that is definitive. It is, in fact, easy to imagine a cosmos without heaven, hell, or God. And indeed, it is sometimes difficult to imagine one with them. But Lennon goes on, "Imagine no possessions. I wonder if you can." Note the contrast here with the first verse. On the one hand, it is easy to imagine a cosmos that is depopulated of all divine agency, but it is a challenge to imagine the *future* that Lennon hopes for. Apparently when God is removed from the cosmic imaginary (as Taylor might put it), the future is removed as well. Now, Lennon's implied sense of turmoil concerning the historical *now* is as old as humankind itself, but the feeling of metaphysical turmoil belongs to us more specifically. Certainly, we sense birth pangs of it in Donne's "Tis all in pieces, all coherence gone, all just supply, and all relation." But as I have argued in the previous chapters, Lennon's 1960s and '70s might be seen as the moment in which unbelief (and correlative with it, therefore, such disorientation) was democratized and popularized. It is worth noting, however, that the whole period ranging from the seventeenth until the twentieth century—in which the future runs away from us—also happens to be the era in which *history* becomes a science (a subject in which there are laws—the study of which will presumably make that future more clear).[77] To reiterate, then, the future seems elusive at precisely the moment that God and his world are. In making this claim, I am influenced by (once again) Jacques Ellul, in his under-studied *Hope in Time of Abandonment*. Ellul writes:

---

77. A classic survey is Löwith, *Meaning in History*. A more recent survey can be found in Ernst Breisach, *Historiography: Ancient, Medieval, and Modern* (Chicago: University of Chicago Press, 2007).

The silence of God means the absence of history. Nothing could be more vainly presumptuous, more ridiculously sad, more profoundly unimpressive, more crucially impertinent, than to say that "man makes his history." Man heaps up nonsense and absurd action. He strings pearls, in other words events, without order or standard. Man reveals himself in his inconsistencies and in his conformities. With his blind and exuberant activism he certainly constructs nothing, especially not history. He creates successive empires and conquers the moon. He kills, then dies. Caught in a Brownian movement, he agitates furiously. He attributes great importance to what he's about to do and to live, only to discover later on that it was worthless. ... Only a completely abstract philosopher could believe in a progressive incarnation of The Idea, in liberation through transition to a classless society, and that such a thing is history. One would have steadfastly to turn his back on the content of lives, of societies, of activities, of events, of politics, on their content and on their reality, to believe that it makes any sense, and that history is made in this way by a piling up of human results. As long as there is no fixed reference point outside this flow, outside this sequence, there is no history. As long as there is no intervention of a factor which is radically other, there can never be anything but combinations of like with like, lacking any possibility of the attribution or the discovery of meaning.[78]

For Ellul, then, the absence of God and modern disorientation (for he speaks of historical disorientation as one of many disorientations) are twin features of the same phenomenon. His own suggestion, that these are evidences of God's abandonment, is idiosyncratic. Drawing on a significant portion of biblical revelation,

---

78. Jacques Ellul, *Hope in Time of Abandonment* (Eugene, OR: Wipf & Stock, 1973 reprint), 89–90.

his case is worth considering, but we need not accept his diagnostic to maintain that he has rightly intuited the relationship between divine and historical absence(s). The God-drained universe is a universe of futural disorientation.

Another diagnostic emphasizes humanity's abandonment of God rather than God's abandonment of humanity. Some, indeed, have traced our sickness to the abandonment of classical theism as such. David Bentley Hart's recent and controversial *The Experience of God* is one such example. Largely a defense of classical theism, Hart's book attempts to capture our abandonment of the metaphysical structures that allegedly warrant the classical view of God. He writes:

> Martin Heidegger ... was largely correct in thinking that the modern West excels at evading the mystery of being precisely because its governing myth is one of practical mastery. Ours is, he thought, the age of technology, in which ontological questions have been vigorously expelled from cultural consideration, replaced by questions of mere mechanistic force: for us, nature is now something "enframed" and defined by a particular disposition of the *will*, the drive toward dominion that reduces the world to a morally neutral "standing reserve" of resources entirely subject to our manipulation, exploitation, and ambition. Anything that does not fit within the frame of that picture is simply invisible to us. When the world is seen this way, even organic life—even where consciousness is present—must come to be regarded as just another kind of technology. This vision of things can accommodate the prospect of large areas of ignorance yet to be vanquished (every empire longs to discover new worlds to conquer), but no realm of ultimate mystery. Late modernity is thus a condition of *willful* spiritual deafness. Enframed, racked, reduced to machinery, nature cannot speak unless spoken to, and

then her answers must be only yes, no, or obedient silence. She cannot address us in her own voice. And we certainly cannot hear whatever voice might attempt to speak to us through her.[79]

For Hart, atheism *willfully* forgets what the word God even means. God is not a being among beings, a first domino in a series of mechanically related causes. And indeed, it is precisely a sort of late modern technological posture that attunes us to the world in such a way that material and efficient causality simply *are* what it means, for us, that a thing is real. This comportment, however, progressively evaporates a sense of the more fundamental meaning of being, being-as-such, existence-as-such, that within which any things are what and as they are at all. For Hart, to know what we talk about when we talk about God is to render God (Being-qua-being, the ground of beings) simply inescapable. Divine absence, then, is actually a symptom of the *willful* move away from classical theism.

If Hart relates the phenomenon of divine absence to the decline of classical theism, Herman Bavinck moves beyond Ellul in relating specifically *classical* theism to the problem of history's elusiveness. In his magisterial *The Philosophy of Revelation*, Bavinck interacts extensively with attempts to discover the laws and meaning of history within the movement of history imminently. He writes:

> The confession of the unity of God is the foundation for the true view of nature and also of history. If this be denied, we must either abide by the multiplicity of reality, by a pluralism of monads and souls, spirits or "selves," demons or Gods; or because man can never find satisfaction in such a multiplicity, we have to search in the world itself for a false unity, as is done by monism in its various forms, and

---

79. Hart, *The Experience of God*, 311–12, emphasis mine. Hart is, of course, drawing on Heidegger, "The Question Concerning Technology."

then all differentiation is sacrificed to this false unity. The souls of men then become parts and phenomena of the one world-soul, and all created things become *modi* of the one substance. Only, then, when the unity of all creation is not sought in the things themselves, but transcendentally (not in a special, but in a qualitative, essential sense) in a divine being, in his wisdom and power, in his will and counsel, can the world as a whole, and in it every creature, fully attain its rights. A *person* alone can be the root of unity in difference, of difference in unity. He alone can combine in a system a multiplicity of ideas into unity, and he alone can realize them by his will *ad extra*. Theism is the only true monism.[80]

Note that for Bavinck, history needs not just a reference point outside of itself but a reference point that lacks the composition that obtains in history specifically and finitude generally. If we deem Hart and Bavinck to be correct, it would seem natural that our instinct might be to evaluate these affairs negatively—lamenting the bygone age when God was clear, the future was secure, and we did not have to traffic around in all this reality-numbing technology. This is, of course, pure nostalgia. What is more, it is a *non-historical* posture. How so? Because if one believes that the future is secure in God's historical plan (as Christians presumably do), it might be worth asking what this current historical moment is meant to accomplish within the divine will. And here, whether we agree or disagree with his particular interpretation, Ellul is asking precisely the right sort of question (at least from a broadly theistic perspective): What might *God* be up to?[81]

---

80. Bavinck, *Philosophy of Revelation*, 136, emphasis in original.

81. For the Protestant, of course, interpreting divine providence cannot be a speculative craft but rather involves fine-grained reading of Scripture, the world, and history in their relation to a fine-grained reading of God's character. The result of this is not a stupid claim to oracle-like insight but rather attunement to patterns and probabilities within an overarching *general* providence, history, and world-structure.

To begin getting at what an orthodox Protestant answer to this might look like, let us recall that to the extent to which human beings are *engaged* in self-possessed labor and are forced to navigate around other agents as well as the activity of the world itself—to this extent the whole cosmos tacitly manifests as agentic.[82] Our most primal experiences are of being spoken to, of wonder at each new object with which we must learn to cope, and of learning to cooperate with other persons whose will and being are different from our own. In such a sense of the world, divine agency is not even an inference but the immediately understood reality within which all other agencies are united—the Agency that transcendentally grounds all others. The world feels very different when most of my experiences of it are mediated by technologies that render it a world "for me"—when I do *not* have to navigate around it, when my relationships with others are mediated simply by my will (moving, unfriending on Facebook, changing jobs, etc.) rather than by necessary confrontation and cooperation, and when even my own labor is more or less absorbed within a system of mechanized exchanges (thereby foreclosing the kinds of cultivation that make people feel as though they are actually changing some small piece of the world). Here we can situate the common sensibility that even one's own agency is ultimately a gear in a machine, an aimless body of impulses and promptings that we do not ultimately *possess*—but in which we *are possessed* in selves and a-histories behind which there is no final Actor. Again, we often experience our own selves as something in which we are carried along. Of course, this is all artifice suspended atop nature, but it is dominating and comprehensive artifice—easily rendering the impression that our itching and unrestful faculties of heart and mind have been scratched when they have rather been numbed.

Here I find myself, once again, contending against any account of our condition that locates primary emphasis on philosophical

---

82. In this emphasis on engagement, I am influenced by Sennett, *The Craftsman*.

movements, whether it be nominalism's parity of being, Cartesian skepticism, or political voluntarism. Certainly, these systems and instincts are not unrelated to anything I am seeking to address, and each could be appropriated in tension with classical theism. But even apart from these movements, the alienation I am attempting to identify occurs and therefore reshapes the instincts *about* and comportment *to* being that make classical theism plausible and natural in the first place. I am thinking specifically of whatever practical features of the world render the world itself silent, broken into thinking subject and silent object (experientially rather than philosophically). Whatever metaphysics we have, this is what the common experience of the world is like. Hume's fact/value distinction is first not a philosophy but a way in which the world seems to us. Lessing's "accidental truths of history" that stand across a wide ditch from the "necessary truths of reason" already sound the birth-pangs of a race alienated from its own sense of belonging (in relation to which more primal phenomenon, reaso*ning* is a second-order activity). It is perhaps difficult for late modern people to imagine what the (practically) cosmic primacy of *volk* or blood or nation might have been like—a sense of heritage, civilization, and connection to land that was instinctively indistinguishable from the realm of necessary truth. Recent political events, indeed, are perhaps vengeance on our inability to grasp this. Conversely, there is danger in our ignorance since we fail to note the modern surrogates of these impulses as just that—potentially violent and superficial late modern forms of belonging.[83] In any case, the point I am emphasizing is that this is largely a practical, rather than an intellectual, shift. To address modern persons, we will have to address ones who live in *this* world.

And yet, this is not quite enough to orient us toward home (or, therefore, to clarify our first steps in that direction). I have

---

83. See Lilla, *The Shipwrecked Mind* and *The Once and Future Liberal*. On the general fragmentation of thought and status quo at the turn of the nineteenth into the twentieth century, see Daniel Borus, *Twentieth-Century Multiplicity 1900–1920* (Lanham, MD: Rowman & Littlefield, 2009).

just summarized anxieties and therapies that exist not only in various branches of Christendom but even outside of them. And what stands out to me is that while this line of thought does get at the metaphysical (and to some extent practical) dimension of our historical and practical alienation, it does not get at the *historical* dimension of our historical alienation. We could conclude that history might have meaning but have little (beyond the generic) sense of what that is. And this, it must be noted, is dangerous. There have been many compelling critiques of modern materialism, defenses of classical theism, and celebrations of virtue or spiritual practices that nevertheless had their *telos* in some legalistic or manualist—which is to say idolatrous—project. The recovery of ancient traditions can most certainly function in this manner, as can the reduction of historical meaning to one's belonging to a certain *volk*. Indeed, the Christian claim is that the human heart is deceptive (Jer 17:9), warranting some watchfulness concerning our distinctive vulnerabilities. To the extent that ecclesiocentric projects, for instance, attempt to recover a belonging that is a kind of Christian identity politics, one fears that we have not yet fully transcended our disorientation—but have rather internalized it more profoundly. Like a gardener who lacks the fitting sense of belonging to the *human* project, we might have some competent tools and the knowledge of how to use them, and we might even accomplish some of the immediate tasks of cultivation (planting, growing food). But one might also relate to a garden in an illicitly imposing way, *merely* dominating rather than unleashing its potential. But to garden is to unleash potential that exceeds my immediate use, to push into the realm of the uncultivated. And so it is with history. As such, it is worth thinking through this historical dimension more carefully.[84]

Of first importance, then, it must be stated that we *are* involved in our history before we understand it. Or, Ellul's alternative

---

84. See (again), Robert Pogue Harrison, *Gardens*, in conversation with his more recent, *Juvenescence*.

formulation is that our generation is "in the grip of the absence of history in a world which is nothing but history."[85] What I want to emphasize here, once again, is that we live in a primal comportment to the human project that is prior to our distorted intellectual/spiritual inflection of it. And so part of the modern Christian's task in recovery is to avoid some clash of narratives (the Christian versus the Islamic versus the Marxist versus the … and so on)— as though the Christian narrative is just one right next to others, one which just so happens (in the judgment of the Christian) to be true. Even if this is not false, it misstates things. There is, in fact, a single collective history to which all humans belong and to which they are all either more fittingly or unfittingly attuned. Indeed, Christians ought not to fancy that those outside their confessional boundaries cannot be caught up in human history in a way that challenges those whose belonging to the Christian faith is a myopic belonging—indistinguishable from a sense of one's ethnicity or a set of enculturated gestures. This is important to emphasize because the modern project in relation to which we feel some large degree of tension is also *itself* an inflection of the project that simply *is* the human project. It is distorted, but what is desired in an idol is a parody of humanity's natural end. And if modern Protestants fail to relate to humans as involved in the same project that simply *is* the human project, they will perhaps (to that extent) fail to recognize their own subtle idols (reducing the Christian faith to a functionally private modern identity) and also fail to come to grips with the Christian claim that Christ is the Desire (and the *telos*) of the nations (Hag 2:7). And perhaps more than any other, the rhetorical posture implicit in this phrase is perhaps more urgent for those of modern Christian persuasion to cultivate since it is especially relevant in an era of pluralism and globalism. I will say more about this in the conclusion.

---

85. Ellul, *Hope in Time of Abandonment*, 17. Ellul saw the student uprisings in the middle of the twentieth century as indicating a felt lack of history.

It is, finally, essential to highlight the relationship between the historical and the practical dimensions of our alienation. Human labor is perhaps the most immediate manner in which the human feels himself to be a part of the human project—of history. An individual life of cultivation can give us a sense of individual history,[86] but a tacit sense of belonging to *History* can only be achieved where our sense of individual project and common project intersect. To the extent that our world does not seem like one in which we take some direct part in these larger motions, precisely to that extent will our history remain enigmatic. What is more, it is precisely to that extent that a divine Author will seem but a projection onto the order of things.

And so this is our situation. Our individual and historical alienation are bound up with one another—and each is bound up with a cosmos in which the God of classical theism is, more than simply implausible, inconsequential. From here, however, we take a perhaps unexpected turn.

B. Beginning the Journey Home

For Dietrich Bonhoeffer, the absence of God from the modern world is not a situation to be lamented but one wherein God himself calls us to religious maturity. Bonhoeffer writes:

> God as a working hypothesis in morals, politics, or science, has been surmounted and abolished; and the same thing has happened in philosophy and religion (Feuerbach!). For the sake of intellectual honesty, that working hypothesis should be dropped, or as far as possible eliminated ... Anxious souls will ask what room is left for God now; and as they know of no answer to the question, they condemn the whole development that has brought them to such straits. I wrote ... before about the various emergency exits that

---

86. See Sennet, *The Corrosion of Character*, 44.

have been contrived; and we ought to add to them the *salto mortale* (death-leap) back into the Middle Ages. But the principle of the Middle Ages is heteronomy in the form of clericalism; a return to that can be a counsel of despair, and it would be at the cost of intellectual honesty. It's a dream that reminds one of the Song *O wüsst' ich doch den Weg zurück, den weiten Weg ins Kinderland* ["Oh, I wish I knew the way back, the long way into childhood"]. There is no such way—at any rate not if it means deliberately abandoning our mental integrity; the only way is that of Matt. 18:3, i.e. through repentance, through *ultimate* honesty. And we cannot be honest unless we recognize that we have to live in the world *etsi deus non daretur* ["as if God did not exist"]. And this is just what we do recognize—before God! God himself compels us to recognize it. So our coming of age leads us to a true recognition of our situation before God. God would have us know that we must live as men who manage our lives without him. The God who is with us is the God who forsakes us (Mark 15:34). The God who lets us live in the world without the working hypothesis of God is the God before whom we stand continually. Before God and with God we live without God. God lets himself be pushed out of the world on the cross. He is weak and powerless in the world, and that is precisely the way, the only way, in which He is with us and helps us. Matt. 8:17 makes it quite clear that Christ helps us, not by virtue of his omnipotence, but by virtue of his weakness and suffering. Here is the decisive difference between Christianity and all religions. Man's religiosity makes him look in his distress to the power of God in the world; God is the *deus ex machina*. The Bible directs man to God's powerlessness and suffering; only the suffering God can help. To that extent we may say that the development towards the world's coming of age

outlined above, which has done away with a false conception of God, opens up a way of seeing the God of the Bible,
who wins power and space in the world by his weakness.[87]

For all the ways in which we might want to counter Bonhoeffer's
claims (especially as appropriated by later theologians), particularly fascinating is his sense that humankind has come of age and
must live without God (apparently) in the way a young person
must ultimately learn to live without a parent. There are all sorts
of ways which this could be modified and contested, but the reflections that follow will perhaps unwittingly vindicate Bonhoeffer as
having captured just the right tension (and in just the right image)
for modern Christians. In *fact*, we still practically move around
in a world wherein we do not have to make explicit reference to
God. This is historically remarkable. Our motions throughout the
day, week, month, and year can aid in our survival, achieve social
success, and even attain some degree of personal fulfillment with
nary a glance beyond the finitude of the finite. Bonhoeffer speaks
of modern people as having come of age.[88] In my judgment, the
best way to capture our age is to say that we are faced with the
malady of young adulthood. Apart from our will (perhaps contra
Hart), we have been kicked out of the house of our cultural childhood into a state of both increased dependence and increased
independence. Of course, juveniles tend to be more aware of the
latter than the former, but our options as it respects our own story
are the options of an un-homed juvenile in relation to his own
heritage. These options are three. On the one hand, there is the
option of a childlike (i.e., uncritical) appropriation of our ancestors' legacy. This option is usually motivated by a longing for the

---

87. Dietrich Bonhoeffer, *Letters & Papers from Prison* (New York: Simon & Schuster,
1997), 360–61, emphasis in original. My reading of Bonhoeffer is significantly dependent
upon Richard Bube's essay, "Man Come of Age: Bonhoeffer's Response to the God-of-the-
Gaps," *Journal of the Evangelical Theological Society* 14, no. 4 (1971), 203–20.

88. Cf. Harrison's recent reflections, *Juvenescence*, 145–51, that we are both "extremely
young" and "extremely old" in the modern America.

simplicities of childhood. And yet, one can never have childhood back. A child does not have a culpable relationship to its heritage, but those who must necessarily *choose* it to preserve it do. Kant might have called this "self-imposed tutelage." Implied in Kant's famous definition of enlightenment is that our freedom is a simple fact and our dependence self-imposed. Turning Kant around, it could be argued that modernity is a state of *other*-imposed agency. Like the forcibly un-homed juvenile, we are free whether we want to be or not, and it is this that the path back to childhood (as Bonhoeffer calls clericalism) can never reckon with.[89] Another path, then, is to entirely reject the project of one's parents. This is the option of much of modernity. It is the alter ego of the first option and arguably the most common path taken in our culture. Here, whatever is new and future stands in little need of justification. But beneath the intensity and speed and the distraction and the advent of thing after thing is an underlying anxiety. It can be numbed and ignored, but the market for dystopian and science fiction suggests to us that we waver in a dialectical motion between the uncritical fetishization of the new and a childish, nostalgic relationship to the primitive.

And yet, for Bonhoeffer, this appears to be more an opportunity than a moment about which we ought to be anxious. The opportunity of imposed agency, of un-homed juvenility, is that we can learn to grow up. And so the final option, the wise option (one might even say the Protestant option), is to stand critically within one's heritage. This is the option of *free* cultivation, of self-possession, of responsible ownership. And this means that whatever prophetic postures we might want to take, whatever disciplines we might want to recover, whatever enchantment we might want

---

89. In my judgment, many Protestants are shame-faced on this point and tend toward ecclesiocentric models of religious authority and orientation. Without discrediting the importance of the church, I would nevertheless argue that the genius of Protestantism is the truly radical insight that the church is just the people—formed by the Word. For principles on this score, see Joseph Minich, ed., *People of the Promise: A Mere Protestant Ecclesiology* (Landrum, SC: The Davenant Trust, 2017).

to "re"—these must not be a *reaction to* alienation from, but *leadership within* the human task (born of love rather than hubris)—pushing us forward in the same project in which we and all of our neighbors are distortedly engaged. We are drawn into and drawing toward the reality to which they (and sometimes we) attempt and fail attunement. Most importantly, we must perform this task in precisely *this* context and in *this* world, which fights against such comportment—whether by intention or accident.

C. The Journey Home Proper

Attempting to explicate the path between our present bulwarks of unbelief and (for Christians) hoped-for and unprecedented bulwarks of belief, however, requires one additional element. From a Christian point of view, one might begin to chart a course home, one might have retooled one's metaphysical ship, reengaged one's historical sails, and untied all one's alienated knots—but we cannot sail without wind. We cannot sail without something beyond us that pushes us toward our destination. The Christian claim is that this wind is a word from beyond. Ellul writes that God "is a God of History, and this discovery about God is Judaism's monumental invention, which has been completely adopted by Christianity. This is the origin of all historical thinking and of History ... God, the World, Time, and History are connected through the Word."[90] God's speech is not seen to be merely a post-lapsarian correction to our misdirection. It is, in Christian theology, an original feature of humanity's world. God speaks, and humanity's attunement to creation and orientation to the future were always meant to exist in concert with that speech. God's speech makes history, and as Ellul claims, speech and words have a distinctive relationship to time—not as an absolute series of moments but as an experienced phenomenon in which we are engaged and in which we develop.[91] Humans cannot navigate the world without language, and

90. Ellul, *The Humiliation of the Word*, 55.
91. See ibid., 5–47.

they have no history without it. But as speakers and as responders to speech, they make history. And just as Genesis portrays God as planting the original garden to be further cultivated by human beings, so (on the Christian account) *God's* speech initiates and drives the history in which human beings are subsequently caught up. As argued in the previous chapter, there is even a prima facie case to be made that we should anticipate divine revelation to take the form of speech rather than vision. Orientation away from modern temptations and toward hoped-for goods, therefore, requires the powerful force of divine speech. Indeed, on the Christian account, it would be strange to expect otherwise.

The history to which humans belong, then, is one that groans for the revelation/word that both is its origin and summons it to its end. Of course, this has always been the case. But the evaporation of agency, history, engagement, and so on has had the effect of rendering revelation itself implausible, and with it, our own futural orientation. And yet we *remain* our own history. And precisely because we *are* our own history, we cannot help but seek to find revelation in surrogate places—whether it be scientists, technocrats, gurus, or anyone who makes sense out of our universal task and end. [92] And so, it is not just the *fact* of agency but the primary agency of *God* that the Christian account would emphasize. The agency of God in history reminds them that the future is not entirely a human achievement. The path from juvenility to adulthood is unpredictable, but for juveniles to learn wisdom means for them to learn their own potentialities *as well as* their limitations. Limitation will never appear as good, however, apart from a strong sense of the manner in which it actually relates to the future that is otherwise forcefully sought in the limit-despising, transgressive seizure of history.

---

92. This is especially important relative to the role that technology is felt to play in the achievement of our future. For examples, see the corpora of Paulo Soleri, Ray Kurzweil, and Robert Wright.

And so, finally, I will briefly consider what a state of imposed agency means in its relationship to three items of concern for modern orthodox persons: (1) the precise shape of the historical hole left in the wake of God's vanishing; (2) how the content of divine speech fills out this gap in precisely the shape of this absence—and therefore illuminates the human project; and (3) how this history to which we belong leads (per the Christian account) the heart and mind to the God who is its ground—and therefore away from the unbelief that has been my object of analysis throughout.

D. Orientation from Divine Speech

And so, first, the evaporation of God could be seen by modern Christians as an opportunity because of the many idols (on their account) that have been evaporated with him. Our being un-homed from the cosmos and from our various traditions has actually demonstrated that most of these traditions are radically contingent and unfit to bear the burden of the human story. This has, of course, happened in other contexts. Just as Augustine treated the tragic fall of Rome as an opportunity for Christians to recognize their chief citizenship in the city of God, modern Christians can recognize, in the heritage-consuming world of modernity, that many of the cultural norms and mores in which we might be tempted to find our ultimate orientation are only contingent pieces of history (able to be removed from the main story).[93] For the Christian, however, what passes through the historical flame of modernity are nevertheless the essential things of God and his word. But this, then, establishes what constitutes our certain *history*, which cannot perish within it. The accidental truths of history are only formally accidental. They are historically essential, and the necessary truths of reason are but the scaffolding atop which they are

---

93. Two important treatments are Marshall Berman, *All That Is Solid Melts into Air*, and Bauman, *Liquid Modernity*.

accomplished. Concerning the manner in which God's revelation actively constructs this history, then, Bavinck writes:

> Revelation gives us a division of history. There is no history without division of time, without periods, without progress and development. But now take Christ away. The thing is impossible, for he has lived and died, has risen from the dead, and lives to all eternity; and these facts cannot be eliminated—they belong to history, they are the heart of history. But *think* Christ away for a moment, with all he has spoken and done and wrought. Immediately history falls to pieces. It has lost its heart, its kernel, its centre, its distribution. It loses itself in a history of races and nations, of nature and culture-peoples. It becomes a chaos, without a centre, and therefore without a circumference; without distribution and therefore without beginning or end; without principle and goal; a stream rolling down from the mountains, nothing more. But revelation teaches us that God is the Lord of the ages and that Christ is the turning point of these ages. And thus it brings into history unity and plan, progress and aim. The aim is not this or that special idea, not the idea of freedom, or of humanity, or of material well-being. But it is the fullness of the Kingdom of God, the all-sided, all-containing dominion of God, which embraces heaven and earth, angels and men, mind and matter, cultus and culture, the specific and the generic; in a word, all in all.[94]

For this reason, the need for revelation ought not to be portrayed as an aimless and unstructured impulse that impels persons to merely compare the world's literatures, like sailors comparing star-charts to a cloudy sky. In the Christian interpretation of history, our lack has *shape*! If (as is the Christian claim) the revelation of the Christ simply *is* our history in its consummate form, for which

---

94. Bavinck, *Philosophy of Revelation*, 141, emphasis in original.

all history before it was prepared and out of which all history from it lives—then God's speech stands on its own. Here I do not mean that it cannot be confirmed by the world into which it speaks. Much the opposite. The claim is that it makes and sustains this world and necessarily, therefore, aligns with it. But the history that culminates here, on the Christian account, just *is* human history—of which we are always already a part. God's speech stands on its own, therefore, because (for those who listen to its announcements) it speaks to us authoritatively, illuminatingly (with fine-grained calibration), and with power.[95] The illumination of what is common distinguishes divine speech from gnostic utterance. Their authority and adequation to our shared world is *public*.[96]

E. Orientation toward Divine Mission

Second, then, how does this word illuminate the human project as such? On the Protestant account, it does so by announcing and accomplishing an inescapable end in precisely the *shape* of our lack. The opportunity of cultural juvenility, of our current alienation, is that we can be reoriented to that from which we can never finally be alienated (and which is more easily obscured in other contexts). So, for instance, even in seeking just modes of labor and the opportunity for normal human cultivation, the Christian can avoid an idolatrous relationship to these projects (i.e., putting one's final hope in them). This is highlighted in the gospel's treatment of human labor and history. To wit, in the Christian account, all of human history is to be given back to God in Christ (1 Cor 15:28). All human cultivation ultimately moves between the poles of Genesis 1 and Revelation 22. But added to this original

---

95. "'Is not my word like fire,' declares the Lord, 'and like a hammer that breaks a rock in pieces?'" (Jer 23:29)

96. A very useful treatment of the relationship between divine discourse and history can be found in Michael Horton, Covenant and Eschatology: The Divine Drama (Louisville: Westminster John Knox Press, 2002).

commission, as its redeemed inflection, is the call to cultivate the nations with the good news of the Christ who interrupted history. That is, to preach and to make disciples by baptism (Matt 28:16–20)—to spread Christ's Way under the King who (again, in Christian conviction) reigns over heaven and earth. This commission touches all aspects of the creation mandate and reorients it to the end of Christ's kingdom (which was its original aim). Rather than erasing all distinction, nation, *volk*, provincial histories, it actually fulfills them by taking them into itself and even serving them by orienting them toward the good.[97] And yet it does this precisely to the extent that it renders them *penultimate* and therefore enables them to serve the good of a collective species that shares a more primal history and a more universal end. Christianity is the original universalism (an ethical and historical rather than political globalism).[98]

In related fashion, the New Testament speaks in a dual fashion about the Christian's penultimate callings. On the one hand, they are called to take freedom if they can achieve it (1 Cor 7:21). And yet, they are also called to love and be Christlike even to unjust masters (1 Pet 2:18). This is not some insensitive neglect of our dignity and humanity. It is rather the heralding of a calling that cannot be suppressed—to belong to the true history that just is seen to be human history. In one's life *coram deo*, even injustice is an opportunity to reflect God's character and to unleash a new order of things (i.e., love) into this world. This calling contextualizes all others. One might be unjustly limited in one's ability to cultivate the creation commission—but one can never be prevented from

---

97. As Eglinton shows in *Trinity and Organism*, the theme of unity-in-diversity is a central theme in the theology of Herman Bavinck and a theme that he applies to the preservation and eschatological integrity of the nations as represented in Revelation 5.

98. Here I echo, albeit from a different perspective, some of the comments of Frederick Turner on the universality of the Christian faith in his *Natural Religion*. See also, on a historical register, Tom Holland, *Dominion: How the Christian Revolution Remade the World* (New York: Basic Books, 2019).

embodying the love that re-animates the world and that commis-sion. And yet inasmuch as this love is unleashed in the world, it leaves a more just world in its wake—masters who care about the alienation of their servants, moral sensibilities about human dig-nity that are arguably the historical legacy of the world Christian movement, and so forth.[99] Moreover, this unleashing is not simply a matter of moral power or persuasion but, in Christian conviction, a matter of divine intrusion in the Holy Spirit working through divine revelation—animating otherwise self-obsessed humans to extraspective love.[100] Each person's sovereignty is one that gives itself to the other in death, like Christ. The dignity of free people, acting in their capacity as prophets, priests, and kings—is to serve unto death.[101] And it is in this death that the Christian finds life (2 Cor 4).

Nevertheless, I want to be careful here. This is a difficult sub-ject in relation to which many Christian practitioners have made sloppy comments. Nevertheless, for the traditional Christian, the following conundrum arises: many persons apparently do what they do for the glory of God but not, apparently (at least con-sciously), for the kingdom of Christ as such. Contrary to pop-ular belief, Muslim eschatology (for instance) is focused not on

---

99. Perhaps no text in the New Testament highlights this with the precision of Colossians 3, wherein Paul encourages the saints to keep their minds on the "things above" where their "life is now hidden with Christ in God" (vv. 2–3). Out of this, like ripples from the epicenter of an earthquake that fixes rather than fragments the world, he unfolds the social implications of this reality. On the impact of Christianity in the development of humanism, see David Bentley Hart, *Atheist Delusions: The Christian Revolution and its Fashionable Enemies* (New Haven: Yale University Press, 2009).

100. On the manner in which God moves persons through his word, see Kevin Vanhoozer, *Remythologizing Theology: Divine Action, Passion, and Authorship* (New York: Cambridge University Press, 2012).

101. Here I am influenced by John Piper, *Don't Waste Your Life* (Wheaton, IL: Crossway, 2018); Joe Rigney, *The Things of Earth: Treasuring God by Enjoying His Gifts* (Wheaton, IL: Crossway, 2014); and the corpus of Andy Crouch, including *Culture Making*. See also the latter's *Playing God: Redeeming the Gift of Power* (Downers Grove, IL: InterVarsity Press, 2013) and *Strong and Weak: Embracing a Life of Love, Risk, and True Flourishing* (Downers Grove, IL: InterVarsity Press, 2016).

attaining a pile of virgins but rather on enjoying the greatness of God. Similar things could be said of Jewish eschatology. And yet, the Christian must presumably account for the fact that Paul seems to treat both philosophical sophistication and religious piety apart from Christ and his body as mere fleshliness (Col 2:16–23). And indeed, Paul can speak of anything beyond eating, drinking, and being merry as foolishness apart from the promise of Christian resurrection (1 Cor 15:32). In attempting to honor these words, the Christian would also want to honor the utterances of Christ when he spoke of those who were "not far from the kingdom of heaven" (a category perhaps echoed in Paul's Mars Hill discourse in Acts 17). The Christian resolution of this tension implicitly looks something like this: Inasmuch as we achieve some good but fail to discover the Christ, we have missed the point of history. We have missed life (John 17:3). It is not that these things are not good. It is that they are all relative. We were not meant to merely contemplate divine simplicity (which mystifies the mind). We were meant to be caught up in a concrete history—involved with a God who acts and speaks within it—all of which centers around the Christ who holds it all together (Col 1). And so inasmuch as any tradition captures our end as in God and his glory and his kingdom, it lives in reality. But inasmuch as it fails to see Christ as the one in whom all of these things are fulfilled, it misses the axis upon which it all turns.[102] Or at least, this seems implicit in Paul's statements that

---

102. One question that might follow from this is precisely what we mean by "Christ." Is the historical Jesus of Nazareth essential to history? Certainly, he is to our *actual* history, but what if there had been no fall? In what sense could we say that Christ is "essential" to history in its character as created rather than in its character as redeemed? Minimally, theologians have often spoken of the Logos as the Mediator between God and humanity in creation. Maximally, theologians have sometimes spoken of the incarnation as an end of history even apart from the fall. In my judgment, this is a somewhat speculative matter about which theologians may differ. I am inclined toward the maximal position for the following reasons: (1) Paul speaks of common marriage (an institution prior to the fall) as intrinsically related to the relationship between Christ and his church; (2) 1 Corinthians 15:42–49 roots the contrast between Adam and Christ not only in the fall but also in Adam's pre-fallen state in contrast to its telos in Christ's state of resurrection; (3) it would seem fitting that the state of final blessedness would involve an embodied relationship with a

God "made known to us the mystery of His will, according to His good pleasure which He set forth in Him, regarding His plan of the fullness of the times, to bring together in Christ, things in the heavens and things on the earth" (Eph 1:9–10), that all things were created for Christ—that he might reconcile all things to himself (Col 1:15–20), or in Jesus's claim that eternal life (which is more than just forgiveness) is to know God *and* to know Christ (John 17:3). Straining at a pithy formulation of the Christian conviction, we might say that *what the Christian faith shares in common with other faiths stands in intrinsic tension with that wherein they differ. And this is because what is shared in common between them is extrinsically fulfilled and consummated in what is distinctive within the Christian faith.*[103] This distinctiveness is fundamentally historical—including an account of the fall, God's promise to overcome humanity's guilt and restore the world, and the consummation of that promise in a new Adam. The history of God, humanity, sacrifice, heroism, war, empire, culture, art, prophet, priest, and king is seen to be fulfilled and then unleashed in history as a new *power* (the Holy Spirit) to love. Christ's telic sense-making of these structures and his resolution of their tensions is underscored, from the

---

divine Person. This is not because of some ontological gap that needs to be overcome but because the manner in which we experience meaning and know others is embodied. The longing that the church experiences to embrace Christ is surely more than a longing for a state of mind; it is a longing to have the Lamb in our midst—to love and to be loved as we love and are loved. In short, the intrinsic relationship between creation and the incarnation is the intrinsic relationship between creation and God's desire to maximally bless creatures in the capacity of their nature to enjoy him (across not a metaphysical but rather a modal gap). This is not to replace traditional emphases concerning our final contemplation of the divine, but rather to add to them. Nevertheless, even if this is misguided, two more points are worthy of attention. First, even if the fall is accidental to human nature as such, it is not accidental in God's plan. As such, the centrality of the historical Christ to our *actual* history still underscores what (or Who) we were made for, whether or not this can be derived from our nature considered in isolation from the history of which it is a part. Second, as I have argued above, divine speech begins prior to the fall—begetting and moving history forward. But this is the particular speech of a particular "Person" who just is the Logos. To miss just *this* speech, then, is to step out of the historical current and its center.

103. A competent treatment of the Christian faith in its relationship to other religions can be found in Gerald McDermott and Harold Netland, *A Trinitarian Theory of Religions: An Evangelical Proposal* (New York: Oxford University Press, 2014).

Christian perspective, by the observation that the Christian move-ment is truly a world movement. The Christian claim is that this is accounted for by Christianity's distinctive role in addressing the human's most deeply suppressed need for forgiveness and redemp-tion from sin and guilt—the profound depth of which is uniquely emphasized in the Christian tradition (thus making its history, which I take to be our history, a history of gratuitous redemption).

Indeed, for this reason, Herman Bavinck claimed that Christian mission was a unique apologetic in the modern era. Writing at the height of the Protestant missionary movement, Bavinck states, "While unbelief increases in Christian countries, mission plants one congregation of Christ after another in the heathen world. Today, mission is probably the strongest apology for the Christian faith ... Mission shows the power of ... Christ."[104] But, per the clas-sical Protestant emphasis on the priesthood of all believers, the most ordinary participation in this mission is to be located in the ordinary love of neighbor. Such charity is not merely a calling but the Christian's chief participation in the history to which all humanity belongs. Faith and hope will cease, but love will never cease (1 Cor 13). This is the center of Christian cultivation and of Christian civilization. Living out of the historical event that is the

---

104. Cited in de Wit, On the Way to the Living God, 12 n. 22. Note the self-conscious historical contingency of Bavinck's claim here (i.e., it is "today" that this is the strongest apology for the Christian faith). The Great Commission advenes on the history that the Cultural Commission builds into human nature. There is an end to and reward for the commission (the earth being filled, its subduing, etc.), and the resultant achievement does not change humanity's essential nature, but resituates them in a different context. This is manifest subliminally in humanity's instinct toward fruitfulness, multiplication, nations, empires, and so forth. These aspirations have existed since the beginning, at least as parody. To the extent that ancient myths treat history as culminating in the present, and do not (as the Hebrew tradition does) have the present as toward the future, humans—via knowing ourselves—can know that we have not written our own story rightly. Its structure is written into our nature and consciousness. We are our own involvement in our development. The Great Commission is not fundamentally new but is rather the redemption of the human commission from sin. It is God's attempt to glorify humanity's labor via redemption rather than to allow it to be reduced to nothing via the disintegrating impact of sin.

epicenter (on the Christian view) of human history, this commission, then, is seen to be its own apologetic.

In order to foreclose a fairly understandable response to the above, of course, it is important to reiterate that I do not here imagine a sort of team of "answer havers" over against pagan masses. One way of making this point (which I have more briefly made above) is that I do not aim to present a Christian variant of identity politics over against other religions. The kind of adequation to our universal history that I highlight is entirely possible for Christians themselves to miss and for non-Christians to more fittingly approximate. Why? Because it is entirely possible for Christian practitioners to miss the essence of their own faith and to reduce it to a mere ideology. But the posture to which Christianity is most adequated is that of the most simple mode of prayer—that universal speaking into the ether for help.[105] And what is claimed to be revealed in Christian discourse is the coming-forward of that Stranger who grounds and elicits such prayers.[106] While dogma is urgent and necessary, that which it describes always and ever exceeds it and is related to all persons immediately as the ground of their being. One might put it this way: precisely to the extent that Christians fittingly grasp their own dogma, they know God to exceed it and (precisely in his excess) to be immediate to all persons—though understood in a more or less confused way. And it is precisely that universal immediacy, which transcends exhaustion in any discourse, that is the appropriate site of contact for persuasion concerning the universal import of Christian claims. In short, the veracity of Christian dogma is not an ideology as opposed to other ideologies in its being but only in its capacity to illuminate

---

105. Internalizing this truth more than perhaps any other theologian, Martin Luther's dying words were, "We are beggars. This is true." The best contemporary introduction to the fullness of Luther's thought is Oswald Bayer, *Martin Luther's Theology: A Contemporary Interpretation* (Grand Rapids: Eerdmans, 2008).

106. On the theme of the Christian faith as "meeting a Stranger," see Horton, *Lord and Servant*, 1–21.

the Way (the original name of Christianity) that all persons find themselves simultaneously reaching for and running away from.

F. Excursus on Progressivism

The obvious secular alternative to the above description of a universal history is, of course, modern progressivism (broadly speaking, modern movements that emphasize the pursuit of global equality through as-equal-as-possible distribution of the fruits of production and the maximum social affirmation and support of lifestyles and identities that do not cause obvious harm to others). Progressivism is attractive precisely to the extent that it cultivates a sense of "common-ness" in which people can be corporately engaged, but it cashes out in something shallow. It inflects the meaning of the historical process—but fails to capture its end. And arguably, this is a felt anxiety for those engaged in it. In its transhumanist variety, for instance, there is both excitement and anxiety concerning what happens when we transcend our bodies, when we inhabit particles, when we achieve some degree of immortality. Mere charges of impossibility or incoherence cannot, of course, easily contest with the fact that *this project gives us a history*! But it navigates with a single sail (the pursuit of freedom) without getting at our fractured relation to far more than this (to wit, the purpose of freedom). The popularity of dystopian and science fiction novels suggests both our fascination with and anxiety about this future. Frequently in their telling(s), we are still ultimately suspended in laws that are less than agentic and are subject to forces that ultimately transcend any personal control. But even if we achieve freedom and the transcendence of our limits—what would we do then? What would our project be then? What would our *history* be then? What happens after you have achieved the brotherhood of man, the lack of possessions, the omega point, the fusing of consciousness, laser vision, and so forth? It is a fascinating question, and while this blank space can be populated sentimentally by words like love or community, very often these are attempts to dignify visions of the good life that do not sub-stantively move us beyond "being free" or "not being told what to do" or "chilling out."[107] But this is only to overcome one alien-ation with another—an alienation of humanity from its projects solved by an alienation of humanity from its natural end—to wit, the enjoyment of the infinite in the mirror of finitude. The latter is arrived at when limits are conceived of as the good that they are and when the transcendence of human nature would be seen as the loss that it is.[108]

Moreover, expanding on this point, there are at least two more fatal problems with this aspiration. First, it assumes that human vice is a matter of software or hardware rather than a cancer of human desire that humans are powerless to change—even with an upgrade. And even if one suspects that such cancer does reduce down to frustration with our limitations (which we might techno-logically overcome), it is extremely unlikely that we are in a posi-tion to know this—enigmatic as our own consciousness is to our very own selves.[109] Any aspiration based upon this confidence is, therefore, foolishly risky. Second, even if this vision were achiev-able, it longs for a mode of life that is more suited to the folkish portrayal of angels rather than men—disembodied individuals that are each a species to themselves and have maximal agency,

---

107. See Germain, *Spirits in the Material World*.

108. Two crucial treatments of our cultural moment can be found in Carl Trueman, *The Rise and Triumph of the Modern Self: Cultural Amnesia, Expressive Individualism, and the Road to Sexual Revolution* (Wheaton, IL: Crossway, 2020), and Joshua Mitchell, *American Awakening: Identity Politics and Other Afflictions of Our Time* (New York: Encounter Books, 2020).

109. Indeed, Mark A. Seifrid, in his essay, "Unrighteousness by Faith: Apostolic Proclamation in Romans 1:18–3:20," in *Justification and Variegated Nomism Volume 2: The Paradoxes of Paul*, ed. D. A. Carson, Peter T. O'Brien, and Mark A. Seifrid (Grand Rapids: Baker Academic, 2004), 105–45, argues (in concert with Martin Luther) that part of Christian conversion is the recognition that God is a better reader of the human than humans are. That is, our fallenness is not to be conflated with our awareness of it but is rather to be measured by God's contention against humans—a contention that humans trust and recognize to be right by faith. Of course, such abyssal readings of the fallen self are also suggested by the most insightful commentary on the nature of finite consciousness, but this is easily overlooked by the naïve optimism that afflicts so much transhumanism.

freedom, and power.[110] But it is precisely humanity's location at the intersection of minerality, biology, spirit, and history (in all its corresponding layers of profound dependence and shocking independence) that renders its experience of reality beautiful and distinctively meaningful. To cast off our embodied limits would be to cast off the opportunity of human nature to enjoy that intersection of being in which the latter is maximally manifest in all its interrelationships via *precisely* these modes of limitation.[111]

Resonant with this, in Protestant Christianity (as recognized by Charles Taylor and others) is an affirmation of *ordinary* life and *ordinary* calling. And this means that both the practical import of the call to love and, therefore, the particular strategy one takes relative to the cultivation of new bulwarks of belief are as diverse as the human race itself. By contrast, the transgression of the limits of our own body, of dealing with others, and so on is the perennial temptation of a (in Christian doctrine) fallen angel—Satan—the animating principle of whom is *mere* libido, will, and power in

---

110. A helpful theological (rather than folk) account of angels can be found in Bavinck, *Reformed Dogmatics Volume 2*), 443–72. Increasingly shorn of limitations, and increasingly reduced to will, one wonders if post-humans would be more rational in one sense but less rational in another. Perhaps a Christian theology of demonic consciousness can see it as a mode of absolute compartmentalization—pure will juxtaposed to maximal rationality and knowledge of the good, but without a unity between these. Humans, on the other hand, cannot live without a sense of synthesis (whether honest or dishonest) and feel quite unstable when their self-narrative is exposed as a bundle of contradictions or as a lie they tell themselves. The ability to delightedly compartmentalize between these two aspects of our consciousness—*especially* if we suffer from distorted wills—could very well be the manufacturing of a demonic mode of being.

111. Trans- and post-humanists, of course, do not necessarily imagine full disembodiment in all cases. And one might object that I am privileging humans over the possibility of other intelligent life forms. Rather, however, I do not deny that human nature can achieve a greater order of perfection. This is a basic Christian claim. But this will always be suspended atop the experience of being not merely a body but a particular kind of body relative to social organisms, descendancy, paternity—with all the dependencies and independencies that this implies. Moreover, the limitations of the body are juxtaposed with the magnanimity and capacity of the human mind to create (especially in conjunction with the aforementioned) a sort of hermeneutical color spectrum for humans such that they represent a mode of life, precisely in their limitations, that has an (as far as we know) unparalleled capacity to savor the infinite from the vantage point of an extraordinarily complex and multilayered finitude.

all their history-consuming potential.[112] But, on the contrary, it is precisely in relation to these experienced limits that history plays out and we experience the motion toward development that gives life meaning. From this perspective, it is morally scandalous that we might deem an end of human aspiration merely in everyone obeying the harm principle. Our most meaningful relationships, rather, call us out of ourselves, demand something of us, and inconvenience us. And while we have largely lost the moral vocabulary and the experience of the world to interpret this fact, the basic moral phenomenon remains.[113]

By contrast, if the finite (i.e., the limited) is suspended in the infinite, we preserve the stages, seismic shifts, and chapters that constitute the narrative we call history—without collapsing the future into a singularity. There is, in Revelation 22, an everlasting dimension to the human project. Because God is infinite, the finite will always be able to press further into him, grow in its capacity to know and to love, be able to cultivate his creation more—and yet never scratch the surface of God's gravity. Imagine, if you will, that Handel's *Messiah* is but the music of children. Both this future and our Handelian past can only finally be held together if there is an (purely) actual infinite. More boldly, non-historical finitude is difficult to even imagine since the mirror of finitude seems superfluous without a mode of being who enjoys and gives utterance

---

112. It is interesting to note that the enigmatic character of Satan, or sometimes "the Satan," is typically the attempted prevention of humanity from achieving its historical end (via derailing it and playing surrogate in Gen 3 and Matt 4). That is, the actions of this character seem to be oriented toward humanity rather than God (as in the famous case of Job). An underexplored thesis is that this is rooted in the jealousy of humankind's historical telos and adventure as compared to the more static and (in some respects) limited existence of angelic life. How ironic, then, that transhumanism is, in some ways, jealous of a creature's mode of life who might be (in turn) jealous of humanity's mode of life and destiny.

113. An element of our moral cynicism is the Freudian or post-Freudian reading of libido and will as the substantive rather than accidental center of human nature. See Dallas Willard's posthumously published *The Disappearance of Moral Knowledge* (New York: Routledge, 2018).

to what is beheld. The classical Christian claim is that this mode of being is humanity—the mouthpiece of creation.

We must here reiterate the importance of transcendence to history. History has meaning precisely as a participation of finitude in the infinite. It is suspended, grounded, and propelled forth from Being, and it is summoned, called into, and drawn up into the same as an end. To the extent that we fail to see this, we will inevitably be addicted to self-imposed (or worse, other-imposed) scripts that attempt to parody this one. Bringing this chapter full circle, however, the link between origin and end moves along the track of human participation—highlighting (once again) the importance of the human will as aligned with the human mind. And this, in turn, underscores the above claim that the human race cannot circumvent the process of persuasion and self-possessed motion toward that end. What the Christian is left with, then, is simply a proclaimed and embodied history that recognizes in divine speech the echo of the eternal Logos.[114] And following its traces, we find ourselves involved in a project from which we cannot be alienated and for which we were made.[115] And, moreover, to the extent that this project involves the persuasion of others, it is only the *tools* of persuasion that are rightly afforded us—not the tools of a coercion that would miss the very point of the project. Perhaps no one understood the relationship between freedom, power, and history better than C. S. Lewis. He writes:

> In order to understand fully what Man's power of Nature, and therefore the power of some men over other men, really means, we must picture the race extended in time from the

---

114. This underscores the importance of the Christian practice of preaching as a means of formation. Preaching is meant to persuade rather than to coerce. The Reformation re-emphasized this fundamental insight. See, for example, Torrance Kirby, *Paul's Cross and the Culture of Persuasion in England, 1520–1640* (Leiden: Brill, 2013).

115. In this vein, we need to recover the language (though not necessarily the substance) of former concepts of universal history. A helpful orienting point can be found in Dru Johnson, *The Universal Story: Genesis 1–11* (Bellingham, WA: Lexham Press, 2018).

date of its emergence to that of its extinction. Each generation exercises power over its successors: and each, in so far as it modifies the environment bequeathed to it and rebels against tradition, resists and limits the power of its predecessors. This modifies the picture which is sometimes painted of a progressive emancipation from tradition and a progressive control of natural resources resulting in a continual increase of human power. In reality, of course, if any one age really attains, by eugenics and scientific education, the power to make its descendants what it pleases, all men who live after it are the patients of that power. They are weaker, not stronger: for though we may have put wonderful machines in their hands we have preordained how they are to use them. And if, as is almost certain, the age which has thus attained maximum power over posterity were also the age most emancipated from tradition, it would be engaged in reducing the power of its predecessors almost as drastically as that of its successors. And we must also remember that, quite apart from this, the later a generation comes—the nearer it lives to that date at which the species becomes extinct—the less power it will have in the forward direction, because its subjects will be so few. There is therefore no question of a power vested in the race as a whole steadily growing as long as the race survives. The last men, far from being the heirs of power, will be of all men most subject to the dead hand of the great planners and conditioners and will themselves exercise least power upon the future. The real picture is that of one dominant age—let us suppose the hundredth century A.D.—which resists all previous ages most successfully and dominates all subsequent ages most irresistibly, and thus is the real master of the human species. But even within this master generation (itself an infinitesimal minority of the species) the

256

CHAPTER FOUR

power will be exercised by a minority smaller still. Man's conquest of Nature, if the dreams of some scientific planners are realized, means the rule of a few hundreds of men over billions upon billions of men. There neither is nor can be any simple increase of power on Man's side. Each new power won by man is a power over man as well. Each advance leaves him weaker as well as stronger. In every victory, besides being the general who triumphs, he is also the prisoner who follows the triumphal car.[116]

G. Arriving Home

We are now in a more secure position to summarize how all of the above relates to atheism. Atheism is the natural manner in which the world manifests when humans have been alienated from it and from their history. And humans are alienated especially from the latter when they are un-homed in their participation in the human project. These three—our alienation from our labor, our loss of history, and the decline of theism—share a history. And what evaporates in our state of imposed agency is any default at-home-ness and engagement in the world. What is demanded, therefore, is a more willful posture toward reality. Via participation in the history of the kingdom of God as it irrupted (in Christ) and irrupts itself into the world, the Christian finds himself caught up in the history in which all persons already participate via ordinary calling (as animated by love). The kingdom of God, then, is not a mere surrogate of what has been lost but the primal history that it never was—that impels the Christian to echo its life into and to cultivate those histories that are suspended in it.[117] To cultivate the world in this way is to cultivate a world in which classical theism is plausible and atheism is not—because it is a world in which we are once

---

116. Lewis, *The Abolition of Man*, 68–69.

117. The best treatment of the kingdom of God is still Herman Ridderbos, *The Coming of the Kingdom* (Philipsburg, NJ: Presbyterian and Reformed, 1962).

again at home in our own nature. Only this time, the will had to choose what was recognized by the mind despite felt and sometimes tempting alternatives. In other words, we had to grow up.

CONCLUSION

The Desire of the Nations in an Age of Pluralism

THE ARGUMENT SUMMARIZED

This book began with the juxtaposition of Herman Bavinck's prospective and John Updike's retrospective response(s) to the phenomenon of modern atheism. To account for the difference in their reactions, I have appropriated Charles Taylor's notion of "bulwarks of belief" (used in his work to describe what rendered religious belief inevitable in medieval Europe) and tried to give a historical and phenomenological analysis of what I have termed "bulwarks of unbelief," or those features of the modern world that render unbelief, again, not inevitable but at least plausible. Specifically, I have claimed that the most fitting access point for getting inside this query is the modern sensibility that divine absence (or invisibility) has something to do with the question of God's existence. To account for the link that obtains between the experience of divine absence and the plausibility of atheism, I have analyzed the manner in which late modern technoculture (i.e., technology as actually *used* in its relationship to labor and culture) has tacitly shaped our pre-cognitive perceptions of what it even means for a thing to be real. While I have claimed that my argument deflates or relativizes the plausibility of atheism, I have also been keen to note (as I do here) that it does not—as such—refute it. Nevertheless, correlated as atheism is with the broader and *common* quandaries that I highlight at the beginning of chapter 4, any sufficient attempt to deal with the "problem" of atheism must therefore deal with these problems as well. Not surprisingly, however, such a response cannot be had in the absence of an orienting vision of the good, the true, and the beautiful. Consequently, I have offered an account of what an orthodox Protestant response (with all the aspirations that this entails) might look like. Moreover, I have tried to posture this analysis in such a way as to highlight its scandalous claim to be a discursive unveiling of the universal history in which all humans are already involved. That is, I have tried to present a vision that is meant to induce those who encounter it (precisely in their being human-qua-human) to say "aha" about their own world and its telos.

Of course, such a presentation cannot but expect a kind of failure—a more frequent response of curiosity (at best) or incredulity (at worst) rather than persuasion. What this conclusion affords me, nevertheless, is one last opportunity to fill out this vision in more immediate practical rather than in broad systematic terms. The elephant in the room of my analysis is the remaining implausibility of Protestant orthodoxy specifically (rather than theism generally) in an era of religious and ideological pluralism. Moreover, one might presumably still query why—if the Christian claim is true—it is not as *obviously* so as one might wish. And if this were not enough, one would be forgiven for the suspicion that any universalizing sort of humanism is not worth the risk of the violence often thought to be inherent in universalisms as such. In the remaining three sections of my conclusion, then, I attempt a final act of rhetorical calibration in sympathy with these three anticipated reactions: concerning pluralism, the non-obviousness of Christianity's claims (especially relative to divine absence), and the dangers inherent in any universal humanism.

JAMES DAVISON HUNTER ON DIFFERENCE
AND DISSOLUTION

In *To Change the World*, cultural theorist James Davison Hunter argues that that the two most immediate challenges faced by traditional Christians in the modern world are what he calls "difference" and "dissolution."[1] Broadly speaking, these refer (respectively) to the problem of pluralism and to the problem of a trust that links social actors to a felt reality outside of themselves. The latter could be attributed to relativistic philosophy or to other intellectual movements, but Hunter argues that modern skepticism about common, public, and universal reality is perpetuated and reinforced by ordinary modern (and even pre-cognitive) experience. In the new communications era, much of our reality is far away, and mediated via artifice and illusion. This is in direct proportion to the increased fracture of more immediate modes of social trust. Combined with an awareness of and intimate contact with a plurality of religious "others," the public (or universal in import) aspect of traditional Christian claims is brought into serious question.

Throughout my extended essay, I have implicitly addressed issues related to each of these points. Here I want to name and address them more directly, albeit tentatively. Perhaps more accurately, I aim to address *persons* who are aware of and want to reflect on this cultural condition. It would not, after all, be so surprising if some of my readers were unpersuaded by the picture of reality that I have painted. Moreover, this cannot but have something to do with the fact that there are so many other voices that relativize my own. Is persuasion still possible, however? Can one craft rhetoric to cut through the numbness created by these two perpetual elephants in the room?

---

1. James Davison Hunter, *To Change the World*, 197–212.

It would be silly not to acknowledge the controversial quality of a claim that privileges the Christian story as the universal story.[2] And even if this were not taken as innately violent or offensive, it might be taken as naïve and thoroughly implausible—a summons to an insufficiently motivated ultimate wager.[3] In my judgment, the next generation of Christian theologians and philosophers need to take this seriously enough to produce work that seeks to demonstrate the manner in which particular Christian claims illuminate common reality and how Christian claims resolve tensions present in what is common to human religion (as their transcendent end).[4] That is, the future of Christianity's public/common plausibility depends (in part) upon the ability of its practitioners to persuade others *not* by ignoring reality or the voices of those outside its pale with a more loudly and confidently shouted bare assertion. It is rather precisely through open and honest engagement with reality and others that we must move through the accomplishments of human thought and the structures of human experience, demonstrating how their outlines and contours belong (consciously or not) to this grand narrative unfolding in (or on) precisely *this* canvas.[5] In the present context, I can only be suggestive toward what

---

2. Concerns of orientalism or imperialism are particularly apt here. On this, see Stephen Neill, *Colonialism and Christian Mission* (Cambridge: Lutterworth Press, 1966); Lamin Sanneh, *Disciples of All Nations: Pillars of World Christianity* (New York: Oxford University Press, 2007); and Philip Jenkins, *The Next Christendom: The Coming of Global Christianity* (New York: Oxford University Press, 2011).

3. It is not my own view that this is a wager. I am simply trying to be sympathetic to what I anticipate a potential reader's response to be.

4. In method, but not necessarily in all of its particular claims, this might look something like the alternative "universal history" captured in Frederick Turner, *Epic: Form, Content, and History* (New Brunswick: Transaction Publishers, 2012).

5. Secular counterparts to this can be found in the project of such global historians of philosophy as John Plott and Hajime Nakamura. The former only penned five volumes of an anticipated much larger global history of philosophy. The latter penned, for instance, *A Comparative History of Ideas* (New Delhi, India: Motilal Banarsidass, 1998). An important corrective to typical Western treatments of philosophy can be found in Peter K. J. Park, *Africa, Asia, and the History of Philosophy: Racism in the Formation of the Philosophical Canon, 1780–1830* (Albany: State University of New York Press, 2013).

this might look like.[6] And I will do so by briefly reflecting upon the materialist consciousness—provisionally overlooking its hubris.

Many modern persons experience a deep and instinctual suspicion of the supernatural, the miraculous, the afterlife, or mind-like properties of reality that are not reducible to mechanical laws. And as I have argued throughout this essay, this is not what reality tacitly *seems like* to us, and we tend to feel viscerally the most "in touch with reality" when we focus on those things that are the most visible and clear to us, positing nothing (even a grand system) beyond what is immediate. This is easily felt to be a completely honest, comprehensive, natural, and obvious posture toward reality. But let us exegete this for a moment. All cynics and doubters know this sensation, but what is it? Is it an intellectual judgment? Is it an instinct? Let us admit for a moment that it functions and seizes us (at least immediately) more in the form of the latter than the former. But it is no mere instinct. It is a feeling about reality that manifests as more than a suggestion but is rather experienced as perfectly fitted to the world as it *actually* manifests. It is, as it were, felt to be a kind of intellectual and volitional submission to reality without adding foreign elements. And yet, there is an irony here. Precisely when the sensation that we live in a materialist cosmos is at its maximum, we experience the greatest haunting, a deep sense of dependence, of the beauty of the particulars of the cosmos, and so on. Added to this is the felt dignity of one's intellectual and moral bravery, the sense of responsibility that comes with our own newfound radical freedom.[7] But what is loved and enjoyed in loving and enjoying this reality? Arguably, it is just the structure of reality (albeit known in part) itself. The irony of these experiences is that we do not just fancy ourselves as simply having a private feeling, but rather we feel ourselves to be *participating* in and rightly valuing something about the world. That is, we are

---

6. My hope is to produce something more robust on this in the future.

7. Cf Taylor's notion of "fullness" and "subtler languages" throughout *A Secular Age*.

having feelings that we think others *ought* to have because the value of the things themselves demands this. The beauty demands a fitting response.

I would argue that in this aesthetic sense of participating in reality, and in this courageous love for truth, lies the beginning of a journey that ends far outside the initial impressions that evoke this haunting—but in a way that honors their integrity and usefulness along the way. This is rightly called a journey or a way because this is precisely how such moral phenomena manifest— as the obvious and most immediate markings that help us press deeper into the denser regions of the forest that constitutes our common world. As one ancient Proverb has it, "It is the glory of God to conceal a matter, but the glory of kings is to search out a matter" (Prov 25:2). But it is exactly that sense of *participation* that acts as a fissure to the transcendent—replacing the initial map of the terrain in the same way that the vantage point of the top of the mountain corrects the misperceptions of one's environment that were provisionally used in climbing it. This philosophical journey is not traversed alone, however, but is co-navigated with others. And especially in light of modern difference and disillusion, the irreducibly narrative character of human self-identity (and world-construction) highlights once again the rhetorical possibilities that obtain in articulating a coherent and post-colonial universal history.[8] Such narrative consciousness, then, is not to be confused with a historicizing relativism that reduces all discourse to local stories. Much the opposite, the point is rather to continue cultivating a universal discourse that makes it clear how particular discourses either miss or approximate the public, common, and objective universal story that grounds and is the end (ultimately

---

8. That is, post-colonial as it pertains to Augustine's city of man, but not to his city of God (understood as transcending any earthly polity). See John von Heyking, *Augustine and Politics as Longing in the World* (Columbia: University of Missouri Press, 2001).

the judge) of all particular tales—including the judge of would-be universal discourse itself.[9]

DIVINE PRESENCE AND ABSENCE AS HISTORY

It is fitting, then—especially in light of the peculiarities of our relationship to it—to query how the phenomenon of divine absence that I have analyzed throughout this essay relates to such a universal (as it claims to be) story. It would be fair to ask, as noted above, something like the following: "Could God not be more obvious than he is? Could he erase all atheism? Could he overcome all intellectual doubt in an instance? Would it ruin the big story if he were a bit more clear?" The classical answer to this is that, of course, God is capable of such things. But he does not apparently do them. Why might this be? Interestingly, answering this well—from an orthodox Protestant perspective—actually gets us back to the human story (in which we always and irreducibly participate) itself. Along these lines, there are at least two important points to be made. First, according to Christian theology, *God is only interested in his revelation being clear enough for the purposes he has in revealing himself.*[10] That is, God's revelation is about God's rather than humanity's goals. And it is not humanity, therefore, who determines what a fitting amount of clarity might be. Humanity's purposes may well be at odds with those of God. God is actually not, in Christian thought, that interested in people simply believing that he exists. Consider the parallel of Jesus in the gospels. How often does Christ actually conceal his teaching and his identity precisely because he knows that people will simply abuse his teaching or seek to manipulate his identity for their own ends (John 6)? Christ is portrayed as most clear to those who pursue, who hunger, who thirst—as in the case of the woman at

---

9. On this, see the important work of Corduan, *In the Beginning God* in relation to the kinds of developments highlighted in Witzel, *The Origins of the World's Mythologies*. See also Larsen, *The Slain God.*

10. On this, see Moser, *The Elusive God.*

the well (John 4). This does not mean that his identity was, as such, unclear. It means that he was not interested in *maximal* clarity. His clarity was fitting to his own purposes in coming and revealing himself and his Father. So it is with God in natural revelation. God is not interested in people merely believing in him (i.e., recognizing the fact of his existence). Why would he then fix what is not, by his standards, broken? Again, was that medieval world (suffused with divine agency, the so-called sacramental universe) a world of godliness, of love for God, of pursuit of His kingdom? Was (in either the Jewish or Christian account) ancient Israel full of faithful Hebrews because God's cloud was in their midst? Was the New Testament church in good shape because, as it is claimed, they had the immediacy of the Spirit's presence? A cursory reading of Paul's Corinthian correspondence would suggest otherwise. In each of these cases, God's presence was more clear in some relevant sense than it is to us. And yet human beings were no different from how they are now. "If they do not listen to Moses and the prophets," Christ says, "they will not be persuaded even if someone rises from the dead" (Luke 16:31). Jesus is, of course, talking not about believing in God's existence or power but about believing "on" God as a child. Following Christ, the Christian claim is that the problem is and always has been the human will. Intellectual distortion has always been a function of this more primal seat of human fallenness. And the deep human memory (which is parodied in some modern constructs) of some juxtaposition between a primal condition and its ruination is crucial here.

But this gives only part of the answer. Another answer involves understanding how divine presence and absence structure the biblical (and therefore the Christian sense of the universal historical) narrative. Even in the Genesis depiction of Paradise, God apparently comes and goes out of the garden even before the fall. There is still some distinction between God's divine heavenly realm and humanity's earthly dwelling place. And while God descends into the garden as he later descended into Israel's tabernacle, God's presence is accompanied by God's absence. This is why God can say, "Where are you, Adam?" And Adam can say, "I heard you coming and I was afraid." In Israel as well, God is portrayed as coming and going. He is silent, and then he speaks. He speaks to Abraham, Isaac, and Jacob, and then he is apparently silent as his people live in slavery for centuries. He shows up and redeems them, sets up a tabernacle, a priesthood, a kingship—then the nation of Israel goes into exile for their rebellion. Not long after the exile, God is apparently absent for several centuries again. And then he, in the Christian view, comes climactically in the person of Christ. And yet even Jesus himself, after the resurrection, ascends into heaven. Just when it would seem that God is finally with humans permanently, he goes away![11] He bridges this absence (in Christian thought) through the Holy Spirit, who feeds the people of God as ancient pilgrim Israel was fed manna in the wilderness through their long pilgrimage to Zion. But even this is often experienced as an absence, a silence, a context that necessitates a trust that the Spirit works in the recipient through Scripture (proclaimed and read), sacrament, and prayer. Christians, therefore, long for that time which Scripture speaks of in Revelation 21–22, when heaven and earth come together, and the presence of God with humanity is permanent, when there is no absence (though perhaps never a lack of development or increasing presence—an ever pleasant aching for "more" of the infinite God in Christ to continually refill the already overflowing receptacle of our soul).

What is the Christian account of what is going on here? Why all this absence? Even in creation? Even in Christ? It would seem that one significant answer is rather simple. We are contingent creatures who develop. We mature. And we mature and change and are perfected by means of shifting circumstances and the trials that they bring. God is portrayed as having given Adam a task,

---

11. Michael Horton reflects extensively on this in *People and Place: A Covenant Ecclesiology* (Louisville: Westminster John Knox Press, 2008), 1–34.

to cultivate and keep the garden, to be fruitful and multiply, to fill the earth, subdue it, and rule over it. Adam was to grow in this. Adam was meant to become a man, to be perfected, and to be crowned with glory. For Christians, Adamic failure (however understood) is the paradigm of our own, which is its echo.[12] But this maturing structure is still built into human nature. The British sociologist Anthony Giddens, for instance, writes about the way in which infants develop through their parents' absence as well as their presence:

> Crucial to the intersection of trust with emergent social capabilities on the part of the infant ... is absence. Here, at the heart of the psychological development of trust, we rediscover the problematic of time-space distanciation. For a fundamental feature of the early formation of trust is trust in the caretaker's return. A feeling of the reliability, yet independent experience, of others—central to a sense of continuity of self-identity—is predicated upon the recognition that the absence of the mother does not represent a withdrawal of love. Trust thus brackets distance in time and space and so blocks off existential anxieties which, if they were allowed to concretise, might become a source of continuing emotional and behavioral anguish throughout life.[13]

Note here that without absence, the very experience of presence is different. It is actually absence that reveals presence to be more than a mere given. It is rendered a personal love, reliability, an agency that will never abandon us or fail to return, and so forth. In Christian thought, God desires his contingent creatures to know this. And so he creates not just beatitude but history—a history that involves a dialectic of comings and goings, presences and

---

12. See, for both a reflection on Adam and the nature of human sinfulness elucidated above, Blocher, *Original Sin*.

13. Giddens, *The Consequences of Modernity*, 97.

absences, our failures and his successes, precisely so that we will develop and be cultivated into the sorts of people he has made us to be. This is built into the very structure of things. And when we failed to mature, Christians claim that God entered into our humanity through Christ to bring it, in him, to its intended perfection and glory. In Christ, the maturity that was always meant to be ours is achieved, human nature achieves its perfection, and humans are given the fruits of Christ's labor through the Spirit, who nevertheless then echoes this same narrative in Christians. Though Christ is the ultimate pattern, like him, the Christian suffers and grows and matures and finally (in Protestant theology) enters the perfection that the Christ has already achieved.[14]

In any case, this might be an especially frustrating answer for humans who find themselves begging for the comfort of divine presence or intervention, only to be met with divine silence. But God (presumably) effectively and providentially says "no." Perhaps it means, if one might butcher a Pauline phrase, "My grace is already sufficient for you." That is, at least on the Christian account, God has already shown up, raised Christ from the dead, forgiven Christians' sins, and promised them future resurrection and beatitude. And just as this can be said to have been done for our good, so (perhaps) one might say that it is good that God would ask us to grow up, mature, and learn strength through trust despite life's suffering. There is much of the Old Testament story of Job in this. Therein, God is portrayed as one who will allow his people to hit the bottom, but not without shepherding them to the conclusion that God (by himself) is enough, *sans* all, to satisfy human longings. Job was reoriented, as it were, to the gravity of God.

And this, ironically, is the counter-ethic to the attractiveness of the atheist "bravery narrative" (exposing its hubris). Perhaps—that

---

14. This underscores the imitation of Christ theme in the New Testament, on which see Herman Bavinck, *Reformed Ethics Volume 1: Created, Fallen, and Converted Humanity* (Grand Rapids: Baker Academic, 2019).

is—it rather takes courage to say that, in spite of evil (like the frightened child in the crib), in spite of war, racism, genocide, rape, and so on, that God is still to be trusted and adored. Not, of course, as wishful thinking, not as calling evil "good," but as receiving reality just as it is and as it must be—despite what the world often feels like. Perhaps, indeed, atheism is not bravery after all, but capitulation. Perhaps it is an intellectual, spiritual, and psychological failure to *endure*. It is a failure to say that God, that the Good, is greater and denser and more fundamental and deeper and wider, that love is higher, that all is grounded in the infinite plentitude of a pure actuality that is love Himself—who is God for us through the trauma of rape to the discomfort of wrist pain. The historical Christ-event is, nevertheless, the moment of divine presence to answer all divine absence—warranting childlike and whole trust in God. This, claims the Christian, is orientation to public common reality despite the accidentally mixed signals of our contingent moment.[15]

LOVING NEIGHBORS, LOVING KINGS

Finally, it is unclear whether the humanism that drives so much modern atheism is abstractable from this sort of narrative construction. It is one thing to live off the inheritance of one's cultural grandparents. It is quite another to generate new moral wealth. One manifestation of this is the late modern secular tendency, therefore, to reject any form of humanism with philosophical teeth. And the increasing displacement, among materialists, of humanism with cynical varieties of identity politics is not heartening along

---

15. This is precisely the sense I get when I meet those who confess God's goodness in the face of a death of a child, for instance. Each of us has met several people who do so from an unthinkable grief. Hauntingly, they often come off not as though they "need a crutch," but as though they are deeply conscious that their story is not ultimate. Rather, God is ultimate, and his goodness and eternal being are still greater realities and contain a greater gravity than death and pain. Resonant with this might be the (for lack of a better term) "cosmic theodicy" of Terrence Malick in his film *Tree of Life* (Open Source University, 2011)—despite Malick's unfortunate conflation of the state of creation with a state of fallenness.

these lines.[16] The resultant moral universe is easily felt to be less humanistic than a matter of historically arbitrary power relationships. This cynicism, nevertheless, is reinforced by the dreadful record of what might be called "humanistic" moral philosophies in the last century. To complicate matters further, as George Steiner says, "The humanities don't humanize." The ability to be moved by a depiction of suffering, says Steiner, is easily (and therefore hauntingly) incubated in the same heart that is calloused to the *actual* cry in the street.[17] How do we respond to people who still feel the burden of divine absence but whose therapy cannot (they think) involve attempted historical orientation—suspicious as they are of both the content and power of moral claims that depend upon a *rejected* universal moral structure and view of (un)common human nature? Only, in my judgment, by direct appeal to the very *nature* they are not sure exists in its prediscursive objective adequation to a beauty they are not sure exists. In other words, to trust that realities that are rejected nevertheless phenomenologically and tacitly exert and impress themselves on those who discursively explain them away.

Admittedly, however, I have not quite gotten at the question of justice that often animates the suspicion in the first place. Are not universal stories, after all, responsible for the world's injustices (i.e., they turn out to not be so universal after all—requiring imposition where persuasion fails)? The answer to this brings us full circle to (once again) getting the story right in such a way that demonstrates both the essential link between humanism and universal history and the tendency of the former, *precisely in its relation to the latter,* to limit injustice and promote love.[18] But this

---

16. While I do not want to deny that there are any legitimate concerns elucidated by identity politics, to the extent that its defenders reduce matters of justice to power, they (in my judgment) risk, and perhaps intend, to undermine the humanitarian impulse that ironically accounts for identity politics' surface appeal. See Rita Felski, *The Limits of Critique* (Chicago: University of Chicago Press, 2015).

17. See his presentation at https://www.youtube.com/watch?v=L-WecwvZZzk.

18. On this point, see Brague, *Eccentric Culture.*

is not merely a matter of getting one's facts straight. Rather, highlighted here must be an orientation of one's will that, in Christian theology, cannot be accomplished by the self.

Getting the story right does not itself accomplish transformation. What is required is both insight and *inclination*. The former (once again) names not some mystical retreat to commitment but (in principle) *public* truth. As it turns out, however, it is the latter where our greatest challenges lie. The importance of getting the story right might be to motivate the cultivation of our inclinations in a particular direction. Here, again, we see the importance of conscious agency and will. But this is a tension in Christian theology to the extent that our distorted wills nevertheless require (per the Christian tradition) animation by divine grace (Eph 2:8–10). Nevertheless, it is only in this way, according to historic Christian doctrine, that God achieves his purposes through humans. As Herman Bavinck writes,

> A freedom that cannot be obtained and enjoyed aside from the danger of licentiousness and caprice is still always to be preferred over a tyranny that suppressed liberty. In the creation of humanity, God himself chose the way of freedom, which carried with it the danger and actually the fact of sin as well, in preference to forced subjection. Even now, in ruling the world and governing the church, God still follows this royal road of liberty. It is precisely his honor that through freedom he nevertheless reaches his goal, creating order out of disorder, light from darkness, a cosmos out of chaos.[19]

---

19. Herman Bavinck, *Reformed Dogmatics Volume 1: Prolegomena* (Grand Rapids: Baker Academic, 2003), 479. On the relationship of divine grace to human responsibility, see Bavinck's treatment in *Reformed Dogmatics Volume 4: Holy Spirit, Church, and New Creation* (Grand Rapids: Baker Academic, 2006), 29–175.

In bringing this book to a close, I am aware that, inevitably, there are remaining threads, and it is certainly the case that there are gaps in many of the arguments (warranting further research or more extended commentary). While the object of my inquiry is mostly the world as phenomenologically manifest, much of my theoretical argument is grounded in intuition as specified in discourse and as "played with" in order to see how it helps to illuminate our experience. The success of my argument, therefore, is to be measured less by its comprehensiveness than by whether its basic outline resonates with the intuitions of the reader as illuminating our common world. Moreover, its success depends upon whether it has illuminated the *common* world—not the inner ring of upper-middle-class intellectual consumers, but rather the ordinary world of the (if I might put it this way) fast food-imbibing masses. This is because, bringing my emphasis on humanism full circle, it is precisely in the ordinary that one participates in the history making of heaven, in a particular piece of a tapestry that is part of a whole. In Christian thought, many never-remembered medieval peasants were nevertheless ornaments in that play, that ceaseless weaving of the infinite of which human history is the parodied finite structure or canvas and in which we approximately know and adore the infinite (echoing God's self-delight) via active participation. That is, in Christian thought, these all played a prominent and important role in history—albeit as yet uncelebrated. And this is where we might hope to move from a mere abstract vision to an immediately concrete task.

It is in the context of the ordinary that our most basic calling is apparent—implying once again (however) that our distinctive modes of loving our neighbor (and the cultural strategies we employ to do this well) are as wide as the human race itself. In any case, the highest mode of our dominion, the most immediate way in which we can participate in history, is in the inalienable calling of being the dutiful servant of all. And this is out of not merely a restored self-dignity but the proper and reverential recognition that when confronting others, we speak to kings. This is chastened humanism and universal history together. The dominion of others (in this view) is not a gift we have given to them but is a birthright that is our duty to recognize—a birthright fitted to their nature. Moreover, it is a birthright that persons must recognize of themselves, for socially invisible persons will inevitably go to extreme lengths to be visible to others (perhaps a way of explaining much recent history and general human behavior). And it is in the vocation of robust charity that this visibility helps to heal the world from both sides. I can end with no finer words, therefore, than those of C. S. Lewis, whose moral vision summons us to that calling from which we cannot be alienated—the embodied enactment of which would simultaneously attune us to the echo of the divine in all beings, as well as help us to understand and endure our historical pilgrimage to Zion.

It may be possible for each to think too much of his own potential glory hereafter; it is hardly possible for him to think too often or too deeply about that of his neighbor. The load, or weight, or burden of my neighbor's glory should be laid daily on my back, a load so heavy that only humility can carry it, and the backs of the proud will be broken. It is a serious thing to live in a society of possible gods and goddesses, to remember that the dullest and most uninteresting person you talk to may one day be a creature which, if you saw it now, you would be strongly tempted to worship, or else a horror and a corruption such as you now meet, if at all, only in a nightmare. All day long we are, in some degree, helping each other to one or other of these destinations. It is in the light of these overwhelming possibilities, it is with the awe and circumspection proper to them, that we should conduct all our dealings with one another, all friendships, all loves, all play, all politics. There are no *ordinary* people. You have never talked to a mere mortal. Nations, cultures, arts, civilization—these are mortal, and their life is to ours as the life of a gnat. But it is immortals whom we joke with, work with, marry, snub, and exploit—immortal horrors or everlasting splendors. This does not mean that we are to be perpetually solemn. We must play. But our merriment must be of that kind (and it is, in fact, the merriest kind) which exists between people who have, from the outset, taken each other seriously—no flippancy, no superiority, no presumption. And our charity must be real and costly love, with deep feeling for the sins in spite of which we love the sinner—no mere tolerance or indulgence which parodies love as flippancy parodies merriment. Next to the Blessed Sacrament itself, your neighbor is the holiest object presented to your senses.[20]

---

20. C. S. Lewis, *The Weight of Glory* (New York: HarperOne, 2001), 45–46.

Bibliography

Adams, Henry. *The Education of Henry Adams.* New York: The Modern Library, 1999.

Ahnert, Thomas. *Religion and the Origins of the German Enlightenment: Faith and the Reform of Learning in the Thought of Christian Thomasius.* Rochester: University of Rochester Press, 2006.

Alexander, Christopher. *The Battle for the Life and Beauty of the Earth: A Struggle Between Two World-Systems.* New York: Oxford University Press, 2012.

Alexander, T. Desmond. *From Paradise to Promised Land: An Introduction to the Pentateuch.* Grand Rapids: Baker Academic, 2012.

Allen, Michael. "Divine Fullness: A Dogmatic Sketch." *Reformed Faith and Practice* 1, no. 1 (2016): 5–18.

Allen, Robert. *The Industrial Revolution: A Very Short Introduction.* New York: Oxford University Press, 2017.

Arnold, John. *Belief and Unbelief in Medieval Europe.* New York: Oxford University Press, 2005.

Asad, Talal. *Formations of the Secular: Christianity, Islam, Modernity.* Stanford: Stanford University Press, 2003.

Augustine. *City of God.* Translated by Marcus Dods. New York: Modern Library, 1994.

———. *Confessions.* Translated by Maria Boulding. Hyde Park, NY: New City Press, 1997.

Backus, Irena. *Leibniz: Protestant Theologian.* New York: Oxford University Press, 2016.

Bailey, Michael. *Fearful Spirits, Reasoned Follies: The Boundaries of Superstition in Late Medieval Europe.* Ithaca, NY: Cornell University Press, 2013.

Ballard, J. G. *The Drought.* New York: Liverlight, 2012.

———. *The Drowned World.* New York: Liverlight, 2013.

Bambach, Charles. *Heidegger's Roots: Nietzsche, National Socialism, and the Greeks.* Ithaca, NY: Cornell University Press, 2005.

Barbour, Ian. *Religion and Science: Historical and Contemporary Issues.* New York: HarperOne, 1997.

Barfield, Owen. *Saving the Appearances: A Study in Idolatry.* Hanover, NH: Wesleyan, 1988.

Barr, Stephen M. *Modern Physics and Ancient Faith.* Notre Dame: University of Notre Dame Press, 2003.

Barthes, Roland. *Mythologies.* New York: Hill and Wang, 2013.

Bartley, William. *The Retreat to Commitment.* New York: Knopf, 1962.

Bauman, Zygmund. *Liquid Modernity.* New York: Polity, 2012.

Bavinck, Herman. *Philosophy of Revelation.* London: Longmans, Green, and Co., 1908.

———. *Reformed Dogmatics Volume 1: Prolegomena.* Grand Rapids: Baker Academic, 2003.

———. *Reformed Dogmatics Volume 2: God and Creation.* Grand Rapids: Baker Academic, 2004.

———. *Reformed Dogmatics Volume 4: Holy Spirit, Church,* and New Creation. Grand Rapids: Baker Academic, 2008.

———. *Reformed Ethics Volume 1: Created, Fallen, and Converted Humanity.* Grand Rapids: Baker Academic, 2019.

Bayer, Oswald. *A Contemporary in Dissent: Johann Georg Hamann as a Radical Enlightener.* Grand Rapids: Eerdmans, 2012.

———. *Martin Luther's Theology: A Contemporary Interpretation.* Grand Rapids: Eerdmans, 2008.

Bayle, Pierre. *A Philosophical Commentary on These Words of the Gospel, Luke 14:23, "Compel Them to Come In, That My House May Be Full."* Indianapolis: Liberty Fund, 2006.

Bellah, Robert N. *Religion in Human Evolution: From the Paleolithic to the Axial Age.* Cambridge: Harvard Belknap, 2011.

Berger, Peter, Brigitte Berger, and Hansfried Kellner. *The Homeless Mind: Modernization and Consciousness.* New York: Vintage, 1973.

Berman, David. *A History of Atheism in Britain: From Hobbes to Russell.* London: Routledge, 1990.

Berman, Harold. *Law and Revolution II: The Impact of the Protestant Reformations on the Western Legal Tradition.* Cambridge: Harvard Belknap, 2006.

Berman, Marshall. *All That is Solid Melts into Air: The Experience of Modernity.* New York: Penguin, 1988.

Bester, Alfred. "Adam and No Eve." *Astounding Science Fiction,* September, 1941.

Birnes, William J., and Joel Martin. *The Haunting of Twenty-First Century America: From the Millennium to the New Age.* New York: Forge, 2014.

Blocher, Henri. *Evil and the Cross: An Analytical Look at the Problem of Pain.* Grand Rapids: Kregel Academic, 2005.

———. *Original Sin: Illuminating the Riddle.* Downers Grove, IL: InterVarsity Press, 1997.

Blumenberg, Hans. *The Legitimacy of the Modern Age.* Cambridge: MIT Press, 1983.

———. "Light as a Metaphor for Truth: At the Preliminary Stage of Philosophical Concept Formation." In *Modernity and the Hegemony of Vision,* edited by David Michael Levin, 30–62. Berkeley: University of California Press, 1993.

Blumin, Stuart. *The Emergence of the Middle Class: Social Experience in the American City, 1760–1900.* New York: Cambridge University Press, 1989.

Boas, George. *Primitivism and Related Ideas in the Middle Ages.* Baltimore: Johns Hopkins University Press, 1948.

Boersma, Hans. *Seeing God: The Beatific Vision in Christian Tradition.* Grand Rapids: Eerdmans, 2018.

Bonhoeffer, Dietrich. *Letters & Papers from Prison.* New York: Simon & Schuster, 1997.

Bookchin, Murray. *The Ecology of Freedom: The Emergence and Dissolution of Hierarchy.* Palo Alto, CA: AK Press, 2005.

Borus, Daniel H. *Twentieth-Century Multiplicity 1900–1920.* Lanham, MD: Rowman & Littlefield, 2009.

Brague, Remi. *Eccentric Culture: A Theory of Western Civilization.* South Bend, IN: Saint Augustine Press, 2009.

———. *The Legitimacy of the Human.* South Bend, IN: Saint Augustine Press, 2017.

———. *The Wisdom of the World: The Human Experience of the Universe in Western Thought.* Translated by Teresa Lavender Fagan. Chicago: University of Chicago Press, 2003.

Breisach, Ernst. *Historiography: Ancient, Medieval, and Modern.* Chicago: University of Chicago Press, 2007.

Briggs, Carolyn. *This Dark World: A Memoir of Salvation Found and Lost.* New York: Bloomsbury, 2002.

Brooke, John Hedley. *Science and Religion: Some Historical Perspectives.* New York: Cambridge University Press, 1991.

Brown, Andrew J. *The Days of Creation: A History of Christian Interpretation of Genesis 1:1–2:3.* Blandford Forum, UK: Deo Publishing, 2014.

Brown, Colin. *Miracles and the Critical Mind.* Grand Rapids: Eerdmans, 1984.

Bruce, Steven, ed. *Religion and Modernization: Sociologists and Historians Debate the Secularization Thesis*. New York: Clarendon, 1992.

———. *Secularization: In Defense of an Unfashionable Theory*. New York: Oxford University Press, 2011.

Bube, Richard H. "Man Come of Age: Bonhoeffer's Response to the God-of-the-Gaps." *Journal of the Evangelical Theological Society* 14, no. 4 (1971): 203–20.

Buckley, Michael J. *At the Origins of Modern Atheism*. New Haven: Yale University Press, 1987.

———. *Denying and Disclosing God: The Ambiguous Progress of Modern Atheism*. New Haven: Yale University Press, 2004.

Burnett, Joel S. *Where Is God? Divine Absence in the Hebrew Bible*. Minneapolis: Fortress Press, 2010.

Burtt, E. A. *The Metaphysical Foundations of Modern Science*. New York: Doubleday, 1932.

Bushman, B. J., and L. R. Huesmann. "Short-Term and Long-Term Effect of Violent Media on Aggression in Children and Adults." *Archives of Pediatrics and Adolescent Medicine Journal* 160, no. 4 (2006): 348–52.

Butler, Lance St. John. *Victorian Doubt: Literary and Culture Discourses*. New York: Harvester, 1990.

Calhoun, Craig, Michael Warner, and Jonathan VanAntwerpen, eds. *Varieties of Secularism in a Secular Age*. Cambridge: Harvard University Press, 2010.

Callenbach, Ernest. *Ecotopia*. New York: Bantam Books, 1990.

Callinicos, Alex. *The Revolutionary Ideas of Karl Marx*. Chicago: Haymarket Books, 2012.

Camus, Albert. *The Stranger*. New York: Vintage, 1988.

Capek, Karel. *R.U.R.* Rockville, MD: Wildside Press, 2010.

Carlson, Allan. *From Cottage to Work Station: The Family's Search for Social Harmony in the Industrial Age.* San Francisco: Ignatius Press, 1993.

Carr, Nicholas. *The Shallows: What the Internet Is Doing to Our Brains.* New York: Norton, 2011.

Casanova, Jose. "The Secular and Secularisms." *Social Research* 76, no. 4 (2009): 1049–66.

Castells, Manuel. *Communication Power.* New York: Oxford University Press, 2013.

Chadwick, Owen. *The Secularization of the European Mind in the 19th Century.* New York: Cambridge University Press, 1975.

Chang, Hasok. *Is Water H2o? Evidence, Realism, and Pluralism.* Cambridge: Springer, 2014.

Channell, David. *A History of Technoscience: Erasing the Boundaries between Science and Technology.* New York: Routledge, 2017.

———. *The Vital Machine: A Study of Technology and Organic Life.* New York: Oxford University Press, 1991.

Ch'eng-en, Wu. *Monkey.* Translated by Arthur Waley. New York: Grove Press, 1970.

Clarke, W. Norris. *The One and the Many: A Contemporary Thomistic Metaphysics.* Notre Dame: University of Notre Dame Press, 2001.

———. *The Philosophical Approach to God: A New Thomistic Perspective.* New York: Fordham University Press, 2007.

Clayton, Philip. *The Problem of God in Modern Thought.* Grand Rapids: Eerdmans, 2000.

Colligan, Colette, and Margaret Linley, eds. *Media, Technology, and Literature in the Nineteenth Century: Image, Sound, Touch.* Burlington, VT: Ashgate, 2011.

Collins, C. John. *Reading Genesis Well: Navigating History, Poetry, Science, and Truth in Genesis 1–11.* Grand Rapids: Zondervan, 2018.

Collins, John H. "Cosmology: Time and History." In *Religions of the Ancient World: A Guide,* edited by Sarah Iles Johnston, 59–70. Cambridge: Harvard Belknap, 2004.

Cooper, John. *Panentheism—The Other God of the Philosophers: From Plato to the Present.* Grand Rapids: Baker Academic, 2006.

Cooper, Jordan, and Dan Lioy. "The Use of Classical Greek Philosophy in Early Lutheranism." *Conspectus* 26 (September 2018), 1–27.

Corduan, Winfried. *In the Beginning God: A Fresh Look at the Case for Original Monotheism.* Nashville: B&H, 2013.

Cronon, William. *Changes in the Land: Indians, Colonists, and the Ecology of New England.* New York: Hill and Wang, 2003.

Crouch, Andy. *Culture Making: Recovering our Creative Calling.* Downers Grove, IL: InterVarsity Press, 2013.

———. *Playing God: Redeeming the Gift of Power.* Downers Grove, IL: InterVarsity Press, 2013.

———. *Strong and Weak: Embracing a Life of Love, Risk, and True Flourishing.* Downers Grove, IL: InterVarsity Press, 2016.

Crouse, Robert. *Two Kingdoms & Two Cities: Mapping Theological Traditions of Church, Culture, and Civil Order.* Minneapolis: Fortress Press, 2017.

Cunningham, Conor. *Darwin's Pious Idea: Why the Ultra-Darwinists and Creationists Both Get It Wrong.* Grand Rapids: Eerdmans, 2010.

Currid, John. "Theistic Evolution Is Incompatible with the Teachings of the Old Testament." In *Theistic Evolution: A Scientific, Philosophical, and Theological Critique,* edited by J. P. Moreland, Stephen C. Meyer, Christopher Shaw, Ann K. Gauger, and Wayne Grudem, 839–78. Wheaton, IL: Crossway, 2017.

Dawkins, Richard. *The Blind Watchmaker: Why the Evidence of Evolution Reveals a Universe Without Design.* New York: Norton, 1986.

———. *The Greatest Show on Earth: The Evidence for Evolution.* New York: Free Press, 2010.

de Fraine, Jean. *The Bible and the Origin of Man.* Staten Island: Alba House, 1967.

de Wit, Willem J. *On the Way to the Living God: A Cathartic Reading of Herman Bavinck and an Invitation to Overcome the Plausibility Crisis of Christianity.* Amsterdam: VU University Press, 2011.

Dennett, Daniel. *Darwin's Dangerous Idea: Evolution and the Meaning of Life.* New York: Simon & Schuster, 1996.

Descartes, Rene. *Discourse on Method and Meditations on First Philosophy.* New York: Hackett, 1999.

Douthat, Ross. *Bad Religion: How We Became a Nation of Heretics.* New York: Free Press, 2013.

Dreyfus, Hubert, and Charles Taylor. *Retrieving Realism.* Cambridge: Harvard University Press, 2015.

Dow, Donald W. "Internal Differences: Secularism, Religion, and Poetic Form." PhD diss., Rutgers University, 2008.

Draper, John William. *History of the Conflict between Religion and Science.* Cambridge: Cambridge University Press, 1874.

Dreher, Rod. *The Benedict Option: A Strategy for Christians in a Post-Christian Nation.* New York: Sentinel, 2017.

Dupre, Louis. *Passage to Modernity: An Essay in the Hermeneutics of Nature and Culture.* New Haven: Yale University Press, 1993.

Durkheim, Emile. *Selected Writings.* New York: Cambridge University Press, 1972.

Eagleton, Terry. *Culture and the Death of God.* New Haven: Yale University Press, 2015.

Eberstadt, Mary. *How the West Really Lost God*. West
 Conshohocken, PA: Templeton Press, 2013.
Edgerton, David. *The Shock of the Old: Technology and Global
 History Since 1900*. New York: Oxford University Press,
 2007.
Eggers, Dave. *The Circle*. New York: Vintage, 2014.
Eglinton, James. *Bavinck: A Critical Biography*. Grand Rapids:
 Baker Academic, 2020.
———. *Trinity and Organism: Toward a New Reading of Herman
 Bavinck's Organic Motif*. New York: Bloomsbury, 2012.
Ellul, Jacques. *Hope in Time of Abandonment*. Eugene, OR: Wipf
 & Stock, 1973 reprint.
———. *The Humiliation of the Word*. Grand Rapids: Eerdmans,
 1985.
———. *The Technological Society*. New York: Vintage, 1964.
Endo, Shusaku. *Silence*. New York: Picador, 2016.
Erdozain, Dominic. *The Soul of Doubt: The Religious Roots
 of Unbelief from Luther to Marx*. New York: Oxford
 University Press, 2016.
———. "A Heavenly Poise: Radical Religion and the Making of
 the Enlightenment." *Intellectual History Review* 27, no. 1
 (2017): 71–96.
Escalante, Peter, with Joseph Minich. "Philosophy as a Way of
 Life: Reforming the Quest for Wisdom." In *Philosophy
 and the Christian: The Quest for Wisdom in the Light of
 Christ*, edited by Joseph Minich, 461–513. Landrum, SC:
 The Davenant Trust, 2018.
Felski, Rita. *The Limits of Critique*. Chicago: University of
 Chicago Press, 2015.
Fenton, Charles A. "The Bell Tower: Melville and Technology."
 American Literature 23, no. 2 (1951): 219–32.
Feser, Edward. *Five Proofs of the Existence of God*. San Francisco:
 Ignatius Press, 2017.

———. *The Last Superstition: A Refutation of the New Atheism.* South Bend, IN: Saint Augustine Press, 2008.

———. *Philosophy of Mind.* Oxford, UK: OneWorld Publications, 2006.

Feuerbach, Ludwig. *The Essence of Christianity.* Amherst, NY: Prometheus Books, 1989.

Feyerabend, Paul. *Against Method.* New York: Verso, 2010.

Fitzgerald, F. Scott. *This Side of Paradise.* New York: Dover, 1996.

Flew, Anthony. *There Is a God: How the World's Most Notorious Atheist Changed His Mind.* New York: HarperCollins, 2009.

Foucault, Michel. *The Order of Things.* New York: Vintage, 1970.

Freud, Sigmund. *Civilization and Its Discontents.* New York: Norton, 2010.

Funkenstein, Amos. *Theology and the Scientific Imagination from the Middle Ages to the Seventeenth Century.* Princeton: Princeton University Press, 1986.

Gaukroger, Stephen. *The Emergence of a Scientific Culture: Science and the Shaping of Modernity, 1210–1685.* New York: Oxford University Press, 2009.

Gay, Peter. *The Enlightenment: The Rise of Modern Paganism.* New York: Knopf, 1966.

———. *The Enlightenment: The Science of Human Freedom.* New York: Norton, 1996.

Gentry, Peter, and Stephen Wellum. *Kingdom Through Covenant: A Biblical-Theological Understanding of the Covenants.* Wheaton, IL: Crossway, 2018.

Germain, Gilbert G. *A Discourse on Disenchantment: Reflections on Politics and Technology.* Albany: State University of New York Press, 1993.

———. *Spirits in the Material World: The Challenge of Technology.* Plymouth, MA: Lexington Books, 2009.

———. *Thinking about Technology: How the Technological Mind Misreads Reality.* Plymouth, MA: Lexington Books, 2017.

Gerrish, B. A. "'To the Unknown God': Luther and Calvin on the Hiddenness of God." *The Journal of Religion* 53, no. 3 (1973): 263–92.

Giddens, Anthony. *The Consequences of Modernity.* Stanford: Stanford University Press, 1990.

Gierke, Otto. *Political Theories of the Middle Ages.* New York: Cambridge University Press, 1987.

Gillespie, Michael. *The Theological Origins of Modernity.* Chicago: University of Chicago Press, 2009.

Gilson, Etienne. *From Aristotle to Darwin and Back Again: A Journey in Final Causality, Species, and Evolution.* San Francisco: Ignatius Press, 2009.

Gourdriaan, Aza. *Reformed Orthodoxy and Philosophy, 1625–1750.* Leiden: Brill, 2006.

Greene, Adam, and Eleonore Stump, eds. *Hidden Divinity and Religious Belief: New Perspectives.* New York: Cambridge University Press, 2016.

Gregory, Brad. *The Unintended Reformation: How a Religious Revolution Secularized Society.* Cambridge: Harvard Belknap, 2015.

Grodal, Torben. *Embodied Visions: Evolution, Emotion, Culture, and Film.* New York: Oxford University Press, 2009.

Hacker, P. M. S., and M. R. Bennett. *Philosophical Foundations of Neuroscience.* New York: Wiley-Blackwell, 2003.

Haidt, Jonathan. *The Righteous Mind: Why Good People Are Divided by Politics and Religion.* New York: Vintage, 2013.

Halberstam, Judith. *In a Queer Time and Place: Transgender Bodies, Subcultural Lives.* New York: New York University Press, 2005.

Halpern, Baruch. *The Hebrew Bible and History.* New York: Harper & Row, 1988.

Halpern, Daniel Noah. "Sperm Count Zero." *GQ*, September 2018.

Hamer, Dean. *The God Gene: How Faith Is Hardwired into Our Genes*. New York: Random House, 2005.

Hardy, Thomas. *Jude the Obscure*. New York: Penguin, 1998.

Harrison, Peter. *The Bible, Protestantism, and the Rise of Natural Science*. New York: Cambridge University Press, 1998.

———. *The Fall of Man and the Foundations of Science*. New York: Cambridge University Press, 2007.

———. "Science and Secularization." *Intellectual History Review* 27, no. 1 (2017): 47–70.

———. *The Territories of Science and Religion*. Chicago: University of Chicago Press, 2015.

———. "Voluntarism and Early Modern Science." *History of Science* 40, no. 1 (2002): 63–89.

———. *Gardens: An Essay on the Human Condition*. Chicago: University of Chicago Press, 2008.

———. *Juvenescence: A Cultural History of Our Age*. Chicago: University of Chicago Press, 2014.

Hart, David Bentley. *Atheist Delusions: The Christian Revolution and Its Fashionable Enemies*. New Haven: Yale University Press, 2009.

———. *The Beauty of the Infinite: The Aesthetics of Christian Truth*. Grand Rapids: Eerdmans, 2003.

———. *The Experience of God: Being, Consciousness, Bliss*. New Haven: Yale University Press, 2013.

Hartley, L. P. *The Go-Between*. New York: NYRB Classics, 2011.

Hatch, Nathan. *The Democratization of American Christianity*. New Haven: Yale University Press, 1991.

Hawking, Steven, and Leonard Mlodinow. *The Grand Design*. New York: Bantam, 2010.

Hazony, Yoram. *The Virtue of Nationalism*. New York: Basic Books, 2018.

Hefner, Veronica. "From Love at First Sight to Soul Mate: Romantic Ideals in Popular Films and Their Association with Young People's Beliefs about Relationships." PhD diss., University of Illinois at Urbana-Champaign, 2011.

Hegel, G. F. W. *The Phenomenology of Spirit.* Translated by Michael Baur. New York: Cambridge University Press, 2018.

Heidegger, Martin. *Being and Time,* Translated by Joan Stambaugh. Albany: State University of New York Press, 2010.

———. *Early Greek Thinking: The Dawn of Western Philosophy.* San Francisco: Harper, 1985.

———. "The Question Concerning Technology." In *Basic Writings,* edited by David Farrell Krell, 307–42. New York: Harper, 1993.

Helgeson, Jeffrey. "American Labor and Working-Class History, 1900–1945." In *Oxford Research Encyclopedia of American History.* Article published August 31, 2016. http://americanhistory.oxfordre.com/view/10.1093/acrefore/9780199329175.001.0001/acrefore-9780199329175-e-330.

Herder, Johann. *Philosophical Writings.* New York: Cambridge University Press, 2002.

Herrick, James. *Scientific Mythologies: How Science and Science Fiction Forge New Religious Beliefs.* Downers Grove, IL: InterVarsity Press, 2008.

Hess, Richard. *Israelite Religions.* Grand Rapids: Baker Academic, 2007.

Hilber, John. *Old Testament Cosmology and Divine Accommodation: A Relevance Theory Approach.* Eugene, OR: Cascade, 2020.

Hochstrasser, T. J. "The Claims of Conscience: Natural Law Theory, Obligation, and Resistance in the Huguenot

Diaspora." In *New Essays on the Political Thought of the Huguenots of the Refuge,* ed. J. C. Laursen, 15–51. Leiden: Brill, 1995.

Holland, Tom. *Dominion: How the Christian Revolution Remade the World.* New York: Basic Books, 2019.

Horton, Michael. *Covenant and Eschatology: The Divine Drama.* Louisville: Westminster John Knox Press, 2002.

———. "The Enduring Power of the Christian Story: Reformation Theology for A Secular Age." In *Our Secular Age,* edited by Collin Hansen, 23–38. Deerfield, IL: The Gospel Coalition, 2017.

———. *Lord and Servant: A Covenant Christology.* Louisville: Westminster John Knox Press, 2005.

———. *People and Place: A Covenant Ecclesiology.* Louisville: Westminster John Knox Press, 2008.

———. Review of Brad Gregory, *The Unintended Reformation.* The Gospel Coalition. February 15, 2016. https://www. thegospelcoalition.org/article/book-reviews-the-unintended-reformation.

Howard-Snyder, Daniel, and Paul Moser, eds. *Divine Hiddenness: New Essays.* New York: Cambridge University Press, 2002.

Hughes, John. *The End of Work: Theological Critiques of Capitalism.* Malden, MA: Wiley-Blackwell, 2006.

Hultkrantz, Ake. *The Religion of the American Indians.* Berkeley: University of California Press, 1979.

Hunter, Ian. *Rival Enlightenments: Civil and Metaphysical Philosophy in Early Modern German.* New York: Cambridge University Press, 2001.

———. *The Secularization of the Confessional State: The Political thought of Christian Thomasius.* New York: Cambridge University Press, 2007.

———. "Secularization: Process, Program, and Historiography."
    Intellectual History Review 27, no. 1 (2017): 7–29.
Hunter, James Davison. *To Change the World: The Irony, Tragedy,
    and Possibility of Christianity in the Late Modern World.*
    New York: Oxford University Press, 2010.
Hunter, Michael, and David Wootton, eds. *Atheism from the
    Reformation to the Enlightenment.* Oxford: Clarendon
    Press, 1992.
Hurth, Elisabeth. *Between Faith and Unbelief: American
    Transcendentalists and the Challenge of Atheism.* Leiden:
    Brill, 2007.
Hyman, Gavin. *A Short History of Atheism.* New York: I. B.
    Tauris, 2010.
Israel, Jonathan. *Democratic Enlightenment: Philosophy, Revolution,
    and Human Rights, 1750–1790.* New York: Oxford
    University Press, 2012.
———. "Freedom of Thought Versus Freedom of Religion:
    An Eighteenth-Century—And Now Also a Twenty-
    First-Century Dilemma." Thomas More Lecture,
    Radbouduniversiteit, November 10, 2006.
———. *Radical Enlightenment: Philosophy and the Making of
    Modernity 1650–1750.* New York: Oxford University Press,
    2001.
———. *A Revolution of the Mind: Radical Enlightenment and the
    Intellectual Origins of Modern Democracy.* Princeton:
    Princeton University Press, 2010.
Jacob, Margaret. *The Radical Enlightenment: Pantheists,
    Freemasons, and Republicans.* Lafayette, LA: Cornerstone,
    2006.
Jacoby, Susan. *Freethinkers: A History of American Secularism.*
    New York: Metropolitan Books, 2005.
———. *The Great Agnostic: Robert Ingersoll and American
    Freethought.* New Haven: Yale University Press, 2013.

Jager, Colin. *The Book of God: Secularism and Design in the Romantic Era*. Philadelphia: University of Pennsylvania Press, 2006.

———. *Unquiet Things: Secularism in the Romantic Age*. Philadelphia: University of Pennsylvania Press, 2014.

James, William. "The Will to Believe." In *William James: Pragmatism and Other Writings*, edited by Giles Gunn, 198–218. New York: Penguin, 2000.

Jameson, Fredric. *The Political Unconscious: Narrative as a Socially Symbolic Act*. Ithaca: Cornell University Press, 1982.

Jenkins, Philip. *The Next Christendom: The Coming of Global Christianity*. New York: Oxford University Press, 2011.

———. *The Great and Holy War: How World War I Became a Religious Crusade*. New York: HarperOne, 2014.

Johnson, Dru. *The Universal Story: Genesis 1–11*. Bellingham, WA: Lexham Press, 2018.

Josephson-Storm, Jason A. *The Myth of Disenchantment: Magic, Modernity, and the Birth of the Human Sciences*. Chicago: University of Chicago Press, 2017.

Kafka, Franz. *The Metamorphosis*. New York: Dover, 1996.

Keener, Craig. *Miracles: The Credibility of the New Testament Accounts*. Grand Rapids: Baker Academic, 2011.

Ketabgian, Tamara S. *The Lives of Machines: The Industrial Imaginary in Victorian Literature and Culture*. Ann Arbor: University of Michigan Press, 2011.

Kippenberg, Hans. *Discovering Religious History in the Modern Age*. Princeton: Princeton University Press, 2001.

Kirby, Torrance. *Paul's Cross and the Culture of Persuasion in England, 1520–1640*. Leiden: Brill, 2013.

———. *Persuasion and Conversion: Essays on Religion, Politics, and the Public Sphere in Early Modern England*. Leiden: Brill, 2013.

Kocka, Jurgen. "The European Middle Classes." *The Journal of Modern History* 67, no. 4 (1995): 783–806.

Kolozi, Peter. *Conservatives against Capitalism: From the Industrial Revolution to Globalization.* New York: Columbia University Press, 2017.

Kors, Alan Charles. *Atheism in France 1650–1729 Volume 1: The Orthodox Sources of Unbelief.* Princeton: Princeton University Press, 1990.

———. *Epicureans and Atheists in France 1650–1729.* New York: Cambridge University Press, 2016.

Krutch, Joseph Wood. *The Modern Temper.* San Diego: Harvest Books, 1957.

Kuhn, Thomas. *The Structure of Scientific Revolutions.* Chicago: University of Chicago Press, 2012.

Kurzweil, Ray. *The Age of Spiritual Machines: When Computers Exceed Human Intelligence.* New York: Penguin, 2000.

Larsen, Timothy. *Crisis of Doubt: Honest Faith in Nineteenth Century England.* New York: Oxford University Press, 2009.

———. *The Slain God: Anthropologists and the Christian Faith.* New York: Oxford University Press, 2014.

Lasch, Christopher. *The True and Only Heaven: Progress and Its Critics.* New York: Norton, 1991.

Latour, Bruno. *We Have Never Been Modern.* Cambridge: Harvard University Press, 1991.

Leech, David. *The Hammer of the Cartesians: Henry More's Philosophy of Spirit and the Origins of Modern Atheism.* Leuven: Peeters, 2013.

Leithart, Peter. *The Baptized Body.* Moscow, ID: Canon Press, 2007.

Lelas, Srdjan. "Science as Technology." *The British Journal for the Philosophy of Science* 44, no. 3 (1993): 423–42.

Lepp, Ignace. *Atheism in Our Time.* New York: MacMillan, 1963.

Levenson, Jon D. *Creation and the Persistence of Evil: The Jewish Drama of Divine Omnipresence.* Princeton: Princeton University Press, 1988.

———. *Sinai & Zion: An Entry into the Jewish Bible.* New York: Harper, 1985.

Levin, David Michael. "Decline and Fall: Ocularcentrism in Heidegger's Reading of the History of Metaphysics." In *Modernity and the Hegemony of Vision,* edited by David Michael Levin, 186–217. Berkeley: University of California Press, 1993.

Lewis, C. S. *The Abolition of Man.* New York: HarperOne, 1974.

———. *The Discarded Image.* New York: Cambridge University Press, 1964.

———. *That Hideous Strength.* New York: Scribner's Sons, 1996.

———. "The Inner Ring." In *The Weight of Glory.* New York: HarperOne, 2001, 116–40.

———. *Miracles.* New York: HarperOne, 2015.

———. *The Weight of Glory.* New York: HarperOne, 2001.

Lilla, Mark. *The Once and Future Liberal: After Identity Politics.* New York: Harper, 2017.

———. *The Shipwrecked Mind: On Political Reaction.* New York: The New York Review of Books, 2016.

Lindberg, David. *The Beginnings of Western Science: The European Scientific Tradition in Philosophical, Religious, and Institutional Context: Prehistory to A.D. 1450.* Chicago: University of Chicago Press, 2008.

Lindberg, David. and Ronald Numbers, eds. *God and Nature: Historical Essays on the Encounter between Christianity and Science.* Berkeley: University of California Press, 1986.

———, eds. *When Science and Christianity Meet.* Chicago: University of Chicago Press, 2003.

Lippmann, Walter. *A Preface to Morals.* Piscataway: Transaction Publishers, 1982.

Littlejohn, W. Bradford. *The Peril and Promise of Christian Liberty: Richard Hooker, the Puritans, and Protestant Political Theology*. Grand Rapids: Eerdmans, 2017.

Liu, Cixin. *The Dark Forest*. New York: TOR Books, 2016.

——. *Death's End*. New York: TOR Books, 2017.

——. *The Three Body Problem*. New York: TOR Books, 2016.

Livingston, James, and Francis Schussler Fiorenza. *Modern Christian Thought: The Twentieth Century*. Minneapolis: Fortress Press, 2006.

Livingstone, David. *Adam's Ancestors; Race, Religion, and the Politics of Human Origins*. Baltimore: Johns Hopkins University Press, 2011.

——. *Darwin's Forgotten Defenders: The Encounter Between Evangelical Theology and Evolutionary Thought*. Vancouver, BC: Regent College Publishing, 1984.

——. *Dealing With Darwin: Place, Politics, and Rhetoric in Religious Engagements with Evolution*. Baltimore: Johns Hopkins University Press, 2014.

London, Jack. *The Law of Life*. Providence, RI: Jamestown Publishers, 1976.

Louth, Andrew. *The Wilderness of God*. Nashville: Abingdon Press, 1991.

Lovejoy, Arthur, and George Boas. *Primitivism and Related Ideas in Antiquity*. Baltimore: Johns Hopkins University Press, 1935.

Löwith, Karl. *Meaning in History*. Chicago: University of Chicago Press, 1949.

Luther, Martin. *Luther's Works, Volume 29: Lectures on Titus, Philemon, and Hebrews*. Edited by Jaroslav Pelikan. St. Louis: Concordia Publishing House, 1968.

——. *Three Treatises*. Minneapolis: Fortress Press, 1990.

Mahmood, Saba. *Religious Difference in a Secular Age: A Minority Report*. Princeton: Princeton University Press, 2015.

Marcuse, Hebert. *One-Dimensional Man: Studies in the Ideology of Advanced Industrial Society.* New York: Beacon Press, 1991.

Marias, Julian. *History of Philosophy.* New York: Dover, 1967.

———. *Metaphysical Anthropology: The Empirical Structure of Human Life.* University Park: Pennsylvania State University Press, 1971.

Martin, Scott. "The Spiritual Dangers of Disconnecting from Creation." The Gospel Coalition. February 4, 2019. https://www.thegospelcoalition.org/article/the-spiritual-dangers-of-disconnection-from-creation/.

Marx, Karl. *Economic and Philosophic Manuscripts of 1844 and the Communist Manifesto.* Amherst, NY: Prometheus Books, 1988.

Marx, Leo. *The Machine in the Garden: Technology and the Pastoral Ideal in America.* New York: Oxford University Press, 1964.

May, Gerhard. *Creation Ex Nihilo: The Doctrine of Creation "Out of Nothing" in Early Christian Thought.* New York: T&T Clark, 2004.

McDermott, Gerald, and Harold Netland. *A Trinitarian Theory of Religions: An Evangelical Proposal.* New York: Oxford University Press, 2014.

McGinn, Colin. *The Power of Movies: How Screen and Mind Interact.* New York: Pantheon Books, 2005.

McGrath, Alister. *The Twilight of Atheism: The Rise and Fall of Disbelief in the Modern World.* New York: Doubleday, 2004.

McKnight, Stephen A. "The Legitimacy of the Modern Age: The Löwith-Blumenberg Debate in Light of Recent Scholarship." *The Political Science Reviewer* 19 (1990): 177–95.

McLaughlin, Joseph. *Writing the Urban Jungle: Reading Empire in London from Doyle to Eliot*. Charlottesville: University Press of Virginia, 2000.

McLellan, David. *Marxism after Marx*. New York: Palgrave Macmillan, 2007.

McClellan, James, and Harold Dorn. *Science and Technology in World History: An Introduction*. Baltimore: Johns Hopkins University Press, 2015.

McLeod, Hugh. *The Religious Crisis of the 1960s*. New York: Oxford University Press, 2007.

———. *Secularisation in Western Europe 1848–1914*. New York: Palgrave Macmillan, 2000.

McQuire, Scott. *The Media City: Media, Architecture, and Urban Space*. Los Angeles: Sage Publications, 2008.

Melton, J. Gordon. "Unbelief: A Historical Bibliography." San Diego State University, 2011.

Michalson, Gordon. *Lessing's Ugly Ditch: A Study of Theology and History*. University Park: Pennsylvania State University Press, 1985.

Miller, Adam. "Enframing and Enlightenment: A Phenomenological History of Eighteenth-Century British Science, Technology, and Literature." PhD diss., Vanderbilt University, 2014.

Miller, Eric. *Hope in a Scattered Time: A Life of Christopher Lasch*. Grand Rapids: Eerdmans, 2010.

Miller, Walter. *A Canticle for Leibowitz*. New York: HarperCollins, 1959.

Minich, Joseph, "Class(ic)ifying Jamie Smith." Calvinist International. May 27, 2013. https://calvinistinternational.com/2013/05/27/classicifying-jamie-smith/.

———. *Enduring Divine Absence: The Challenge of Modern Atheism*. Landrum, SC: The Davenant Trust, 2018.

———, ed. *People of the Promise: A Mere Protestant Ecclesiology.* Landrum, SC: The Davenant Trust, 2017.

———, ed. *Philosophy and the Christian: The Search for Wisdom in the Light of Christ.* Landrum, SC: The Davenant Trust, 2018.

Minich, Joseph, and Onsi A. Kamel, eds. *The Lord Is One: Reclaiming Divine Simplicity.* Landrum, SC: The Davenant Trust, 2019.

Mitchell, Joshua. *American Awakening: Identity Politics and Other Afflictions of Our Time.* New York: Encounter Books, 2020.

Mitchell, Stephen, trans. *The Epic of Gilgamesh.* New York: Free Press, 2004.

Mokyr, Joel. *The Enlightened Economy: An Economic History of Britain 1700–1850.* New Haven: Yale University Press, 2012.

Mokyr, Joel, Chris Vickers, and Nicholas L. Ziebarth. "The History of Technological Anxiety and the Future of Economic Growth." *Journal of Economic Perspectives* 28, no. 3 (2015): 31–50.

Moore, Ben. "Invisible Architecture: Ideologies of Space in the Nineteenth-Century City." PhD diss., University of Manchester, 2014.

Moots, Glenn. *Politics Reformed: The Anglo-American Legacy of Covenant Theology.* Columbia: University of Missouri Press, 2010.

Moran, Dermot. *Introduction to Phenomenology.* New York: Routledge, 2000.

Moser, Paul. *The Elusive God: Reorienting Religious Epistemology.* New York: Cambridge University Press, 2008.

———. *Understanding Religious Experience.* New York: Cambridge University Press, 2019.

Muller, Richard. "Not Scotist: Understandings of Being, Univocity, and Analogy in Early-Modern Reformed Thought." *Reformation and Renaissance Review* 14, no. 2 (2012): 127–50.

———. *Post-Reformation Reformed Dogmatics.* Four volumes. Grand Rapids: Baker Academic, 2003.

Mumford, Lewis. *The City in History: Its Origins, Its Transformations, and Its Prospects.* Orlando: Mariner Books, 1968.

———. "Science as Technology." *Proceedings of the American Philosophical Society* 105, no. 5 (1961): 506–11.

Nagel, Thomas. *Mind and Cosmos: Why the Materialist Neo-Darwinian Conception of Nature Is Almost Certainly False.* New York: Oxford University Press, 2012.

Nakamura, Hajime. *A Comparative History of Ideas.* New Delhi, India: Motilal Banarsidass, 1998.

Neill, Stephen. *Colonialism and Christian Mission.* Cambridge, UK: Lutterworth Press, 1966.

Nelson, Eric. *The Hebrew Republic: Jewish Sources and the Transformation of European Political Thought.* Cambridge: Harvard University Press, 2001.

New American Standard Bible. Grand Rapids: Zondervan, 2002.

Nobel, David, and Jeff Myers. *Understanding the Times: A Survey of Competing Worldviews.* Colorado Springs: Summit, 2013.

Noll, Mark, and David Livingstone, eds. *B.B. Warfield: Evolution, Science, and Scripture—Selected Writings.* Grand Rapids: Baker, 2000.

Nongbri, Brent. *Before Religion: A History of a Modern Concept.* New Haven: Yale University Press, 2013.

Numbers, Ronald. *The Creationists: From Scientific Creationism to Intelligent Design.* New York: Harvard University Press, 2006.

———, ed. *Galileo Goes to Jail and Other Myths about Science and Religion*. Cambridge: Harvard University Press, 2009.

O'Connor, Charles. "The Great War and the Death of God: Postwar Breakdown of Western Culture, Retreat from Reason, and the Rise of Scientific Materialism." PhD diss., Georgetown University, 2012.

Oden, Thomas. *The Rebirth of Orthodoxy: Signs of New Life in Christianity*. New York: HarperCollins, 2003.

Oderberg, David. *Real Essentialism*. New York: Routledge, 2007.

Olson, Roger, and Stanley Grenz. *Twentieth Century Theology: God and the World in a Transitional Age*. Downers Grove, IL: IVP Academic, 1992.

Ong, Walter. *The Presence of the Word*. Albany: State University of New York Press, 2000.

Orsi, Robert. *History and Presence*. Cambridge: Harvard Belknap, 2016.

Ortega y Gasset, Jose. *History as a System: And Other Essays Toward a Philosophy of History*. New York: Norton, 1941.

Osterhammel, Jurgen. *The Transformation of the World: A Global History of the Nineteenth Century*. Princeton: Princeton University Press, 2015.

Ott, Walter. *Causation & Laws of Nature in Early Modern Philosophy*. New York: Oxford University Press, 2009.

Park, Peter K. J. *Africa, Asia, and the History of Philosophy: Racism in the Formation of the Philosophical Canon, 1780–1830*. Albany: State University of New York Press, 2013.

Paul, Darel. "Diversity: A Managerial Ideology." *Quillette.* February 19, 2018. http://quillette.com/2018/02/19/diversity-managerial-ideology/.

Pelletier, Arnaud, ed. *Leibniz's Experimental Philosophy*. Stuttgart: Franz Steiner Verlag, 2017.

Perez-Gomez, Alberto. *Attunement: Architectural Meaning after the Crisis of Modern Science*. Cambridge: MIT Press, 2016.

Perl-Rosenthal, Nathan. "Modern Times." *The New Republic.* May 5, 2010. https://newrepublic.com/article/74617/modern-times.

Peterson, Derrick. *Flat Earths and Fake Footnotes: The Strange Tale of How the Conflict of Science and Christianity Was Written into History.* Eugene, OR: Cascade, 2021.

Pettegree, Andrew. *The Reformation and the Culture of Persuasion.* New York: Cambridge University Press, 2005.

Piketty, Thomas. *Capital in the Twenty-First Century.* Cambridge: Harvard Belknap, 2014.

Pinker, Steven. *The Better Angels of Our Nature: Why Violence Has Declined.* New York: Penguin Books, 2012.

Piper, John. *Don't Waste Your Life.* Wheaton, IL: Crossway, 2018.

Pippin, Robert. *Modernism as a Philosophical Problem.* Malden, MA: Blackwell, 1999.

Placher, William. *The Domestication of Transcendence: How Modern Thinking about God Went Wrong.* Louisville: Westminster John Knox Press, 1996.

Plott, John C. *A Global History of Philosophy.* Five volumes. New Delhi, India: Motilal Banarsidass, 1977.

Polanyi, Michael. *Personal Knowledge: Towards a Post-Critical Philosophy.* Chicago: University of Chicago Press, 1974.

Popkin, Richard. *The History of Scepticism: From Savonarola to Bayle.* New York: Oxford University Press, 2003.

———. "Skepticism and the Counter-Reformation in France." *Archive for Reformation History* 51 (1960): 58–88.

Postman, Neil. *Technopoly: The Surrender of Culture to Technology.* New York: Knopf, 1992.

Priestman, Martin. *Romantic Atheism: Poetry and Freethought.* Cambridge: Cambridge University Press, 1999.

Provan, Iain. *Convenient Myths: The Axial Age, Dark Green Religion, and the World that Never Was.* Waco, TX: Baylor University Press, 2013.

Puckett, Joe. *The Apologetics of Joy: A Case for the Existence of God from C. S. Lewis's Argument from Desire*. Eugene, OR: Wipf & Stock, 2012.

Pufendorf, Samuel. *On the Duty of Man the Citizen According to the Law of Nature*. New York: Cambridge University Press, 1991.

Purdy, Jedediah. *After Nature: A Politics for the Anthropocene*. Cambridge: Harvard University Press, 2018.

———. *For the Common Things: Irony, Trust, and Commitment in America Today*. New York: Vintage, 2000.

Ratner-Rosenhagen, Jennifer. *American Nietzsche: A History of an Icon and His Ideas*. Chicago: University of Chicago Press, 2011.

Rea, Michael. *The Hiddenness of God*. New York: Oxford University Press, 2018.

Ricoeur, Paul. *Figuring the Sacred: Religion, Narrative, and Imagination*. Minneapolis: Fortress Press, 1995.

Ridderbos, Herman. *The Coming of the Kingdom*. Philipsburg, NJ: Presbyterian and Reformed, 1962.

Rigney, Joe. *The Things of Earth: Treasuring God by Enjoying His Gifts*. Wheaton, IL: Crossway, 2014.

Rogan, Tim. *The Moral Economists: R. H. Tawney, Karl Polanyi, E. P. Thompson, and the Critique of Capitalism*. Princeton: Princeton University Press, 2017.

Rose, Jonathan. *The Well-Tempered City: What Modern Science, Ancient Civilizations, and Human Nature Teach Us about the Future of Urban Life*. New York: HarperWave, 2016.

Rose, Matthew. "Tayloring Christianity: Charles Taylor Is a Theologian of the Secular Status Quo." *First Things*. December 2014. https://www.firstthings.com/article/2014/12/tayloring-christianity.

Royle, Edward. *Radicals, Secularists, and Republicans: Popular Freethought in Britain 1866–1915*. Lanham, MD: Rowman & Littlefield, 1980.

———. *Victorian Infidels: The Origins of the British Secularist Movement 1791–1866*. Lanham, MD: Rowman & Littlefield, 1974.

Rykwert, Joseph. *The Seduction of Place: The History and Future of Cities*. New York: Vintage, 2002.

Salatin, Joel. *The Marvelous Pigness of Pigs: Respecting and Caring for All of God's Creation*. New York: FaithWords, 2017.

Samuel, Sigar. "Artificial Intelligence Shows Why Atheism Is Unpopular." *The Atlantic*. July 23, 2018. https://www.theatlantic.com/international/archive/2018/07/artificial-intelligence-religion-atheism/565076/.

Saner, Andrea D. *"Too Much to Grasp": Exodus 3:13–15 and the Reality of God*. Winona Lake, IN: Eisenbrauns, 2015.

Sanneh, Lamin. *Disciples of All Nations: Pillars of World Christianity*. New York: Oxford University Press, 2007.

Schaffer, Simon, and Steven Shapin. *Leviathan and the Air-Pump: Hobbes, Boyle, and the Experimental Life*. Princeton: Princeton University Press, 2011.

Schindler, D. C. *The Perfection of Freedom: Schiller, Schelling, and Hegel Between the Ancients and Moderns*. Eugene, OR: Cascade Books, 2012.

Schellenberg, J. L. *The Hiddenness Argument: Philosophy's New Challenge to Belief in God*. New York: Oxford University Press, 2015.

Schmidt, Leigh Eric. *Village Atheists: How America's Unbelievers Made Their Way in a Godly Nation*. Princeton: Princeton University Press, 2016.

Schreiner, Susan E. *Are You Alone Wise: The Search for Certainty in Early Modern Europe*. New York: Oxford University Press, 2011.

Seifrid, Mark A. "Unrighteousness by Faith: Apostolic Proclamation in Romans 1:18–3:20." In *Justification and Variegated Nomism Volume 2: The Paradoxes of Paul*, edited by D.A. Carson, Peter T. O'Brien, and Mark A. Seifrid, 105–45. Grand Rapids: Baker Academic, 2004.

Seigel, Jerrold. *Modernity and Bourgeois Life: Society, Politics, and Culture in England, France, and Germany Since 1750*. New York: Cambridge University Press, 2012.

Sennett, Richard. *Building and Dwelling: Ethics for the City*. New York: MacMillan, 2018.

———. *The Corrosion of Character: The Personal Consequences of Work in the New Capitalism*. New York: Norton, 2000.

———. *The Craftsman*. New Haven: Yale University Press, 2008.

———. *Flesh and Stone: The Body and the City in Western Civilization*. New York: Norton, 1996.

———. *Together: The Rituals, Pleasures and Politics of Cooperation*. New Haven: Yale University Press, 2012.

Shain, Barry. *The Myth of American Individualism: The Protestant Origins of American Political Thought*. Princeton: Princeton University Press, 1996.

Shapin, Steven. *Never Pure: Historical Studies of Science as if It Was Produced by People with Bodies Situated in Time, Space, Culture, and Society, and Struggling for Credibility and Authority*. Baltimore: Johns Hopkins University Press, 2010.

———. *The Scientific Revolution*. Chicago: University of Chicago Press, 1996.

Shepard, Paul. *Nature and Madness*. Athens: University of Georgia Press, 1998.

Siedentop, Larry. *Inventing the Individual: The Origins of Western Liberalism*. Cambridge: Harvard Belknap, 2014.

Smith, Christian. "National Studies of Youth and Religion." Association of Religion Data Archives. http://www. thearda.com/Archive/NSYR.asp.

Smith, James K. A. *Awaiting the King: Reforming Public Theology.* Grand Rapids: Baker Academic, 2017.

———. *Desiring the Kingdom: Worship, Worldview, and Cultural Formation.* Grand Rapids: Baker Academic, 2009.

———. *How (Not) to Be Secular: Reading Charles Taylor.* Grand Rapids: Eerdmans, 2014.

———. *Imagining the Kingdom: How Worship Works.* Grand Rapids: Baker Academic, 2013.

———. *Introducing Radical Orthodoxy: Mapping a Post-Secular Theology.* Grand Rapids: Baker Academic, 2004.

———. *You Are What You Love: The Spiritual Power of Habit.* Grand Rapids: Brazos, 2016.

Sokolowski, Robert. *Introduction to Phenomenology.* New York: Cambridge University Press, 1999.

Soleri, Paulo. *Matter Becoming Spirit.* New York: Anchor Press, 1973.

Spinoza, Baruch. *Ethics.* New York: Penguin, 1994.

Spitzer, Robert. *New Proofs for the Existence of God: Contributions of Contemporary Physics and Philosophy.* Grand Rapids: Eerdmans, 2010.

Spurr, David. *Architecture and Modern Literature.* Ann Arbor: University of Michigan Press, 2012.

Steiner, George. *Real Presences.* Chicago: University of Chicago Press, 1989.

Stenger, Victor. *God and the Folly of Faith: The Incompatibility of Science and Religion.* Amherst, NY: Prometheus Books, 2012.

Stephany, Timothy J., ed. *Enuma Elish: The Babylonian Creation Epic.* CreateSpace, 2014.

Stivers, Richard. *Technology as Magic: The Triumph of the Irrational*. New York: The Continuum Publishing Company, 1999.

Strenski, Ivan. *Thinking about Religion*. Malden, MA: Blackwell, 2006.

Sussman, Herbert L. *Victorians and the Machine: The Literary Response to Technology*. Cambridge: Harvard University Press, 1968.

Svensson, Manfred, and David VanDrunen, eds. *Aquinas among the Protestants*. Oxford: John Wiley and Sons, 2017.

Swartz, David. "Review of Max Weber's Theory of Modernity: The Endless Pursuit of Meaning, by Michael Symonds." *Contemporary Sociology* 46, no. 2 (2017): 221–23.

Symonds, Michael. *Max Weber's Theory of Modernity: The Endless Pursuit of Meaning*. Burlington, VT: Ashgate, 2015.

Taylor, Charles. *The Language Animal: The Full Shape of Human Linguistic Capacity*. Cambridge: Harvard Belknap, 2016.

———. *Modern Social Imaginaries*. Durham, NC: Duke University Press, 2003.

———. *A Secular Age*. Cambridge: Harvard Belknap, 2007.

———. *Sources of the Self: The Making of Modern Identity*. Cambridge: Harvard University Press, 1992.

Thomas, Keith. *Religion and the Decline of Magic*. New York: Scribner's Sons, 1971.

———. *Man and the Natural World: Changing Attitudes in England 1500–1800*. New York: Oxford University Press, 1996.

Thomasius, Christian. *Institutes of Divine Jurisprudence*. Indianapolis: Liberty Fund, 2011.

Thrower, James. *The Alternative Tradition: Religion and the Rejection of Religion in the Ancient World*. The Hague: Mouton Publishers, 1980.

———. *A Short History of Western Atheism*. Bungay: Pemberton Books, 1971.

Toulmin, Stephen. *Cosmopolis: The Hidden Agenda of Modernity.* Chicago: University of Chicago Press, 1990.

Trigg, Jonathan. *Baptism in the Theology of Martin Luther.* Leiden: Brill, 2001.

Trueman, Carl. *The Rise and Triumph of the Modern Self: Cultural Amnesia, Expressive Individualism, and the Road to Sexual Revolution.* Wheaton, IL: Crossway, 2020.

Turner, Frederick. *Culture of Hope: A New Birth of the Classical Spirit.* New York: Free Press, 1995.

———. *Epic: Form, Content, and History.* New Brunswick: Transaction Publishers, 2012.

———. *Natural Religion.* New York: Routledge, 2006.

Turner, James. *Without God, without Creed: The Origins of Unbelief in America.* Baltimore: Johns Hopkins University Press, 1985.

Ulrich, Ferdinand. *Homo Abyssus: The Drama of the Question of Being.* Washington, DC: Humanum Academic Press, 2018.

Updike, John. "The Christian Roommates." *The New Yorker.* April 4, 1964.

———. *In the Beauty of the Lilies.* New York: Fawcett Columbine, 1996.

———. "Seven Stanzas at Easter." In *Telephone Poles and Other Poems.* London: Andre Deutsch, 1964.

van Asselt, Willem. *The Federal Theology of Johannes Cocceius.* Leiden: Brill, 2001.

van Leeuwen, Henry. *The Problem of Certainty in English Thought 1630–1690.* The Hague: Martinus Nijhoff, 1963.

van Ruler, J. A. *The Crisis of Causality: Voetius and Descartes on God, Nature, and Change.* Leiden: Brill, 1995.

Van Vleet, Jacob E. *Dialectical Theology and Jacques Ellul: An Introductory Exposition.* Minneapolis: Fortress Press, 2014.

Vanhoozer, Kevin. *Remythologizing Theology: Divine Action, Passion, and Authorship*. New York: Cambridge University Press, 2012.

Verbeek, Theo. *Descartes and the Dutch: Early Reactions to Cartesian Philosophy 1637–1650*. Carbondale: Southern Illinois University Press, 1992.

Vitz, Paul. *Faith of the Fatherless: The Psychology of Atheism*. Dallas: Spence Publishing Company 2000.

von Heyking, John. *Augustine and Politics as Longing in the World*. Columbia: University of Missouri Press, 2001.

Vonnegut, Kurt. *Player Piano*. New York: The Dial Press, 1999.

Wagar, W. Warren. "World's End: Secular Eschatologies in Modern Fiction." In *The Secular Mind*, edited by W. Warren Wagar, 220–38. New York: Holmes & Meier, 1982.

Walsham, Alexandra. "The Reformation and 'The Disenchantment of the World' Reassessed." *The Historical Journal* 51, no. 2 (2008): 497–528.

Walter, George, ed. *The Penguin Book of First World War Poetry*. New York: Penguin, 2006.

Walton, John. *Ancient Near Eastern Thought and the Old Testament: Introducing the Conceptual World of the Hebrew Bible*. Grand Rapids: Baker Academic, 2006.

———. *Genesis 1 as Ancient Cosmology*. Winona Lake, IN: Eisenbrauns, 2011.

Watson, Peter. *The Age of Atheists: How We Have Sought to Live Since the Death of God*. New York: Simon & Schuster, 2014.

Weber, Max. *The Protestant Ethic and the Spirit of Capitalism*. New York: Scribner's Sons, 1976.

———. "Science as a Vocation." In *Essays in Sociology*, 129–56. New York: Oxford University Press, 1946. Accessed at (and pagination derived from) http://anthropos-lab.net/wp/wp-content/uploads/2011/12/Weber-Science-as-a-Vocation.pdf.

———. *The Sociology of Religion.* New York: Beacon Press, 1993.

Wendling, Amy. *Karl Marx on Technology and Alienation.* New York: Palgrave Macmillan, 2009.

West, David. *Continental Philosophy: An Introduction.* New York: Polity, 2010.

Wheatley, Paul. *The Pivot of the Four Quarters: A Preliminary Enquiry into the Origins and Character of the Ancient Chinese City.* Chicago: Aldine Publishing Company, 1971.

White, Andrew Dickson. *A History of the Warfare of Science with Theology in Christendom.* London: Macmillan and Company, 1898.

White, Lynn. "The Historical Roots of Our Ecologic Crisis." *Science* 155 (1967): 1203–7.

Whitehead, Fred, and Verle Muhrer, eds. *Freethought on the American Frontier.* Amherst, NY: Prometheus Books, 1992.

Whitmarsh, Tim. *Battling the Gods: Atheism in the Ancient World.* New York: Knopf, 2015.

Wilder, William. "Illumination and Investiture: The Royal Significance of the Tree of Wisdom in Genesis 3." *Westminster Theological Journal* 68, no. 1 (2006): 51–69.

Willard, Dallas. *The Disappearance of Moral Knowledge.* New York: Routledge, 2018.

Wilson, A. N. *God's Funeral: The Decline of Faith in Western Civilization.* New York: Norton, 1999.

Wilson, Joshua Daniel. "A Case for the Traditional Translation and Interpretation of Genesis 1:1 Based upon a Multi-Leveled Linguistic Analysis." PhD diss., The Southern Baptist Theological Seminary, 2010.

Witte, John. *The Reformation of Rights: Law, Religion, and Human Rights in Early Modern Calvinism.* New York: Cambridge University Press, 2008.

Witzel, E. J. Michael. *The Origins of the World's Mythologies.* New York: Oxford University Press, 2012.

Wood, Ralph. "Everything, Something, Nothing: The Modern Novel and the Departure of God." ABC (Australian Broadcasting Corporation) Religion & Ethics. November 26, 2015. http://www.abc.net.au/religion/articles/2015/11/26/4360472.htm.

Wright, Robert. *Nonzero: The Logic of Human Destiny*. New York: Vintage, 2001.

Wright, William. *Martin Luther's Understanding of God's Two Kingdoms: A Response to the Challenge of Skepticism*. Grand Rapids: Baker Academic, 2010.

Yasukata, Toshimasa. *Lessing's Philosophy of Religion and the German Enlightenment*. New York: Oxford University Press, 2002.

Zuckerman, Phil. "Atheism, Secularity, and Well-Being: How the Findings of Social Science Counter Negative Stereotypes and Assumptions." *Sociology Compass* 3, no. 6 (2009): 949–71.

Zuckerman, Phil, Michael Martin, Steven Bruce, Russell J. Dalton, Paul S. Froese, Ronald F. Inglehart, Charles E. Lachman, and Peter M. Nardi. "Atheism: Contemporary Rates and Patterns." 2008. https://pdfs.semanticscholar.org/f379/ed99e57782aca6391ef5f666da7ba41f1333.pdf.

General Index

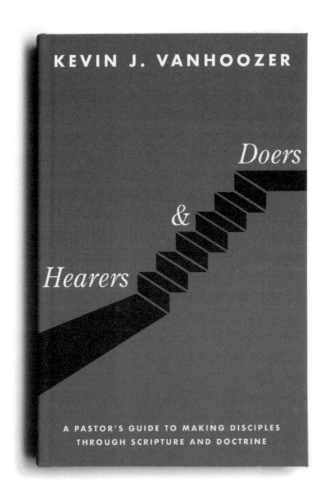

ALSO AVAILABLE FROM LEXHAM PRESS

Hearers & Doers: A Pastor's Guide to Making Disciples Through Scripture and Doctrine

---

Visit lexhampress.com to learn more